JACKEE H

SOUL
PURPOSE

**Self affirming rituals, meditations and
creative exercises to revive your spirit**

PIATKUS

To Aida and Sharron

In memory of Avanda J. Layne
I know you will return

'Ask, and it shall be given you,
seek and ye shall find;
knock, and it shall be opened unto you.'

MATTHEW 7:7

© 1999 by Jackee Holder

First published in 1999 by
Judy Piatkus (Publishers) Ltd
5 Windmill Street, London W1P 1HF

The moral rights of the author have been asserted

A catalogue record for this book is available from the British Library

ISBN 0 7499 1961 2

Designed by Paul Saunders

Data capture by Phoenix Photosetting, Chatham, Kent
Printed and bound in Great Britain by
Biddles Limited, Guildford and King's Lynn

Contents

ACKNOWLEDGEMENTS

To the infinite and unconditional love of God the Mother and God the Father who made it all possible.

To my birth mother and father Celestine Glendora Holder and Carlisle Sylvian Holder.

To my brothers and sisters Calvin, Ronald, Mavrin, Carson, Peter, Mary and Martha.

To my inspirational nephew Dwayne Holder. God gave you your life back and since then you have filled our family with so much joy. Thank you for touching our hearts.

To Dwayne's mother Maxine Goulbourne. Your place is definitely reserved in the heavens.

To the wisdom of the ancestors of my family.

To the memory of my great-aunt, Delcina Braithwaite.

For the wisdom and the goodness of my grandparents Joseph Tate, Ursula Holder, Cleopatra Earle and Stanley Morgan.

To Udean Charles who gave it her all when typing up this manuscript. Thank you for your meticulousness and for teaching me a thing or two.

Thank you Loreen Mckeller for your support in getting this manuscript typed up. And for your vision in the early days of the Face to Face workshops.

To Yvonne Witter who so gracefully and willingly saved the day. Thank you. PS: You are such good company.

To my dearest, best friend Pauline Thomas. I love you as much as I did when I became friends with you at the age of five.

For Valerie Wallace. I love you.

Jawanza, Ezolaagbo and Caroline Shola Arewa – thank you.

For some of my dearly beloved friends – Veronica Hill, Patricia St. Hilaire, Jacquie Moses-Rhoden and Alex Rhoden, Susi Miller, Donovan Bean and Delroy Peters.

For the unconditional love and support of the wise one – Hazel Sage. Your commitment and support have been outstanding.

For the early pioneers who lovingly helped me map my way: Doreen Baidoo, Sharon Jennings, Magna Aidoo, Barbara Love, Doran Van Heeswyck, Janet Hibbert, Ella Jess, Nefertiti Gayle, Yvonne

Fearon, Lorna Robotham, Gene Huie, Jennifer Adedipe, Glen Scott-Thomas, Eden Charles, June Ferrell, Ella Matheson, Christine Matheson, Oveta Mcinis, Marcia Morgan and Sharon Simpson.

For my sisters overseas: Pamela Maragh, Kim Caravan Jones, Catherine Smith Jones, Pamela Payton, Beverley East and Muhsinah Berry
Dawan.

For the teachings and guidance of Nehanda Moyo, Iyanla Vanzant, Jasminder Kaur Love and Namonyah Soipan.

For my moon sisters: Omisade Mills, Mojisola Sonoiki and Donnette Austin.

For the continued love and support of Lorna Lesley, Denise Dupont, Sylvana Chiappa and Charlee Chiappa-Campbell.

For Chris Grant – a shining role model and guiding light.

Thank you Dee Makala for being a true inspiration.

For every single sister and brother who attended and supported the Face to Face and Visions for Black Men workshops – where would I be without you?

For all the women and men who back-rowed as angels on the Face to Face and Visions for Black Men workshops. This thank-you comes from the deepest place in my heart.

To Malcolm Phillips, who trusted me enough and provided the most beautiful venue in which to birth the first Face to Face course, thank you.

For the sheer brilliance of three young people I have had the joy of knowing and being deeply touched by: Camille Curtis Y. Van Dyke, Tokunbo Oluwa and Kwadjo Dajan.

For all the students who worked with me on the BBC Mentor programmes.

To Audrey Walker for the deeper understanding of self you gave me by being in my life.

For Leone Ross who supported me when I wanted to give up being a writer.

For Mrs Hinds, my primary school teacher – you are just as inspirational as you were then.

For Mrs Higgins, my sociology teacher at Westminster College from 1978 to 1979. I wish I could find you to say thank you.

For the courage and sheer determination of Tony Fairweather (of The Write Thing). What a journey. Starting back in 1989, you've kept the show on the road.

To Paul Reid and Ella Jess – thank you.

To Catherine Itzin, Corinne Sweet, Hyacinth Fraser, Geraldine Brennan and Leah Thorn, the members of the writers' group. All the work we did paid off. Thank you.

To Ruth Bothwick, from Spread the Word, who so gracefully one day suggested I send my manuscript to Piatkus Books. What you said about them was right.

To Judy Piatkus who answered my call for help. Thank you. For the endless support and encouragement of Sandra Rigby, Gill Bailey and everyone else at Piatkus Books. Thank you.

To all those I have not mentioned, you are not forgotten, you are dearly remembered.

I Knew the Spring
Would Come

As a young girl growing up in South London, I made a pact with paper and pen. They were my friends. I found it easy to express myself on paper, writing stories and poems and dreaming about one day becoming a writer. That friendship and desire came to a sudden halt at the age of seven when I was sexually abused.

The abuse had a devastating effect. I closed in on myself and put up shutters against much of the world. I threw my dream of one day becoming a writer out of the window. This book is a manifestation of that seven-year-old girl talking from her heart about the journey to reclaim who she truly is. *Soul Purpose* is my way of reminding myself that I chose to live and thrive rather than merely survive. Whatever our experiences in life, we *can* overcome them.

Before I was abused, I had a strong sense of myself and the world I lived in. I had a zest for life, a love of people and a love of myself. After the trauma of the abuse I buried my head in the sand. I believed that I was ugly and that no one could love me. My self-esteem was so low it was pitiful. I believed that those who succeeded were special people and that I was not. How wrong I was.

Each of us receives a great gift from the time we enter this world, a special life mission, a unique assignment – like a fingerprint on the face of our soul. In it is housed the sacred content – our Soul Purpose. Our Soul Purpose has been designed so that we can give the very best of ourselves to the world. It is our doorway to greater fulfilment in life. We need to remember and reclaim our Soul Purpose and to manifest it here on earth. This has been my greatest challenge.

Life has kept me on my toes. The experience of sexual abuse was just one of the dramas I went through. At the age of 21 I was violently attacked by my boyfriend at the time. During this encounter I received a black eye and a deep cut under my eye and I lost a tooth. Eight years later, my six-month-old daughter was sent flying across a room as the result of a blow to my head from her father.

These experiences and many more made me wake up to who I really was. Deep down inside, I knew that playing the role of victim was not the truth for me, yet I was allowing myself to do so. Even though my inner voice was barely audible, my soul constantly played out the message of my true purpose in the back of my mind. It took courage and self-love for me to finally answer that call. For the soul knows that, whether it is in this lifetime or another, each one of us will eventually awaken to the truth of who we are.

Over the years, I have grown stronger and wiser. The seeds of change have turned into a sturdy tree which has gradually blossomed and borne fruit.

In this book I share with you some of my life experiences, spiritual insights and the many lessons I have learnt along the way. It explores what happens when we tap into our inner wisdom. I talk from my own heart with you, the reader, so that I can be inspired to continue on my life path. By joining with me, I hope you too will be encouraged to tune into the truth of your divine being. Through personal sharing, my deepest desire is to inspire and motivate others to reclaim their true purpose in life.

I wanted to write a book that would require you, the reader, to do more than simply read what I had written. From my own experience, I knew that reading alone would not be enough to promote change. There was a time in my life when all I did was read. I'd read any book on spirituality and personal growth that I could get my hands on. But the reality was that I read so much and did so little. It was only when I had hit rock bottom – and all that was left was me, the pen and the paper – that I really began to connect with the truth of my being.

I know, from experience, that I am responsible for the way I have chosen to live my life. We all have the ability to call into existence experiences which shape us, test our patience and faith, test our resilience and mould us. We only need to pluck the useful information, insights and lessons from these experiences and move on. But, instead, we hang around, and throw ourselves deeper and deeper into the negative energy, until it takes over our minds and our lives.

I know – because I have been there many times. I grew resentful and frustrated as I watched my purpose slip further and further away. Yet this resentment and frustration always magically lifted as soon as I took action to fulfil my purpose.

Soul Purpose calls on you to take action – it contains a series of creative spiritual exercises to assist all of us on our journey. In its pages you will find moving meditations, like the Baobab Tree Moon meditation, the inspiring Moon Writing ritual or the creation of your own pocket-sized dream book filled with images to inspire the life you want. You will find writing exercises encouraging you to connect with your passions in life, and prayers to feed your spirit and plug you into the higher source. You will even find bath rituals to help you deal with the everyday stresses of life.

Right now, as I write these words, I am happy and at peace. I have no money in the bank; I have no idea how I will survive or live over the next three months, but I am not afraid. When I write it fills me with a great satisfaction that eases worry and fear. I have peace of mind and I feel excited each time I turn the page. I realise, as the days slip into months, that I love to write, I love to create. This is where I want to be. I know that what matters is what I am doing now and that I love it.

I do not spend time thinking about the house I want, or the car I desire. Right now they are not essential requirements for the journey I am taking. Jesus said, 'In my Father's house there are many mansions.' I know that all my needs have already been taken care of. My mission is far greater. It is to make peace with the purpose assigned to my soul, to fully accept the spiritual side of my being.

Soul Purpose needs you to be present in this process. We do this through the writing and creative processes. To reap the benefits, you will need to purchase a brand new Soul Purpose Journal that you will use throughout this book (more details are included in How to Use This Book page 7). An A4-sized hardback notebook is recommended. If the cover is plain, cover your journal with an image you find inspiring. This is where you will make your daily entries, write down your responses to the exercises, and hopefully create your own exercises.

There is something magical about writing that is not just for those who see themselves as writers. Writing is a creative process that is open to us all. Writing brings our innermost thoughts and desires to life. Writing opens the door to our creative abilities, many of which we may be unaware of.

Your Soul Purpose Journal will become a 'computer database' that documents the inner you. It will hold all the information in your mind. Through the writing and the exploration, you will discover who you really are and what you want. Your journal will become a treasure trove. By working through the exercises you will open yourself to greater spiritual insight and understanding. You may find that the inner you is very different from the person your project externally.

The process begins with picking up your journal and making your first entry. By beginning, you are making a commitment to activate the information that is inside you.

When I put together the synopsis for *Soul Purpose* two years ago I did not realise I would share so much of myself on the page. The book I had visualised was completely different. Even the synopsis I handed in to my publishers in May 1998 does not fully reflect the book you now have in your hands. As I surrendered to the writing, it took me to places I had not planned to visit. I handed over control and started to simply trust the process. As I trusted, I found I had spontaneous conversations with people who had direct links with what I was writing. Visits to the library, which I had not regularly used for a long time, would lead me to just the book I needed for my research.

I learnt to trust and understand the meaning of 'everything in its own time'. I started writing this book in the summer of 1996. Two years on, when it was nowhere near completion, I started to get frustrated. It was this frustration that finally led me to send the synopsis out in May 1998. I sent out ten synopses in all. A chance conversation with someone led me to send the final synopsis to a publisher I had never heard of. I rang and left a message and sent the synopsis through the post the next day. I received a phone call from them almost immediately. They are the publishers of my book.

Even though I wanted this book to be written before now, it was not meant to be. What is included in *Soul Purpose* would not have been there in 1996 or 1997. Two spiritual readings confirmed this. As I lamented about not getting the book finished I was told each time that my book had 'already been written'. A chance conversation with an old friend confirmed this. We both acknowledged that the future is already the past. I could not force my seeds to bear fruit before they were ready. This was a great lesson for my ego. Especially as two sister friends working in the same field finished and published their books months before I did. This lesson taught me the grace of not comparing, the joy of being happy for other people's successes, and the strength and conviction to truly value what is yours.

I want to share this because I know how easy it is for all of us to give up at the first sign of someone doing what we would love to do. I know the resentment that can come when we have procrastinated about following through on a goal, only to see someone else manifest it. But no two products will ever be the same. Remember, whatever you manifest through your Soul Purpose has your own personal stamp on it. Staying focused and committed to your Soul Purpose, regardless of what others are doing, keeps the vice of comparison at bay.

As the days of writing stretched on, I began to love the way in which ideas would flow through me. I began to accept my moods as a writer. Dark intense periods always took my writing to a deeper place. Once out of this, I was like a jack-in-the-box, alive, abundant with ideas, and writing like a flowing waterfall.

The tools in this book include writing, creating collages, writing under the moon, performing rituals and guided meditations. More than anything, I want to share with you the experiences that have helped me make that deeper connection to my Soul Purpose. As human beings, collectively, we are all one. When you live your life as the blessing it truly is, it automatically touches the lives of so many others.

As we enter the 21st century, I dream of a world where we are no longer afraid to follow our dreams; where we naturally act on our positive thoughts; where our lives are living testimonies to our Soul Purpose here on earth. I want more inspiration, more awe in my life. I want to be moved, through all my senses, as I connect with other human beings. Too many of us are leaving this earth with unfulfilled and broken dreams. If you believe in the afterlife you will know that the next time you return to earth you will complete what you did not complete the first, second or third time around. Live your life fully so that, each time you return, it can only get better and better.

You are never alone on this journey. Your god/goddess is always with you. If you look within, you will find all the tools you need to cultivate your Soul Purpose. I send you from my heart an abundant stream of love and blessings, as you reach within, with all your might, to meet your higher good through the manifestation of your Soul Purpose.

May the loving force of God be with you and around you always.

How to Use This Book

IF I WERE TO describe myself as a reader I would say that I'm a bit of a skimmer – someone who reads fast, surveying the terrain as I go along for any words, phrases or sentences that speak to me. Firstly, I realised that, by reading fast, I was not truly digesting the information. Secondly, I was missing information that would be useful to my own personal development. And thirdly, I was ignoring the message, the call to take practical steps, which many books encourage the reader to do.

Reading a book from cover to cover is simply not enough. The way you, the reader, will be kept engaged is by actively participating in the practical application of what you have read. As you read *Soul Purpose*, you are both the reader and the writer. As you engage in the exercises, you will evolve as the writer and creator of your own story.

I have a few rules but they are not like the rules back at school, where you were punished if you didn't stick to them. These rules are really guidelines – they simply provide a healthy structure to support your creative and spiritual development.

With this in mind, I suggest three readings of *Soul Purpose*. The first time, read it through to get a feel of the spirit of the book. The second time, re-read the Introduction and How to Use This Book to gain a good understanding of what is required of you. If you have time, continue reading through the entire book, making notes of any items you may wish to have on hand for particular exercises. You will require four journals for the journey. By the end of your second reading you should have purchased at least one journal. The first will be your Soul Purpose Journal, the second will be your Gratitude and Loving Yourself Journal, the third will be your Moon Journal and the final will be your Dream Journal.

Your third reading is the long haul, the adventure. Through your journal entries, and your responses to the different self-discovery exercises, meditations and rituals, you will gain a deeper understanding of yourself, and cultivate a more meaningful relationship with the world around you.

Allow your Soul Purpose Journal to become a daily companion. As you write your responses to many of the exercises you will find that ideas often flow just as you close your journal or when you have left it behind. Carry it with you, so that you can savour and capture your thoughts and ideas. Remember, the best thinking comes through any time, anywhere.

Once I began writing *Soul Purpose* I thought I had the order neatly worked out. But the writing had its own ideas. I wrote from front to middle, middle to back, front to middle, over and over again. I could not control where the writing took me. All I knew was that I had to follow. I suggest you do the same. Dip in and out of the chapters. You may find that, as a result of completing a forgiveness ritual, you are now ready to tackle your creativity. Or an incident on the night of a full moon may draw you to Chapter 13, The Rhythmic Moon.

For those who wish to proceed in a more orderly fashion, I will explain the order of the chapters and the overall structure of the book.

In this first section, common terms that I use throughout the book are explained. You are then introduced to the Soul Purpose commitment and given an opportunity to complete a rough guide questionnaire to finding your purpose.

The first seven chapters relate to the early years of my quest for greater self-discovery, exploring some of the experiences I went through.

In Chapter 1 I explore the issue of self-esteem. Chapter 2 looks at my experience of earlier relationships. Chapter 3 examines our relationship with our bodies. Chapter 4 looks into how the busyness of our lives often reflects a dis-ease with self. Chapter 5 focuses on how we can and should take on more leadership in our lives. Chapter 6 examines the word 'empowerment' and Chapter 7 (the final chapter in the first part of the book) looks into the healing power of prayer.

Each chapter ends with a series of self-discovery exercises or soul work exercises, your tools for the journey.

A self-discovery exercise is, as the name suggests, an opportunity to discover more about self. It can be anything from a writing exercise, to taking a walk in the park. Each activity will help you make a deeper connection with self. Your Soul Purpose Journal will house your written responses to these self-discovery exercises.

You will also find guided meditations and/or rituals which will give you space to make contact with your spirit self and open the gateway to your creative powers. I have always found that, the more I apply myself to practical tasks to support my growth, the more I discover about myself. Regularly writing in my journal, practising my meditations and carrying out individual rituals empower me to be true to my Soul Purpose.

After Chapter 7 we arrive at the halfway point of *Soul Purpose*. I refer to this stage as 'crossing the bridge' – a point of major transformation, often a time in your life where you reach breaking point but which inevitably leads to a breakthrough.

In the second half, Chapters 8 to 16, the journey becomes more spiritually focused. However, it is by no means a template for the way your life should proceed. It is more of a guide through a series of life experiences which brought me into closer contact with my Soul Purpose.

I have shown you the wrapping. Now it is time for you to unpeel the layers. What lies underneath will be unique to each reader. Do whatever it takes. There is no right or wrong way – the only requirement is that you ACT.

Let me know how you get on. You can write to me at the address at the back of the book. I am excited at the prospect of what awaits you. I hope you are too . . .

YOUR SOUL PURPOSE JOURNAL

An important element of your journey to reclaim your Soul Purpose requires your commitment to keeping a daily (or at the very least a weekly) journal.

Writing in your journal will become your daily artist's ritual, regardless of whether or not you see yourself as an artist. By writing you will be creating sacred time, in silence, to be with yourself and yourself only. Your words will become your own personal guide –

they will show you the feelings you need to let go of and highlight the ones you need to cherish.

Your journal will tell you so much about yourself. Your everyday thoughts will seep out onto the page. The deeper you go, the more the words will uncover the lost and buried parts of who you are. As you write your journal, you will gradually break down the barriers that prevent you from manifesting the fullness of your Soul Purpose here on earth.

Many of the exercises in the following chapters may appear strange or even pointless.

Trust me, they are not. Our society has a deeply entrenched belief that a thing is only worthwhile if it is difficult or challenging. I urge you to suspend this belief. There is great power and magic in the simple things in life. Writing in your Soul Purpose Journal will sharpen your awareness of how simple things can bring awe and sacredness into our everyday lives.

Your Soul Purpose Journal should become your constant companion, waiting to capture your ideas and thoughts as they leap from the crevices of your creative mind. Insert significant images of your Soul Purpose into your journal. Your pocket book of dreams (see Chapter 12) will assist you in developing this.

You may wish to place a small photograph of yourself on the inside cover when you make your first journal entry. Sign it and date it. Do the same for your last journal entry. When you have completed your journal take a look back at the two faces. How have they changed? Use the photographs as markers of the journey you have made.

The key to journal writing is to write when you feel bad and to write when you feel good. Often when we are at our lowest point we are also on the brink of making a breakthrough in connecting with our Soul Purpose.

Some days you may feel as if you have failed. I used to have days of feeling hurt when my writing was criticised or rejected by magazines I wrote for. At that point it is so easy to give up. But the strength and the breakthrough comes with continuing. So when it feels rough, when it feels like you are failing, or when you feel you have nothing to say, see these times simply as stepping stones to spiritual success, to the place of your divine life assignment. By writing each day, no matter what you are feeling, you are clearing the way.

Now that you are committed to keeping a Soul Purpose Journal (and I hope you are), you are ready to work on manifesting your life assignment. Be open to where this leads you. You may find that a leisure activity you sometimes pursue is actually a really important part of your life, helping you fulfil your Soul Purpose.

It's best to write your journal entries in longhand. For example, I could not type the first draft of this book on my computer. Writing in longhand reminds me of when I was a young girl and my creativity seems to flow much more easily.

Once I get it on the computer, that is when my inner critic comes into play, and I feel the need for properly constructed phrases and sentences. This is the role of the editing critic, who polishes the creative word, helping it shine more brightly.

Julia Cameron, in her book *The Artist's Way*, coined a beautiful phrase, describing daily journal entries as 'the morning pages', to be completed each morning after you wake. I therefore suggest that you lovingly make a commitment to write in your journal every morning.

THE HEALING ART OF WRITING

For me, writing *Soul Purpose* was the equivalent of making a daily entry in my own Soul Purpose Journal. Writing can sometimes be a difficult task. The most challenging aspect is expressing what we really feel on the page. I used to hide myself behind other people's words and stories, frightened to reveal what I really believed. When other people expressed in writing what I felt, I became angry with myself.

Yet I know the feeling of elation when the helping hand of God touches my own, works through me, speaks the words as I write. I know the energy that comes when I stop whatever I am doing to write because God has sent a meditation or a new exercise to me.

On bad days I used to judge my work with the harshest, most critical eye. I refused to show it to friends for fear of their feedback. I told myself it would never be good enough. But I kept showing up on the page. And, I kept on pushing and digging, the soil I unearthed got deeper and deeper and richer and richer.

When we surrender ourselves to the creative act messages come from all sorts of places – films, books, people we meet – where we least expect to find them. As creative artists, the earth's holy people, we need to be open and willing to receive the divine hand of God at any time and anywhere. Just be willing to do what you have to do. Give up control. Surrender and let God take care of the rest.

As I have found, and I am sure you will too, the content of the journey, the terrain that we travel, far surpasses our ultimate destination. It is the discoveries along the way that make it all worthwhile. As someone once so perceptively said, 'Failures are our stepping stones to our successes.' I latched on to that quote because the whole of me understood its deeper meaning.

In my own life, my failures have quietly, and graciously paved the way for my successes. For example, I once lost a big training contract because of a poor report I wrote. No so long ago, I agreed to take on a huge contract with a consultancy I regularly worked with. I knew in my heart that this was not my soul work, that I really needed the time to devote to my book. But of course I didn't listen. The planning of the workshop was long and laborious. The more planning I did, the more was demanded of me. My inner voice kept telling me something was wrong. The voice got louder and louder but I convinced myself that the meetings we had regarding the training would guarantee its success.

I ran what I believed was a good workshop. The organisation did not feel the same way. We lost the contract and I didn't get paid. It was a painful and expensive lesson. Yet it was this apparent failure that helped me make my final decision.

After nearly 12 years as a professional corporate trainer, I finally said goodbye to the work that was no longer my soul work. As I did, I made room for my Soul Purpose Journal – my 'morning pages'.

Now I can devote more time to developing and nurturing my spiritual and creative, holistic practice. And I can commit to my life as a writer. This is just the beginning. Our failures teach us about what we do not want. When a seeming failure appears in your life, bless it, seek the gift in the experience, receive it, give thanks and move on.

In her *Daybook of Comfort and Joy* Sarah Ban Breathnach begins her 16 August entry with 'You can't be original – You can be authentic.' As I wrote *Soul Purpose*, it dawned on me that in my pursuit of perfection I kept wanting to be the original writer, the original creator. In doing so, I silenced the authenticity of my own valid and useful life experiences. Part of my healing, as I wrote *Soul Purpose*, was the realisation that I was not alone, that – to all intents and purposes – everything had been said and done before. But it had not been said and shared by me. It is our collective voices, and all our individual stories, that really count.

Bear all this in mind as you write, and are healed by your own writing, in your Soul Purpose Journal.

SOUL PURPOSE COMMITMENT

You may have to experience many different career paths before you are clear about what you really desire to spend your life doing. Don't give up. Commitment is essential because, as Goethe said, 'Until one is committed there is always hesitancy, the chance to draw back, always ineffectiveness.'

Listen to your inner voice. At birth your purpose was declared to you and the universe. Your purpose is contained in invisible words carried in the wind. Both you and the universe know why you are here and what you have been sent to do. You may have forgotten but the message is imprinted in your soul. Keep clearing your way through your life's experiences until you are ready to reclaim your purpose.

Don't wait for other people to give you permission to follow your heart's desire. Too many of us fall from our path and our purpose because we judge our success according to other people's expectations of us. This will eventually lead to a dead end. You will know because, deep down inside, you will feel the deadness in your life. Be courageous. Feel the fear and do it anyway. Take heart from the words of Dr Martin Luther King: 'Courage faces fear and thereby masters it.'

Work out what skills you have been uniquely endowed with, through which you can manifest your divine purpose. These skills are your equipment for your life journey. Nurture them. Feed them so they grow and they, in turn, will feed you. Your skills are your gifts and no one else's. It doesn't matter if you are a homemaker, an engineer, a sales assistant or a teacher. Your skills will shine through when you are in touch with your true purpose.

Seek alternative solutions. Don't allow blocks, challenges or brick walls to deter you from following your path. Get to know people who are out there in the world doing what you also desire for yourself. Listen carefully to how they have overcome internal and external conflicts. Use their experiences to motivate you to keep on moving towards your divine purpose, no matter what.

Learn how to transform any hurt, disappointment or other painful emotion that you may feel as a result of criticism or harsh feedback. Allow this to drive you to move beyond other people's misconceptions of your true purpose and capabilities. Someone once summed criticism up beautifully – 'Criticism is the way some people cry!'

Take responsibility for your own learning and education. Don't sit back and wait for things to be handed to you on a plate, only to hear yourself say in later life, 'If only I had . . .' Embrace learning and your life experiences. Always be prepared to be one moment the teacher, and the next moment the student. The roles are interchangeable and valuable to learning and growing throughout our lives.

Commit yourself to a lifetime apprenticeship. You will continue this apprenticeship until you die. As an apprentice, you can learn how to master your Soul Purpose. We will always remain apprentices because, in God's eyes, we are His/Her children.

How will you know when you have found your Soul Purpose? You will feel constantly energised by what you are doing. Creative ideas will flow abundantly. Opportunities will suddenly be presented to you, without you having to do very much. You will feel blissful and contented. You will develop a glow. Other people, particularly strangers, will be drawn to you and will want to know what you do.

Without thinking, you will effortlessly and with grace and ease give thanks daily for the blessings that have been bestowed upon you. You will do this even when storm clouds loom over your life.

You will embrace the spirit of your being. You will rejoice in the living of your purpose.

You will feel free to be.

You may wish to write out your Soul Purpose commitment in your journal. You may also wish to repeat it from time to time.

THE VOICE OF THE SOUL

The soul is a sacred vessel housed in the deepest parts of ourselves. The soul knows who we are and what we are. It is the soul which holds the memories and records of our purpose, the life mission we were assigned at birth. It is to the soul that we return, when all else fails. The soul pours love on us, regardless of what we are going through.

The soul knows the truth of our existence. It knows that we have the power to create the life we desire. The soul is eternal, it holds the records of our ancestral heritage.

It has been assigned a lifetime mission to support us in achieving our purpose. It will assist us in our greatest hour of need. The soul knows the lessons we must learn in this lifetime. It is through the soul that the voice of God speaks to us. It is the same voice that sends us messages when we are born.

It is to the soul that we retreat when everything crumbles around us. It is the voice of the soul that counsels us in our hour of need. It is the soul that guides us out of darkness. Without a connection to the soul we are lost, for it is the keeper of the eternal memory of who we are.

When the physical body dies the soul lives on. What is not achieved in this lifetime, the soul journeys into another life to complete.

When we do our soul work we make contact with our authentic self. It is through the soul that we deepen our relationship with ourselves and with our higher power. When we honestly strip away the layers of pretence we begin to see and feel our essential selves.

The soul has no need for money, titles or material things to feel its greatness. Its greatness comes when we are truly connected to the source of who we are. This book takes you on a healing journey to reconnect with the soul. Your soul joyfully awaits you.

YOUR PURPOSE IN LIFE

Your purpose has been divinely ordained for you and for you alone. Your purpose will put you in touch with who you are. It will have a deep impact on the lives of others as well as on your own. When you manifest your soul's purpose here on earth it moves your spirit self to a higher level.

Purpose is where you make contact with your soul, the holder of your lifetime memories. Your soul and your purpose work hand in hand. This book has been written to reawaken the passion of your purpose in you. When you think about your purpose it should trigger thoughts of excitement, happiness, enthusiasm. Your purpose will be on your mind when you sleep, when you eat, whatever you do. Connecting with your purpose will require you to go much further in the way you live your life. It will move you beyond the comfort zone, the dead zone which contains your buried dreams. In most cases your purpose will feel like something you just have to do, even if others say you are mad, not good enough, not qualified enough, or whatever.

One morning I watched a programme on BBC News, *Face in the Crowd*. This particular programme centred on a supermodel who, because of an accident, had to have a leg amputated. This had not stopped her living her life. She established an organisation that distributes artificial limbs to countries where people cannot afford to pay for this treatment themselves. During the interview she said, 'This world would be such a different place if we all acted on our positive thoughts, if we just responded to what we felt in our hearts.' That feeling in our hearts is pointing us in the right direction – the direction of our purpose.

So if you are a writer, your purpose is to write. The areas that you can write about are endless. If you have been blessed with the gift of a beautiful voice, use it to sing, use it to heal. Your purpose may be to bring heaven to earth with your smiling face, or to extend a helping hand in an hour of need. Whatever gifts you have been given it is up to you to use them. For it is through the manifestation of your gifts that your purpose will come alive.

By exploring the chapters and exercises in *Soul Purpose* you will start opening up to your divine purpose and unearthing your soul's mission.

Whether it be a written exercise, an affirmation, a ritual, a prayer or a blessing – each will take you to a place of deeper intimacy with your true essence. By committing to writing in your Soul Purpose Journal, you will begin to remove the cobwebs and dust from the seemingly blank canvas on which is painted the most beautiful picture of the inner you.

Open yourself to your spirit, allow yourself to embrace the true direction of your Soul Purpose.

BLESSINGS, THANKS AND PRAYERS

In our family, when we were growing up, it was traditional always to bless our food before we began to eat. Blessing our food gave us an opportunity for a moment's stillness and reflection each day. A time and space in which to give thanks. For the same reason, at both the start and the end of each ritual or meditation that you perform as you work through *Soul Purpose* requires you to perform a blessing, a recitation of thanks or a prayer.

In this way you are acknowledging the present moment, inviting spirit in, and giving thanks in advance. You are declaring your appreciation by expressing your thanks before you have fully received the rewards of the sacred process you will experience.

A blessing is an expression of thanks or a prayer sent directly to God. A blessing, thanks or prayer can come straight from your heart or you can recite one that you have already prepared. In Chapter 7 you will find a selection of prayers. But, as this is your journey, I would strongly encourage you to create prayers and blessings of your own. Keeping your Soul Purpose Journal close at hand will assist you in writing down words or thoughts as they appear in your mind.

You don't have to be religious to write your own prayer or blessing. Think of it as having an honest heart-to-heart with God. What you choose to call that higher power is up to you. Using your own words will help keep it simple and relevant to you. But always remain open to deeper, more salient words or language that may come through you. For example, I see a poem as the way many poets pray. Say your prayer or blessing as a sacred poem to the Most High. Perform your prayers or blessings in silence at the start or end of your rituals and meditations.

You, like me, might have thought that blessings should only be performed in the anticipation of bringing about good. Yet a blessing can also be poured into a challenging or difficult situation. It can open the way for you to understand what you are being taught and the gift the person or the situation is bringing to you. You can bless the situation, even if the person you are trying to get through to is not being receptive to your efforts. Blessing the situation helps you to understand and unearth the good in the experience. When I perform a blessing I remind myself that I, like you, have the power, through the divine intervention of God, to heal and be thankful for every moment of this precious life.

Blessing what appears to be negative or difficult enables the divine to shine its light on the gift that awaits us. It allows us to move on with grace and humility, and to rise above all that seems negative, to claim the goodness that is often hidden deep underneath. If you are fluent in your original mother tongue say your prayers in this language. This not only honours the divine but also honours the spirit of your ancestors.

Add beauty to your rituals and meditations by singing your blessings and prayers. Hymns are the musical versions of prayers. Many hymns move me to tears because their words speak to my heart.

Welcome each day with a blessing, give thanks or say a prayer. Embrace the miracle each one of us is privileged to witness every day of our lives.

Opening blessing for your rituals, meditations and sacred spaces

May the power of God walk with me,
May the eyes of God guide me,
May the arms of God protect me,
May the presence of God watch over me.

Closing blessing for your rituals, meditations and sacred spaces

I salute the air that is our life force,
I bless Mother Earth that is my mother – she takes care of me.
I give thanks for the burning fires of our souls,
Lighting the magnificence of our spirits;
And the flowing waters of our emotions, our eternal life force.
We who are joined here declare the circle open but never broken.
We meet and join in love.
We part in love.
And we look forward to meeting in love again.

Prayer of Thanks to Mother Earth

For the healing element of water that quenches my soul when I
  am thirsty,
For fire that warms me and rekindles my spirit,
For air that brings the voices of my ancestors and the miracle of
  breath,
For the creation of Mother Earth who nourished and fed me,
I give thanks to life because it is a gift,
A perfect present for today.

YOUR SACRED SPACE

It is 5am. Apart from the shrill birdsong outside my window my home is embraced in a comforting silence. Before I begin, I give thanks for the day and bless the gifts the day will bring me. From this space I can hear my inner voice. There is little or no distraction from the messages I receive and I am able to give my undivided attention to the sacred task of writing these words.

Before your begin your meditations or rituals you need to enter sacred space. When you enter sacred space you are declaring your intention to go within and connect with spirit.

Begin by being silent, paying attention to your breathing and reflecting on your intention, the purpose of what you are about to do. You may wish to perform one of the breathing exercises in Chapter 11, Still Waters Run Deep. As you relax and go deeper, allow yourself to tune into your internal self. In much the same way as an athlete tones up for a race, or a singer exercises his or her voice before a performance, this is your preparation before you embark on your creative and spiritual journey.

It is so easy, once we have made this sacred commitment to ourselves, to get distracted, lose enthusiasm and begin to feel self-doubt. This is why we need to protect ourselves when we are doing our spiritual work.

What you are drawing around you is an invisible field of protective energy with which to support and protect your sacred work. There are several ways you can do this. I was taught by one of my spiritual teachers, Jasminder Kaur Love, to protect sacred space by visualising myself surrounded by an invisible circle of intense white light. The light can be white, gold or any colour you believe offers protection at the highest level. Declare the circle of light closed as you begin your work and declare it open when your work is complete (see the blessing on page 18).

Having an understanding of the sacred and symbolic nature of circles will help you integrate healing energy into your exercises.

Our first home is a protective shield of circle energy. Surrounded by fluid, we live for nine months in the womb. The circle gives us room to grow and evolve. We slide from this circle into life on a circular planet. The solar system's fantastic elements are all formed in circles – the sun, the moon and the orbits of the planets. The Native Americans honoured the four compass points, mapping them out in the form of a circle. For all these reasons, you should visualise a circle of light around you as a shield of protection.

Performing your meditations and rituals in sacred space helps prepare you for your spiritual work. It also protects you against negative forces. It is your personal way of honouring the work that you are doing.

When I run weekend workshops and we don't have access to a garden we use the nearest local park. Because of the nature and intensity of the work, it is crucial that the group enters sacred space. We do this by preparing ourselves before we leave the building by praying, meditating or grounding and centring ourselves through a series of breathing exercises. To maintain our sacred space, we walk to the park in silence.

If you are working directly on the earth, sprinkle salt in the shape of a circle around you to denote your sacred space. Or you can follow the tradition of the Native Americans and mark your sacred space by building a circle of stones. Use singing and prayer to mark your sacred space (see the opening blessing on page 18).

Remember, you don't have to be alone to enter sacred space. You may enter sacred space in a crowded room simply by going within and visualising yourself surrounded by white light.

If you are distracted whilst you are in sacred space and you are forced to stop, do a short closure by saying a blessing (see the closing blessing on page 18). Respond to the distraction if necessary. Afterwards review the situation. Ask yourself these questions in order to understand why the distraction may have come about:

– What stage of the process were you at?
– Did you subconsciously call in the distraction as a way of avoiding the next step?
– Intuitively, ask yourself what the reasons for the interruption were.

THE MEANING OF RITUAL

'Ritual' is a word that often brings up a lot of resistance in people. I believe we need to reclaim it and elevate it to its original meaning – a significant sacred act in our everyday lives. The performance of rituals transforms our spiritual understanding into practical reality – the movement of spirit into matter.

In ancient times rituals were often performed in secret by priests or shamans. The content of a ritual would not be disclosed because of the power, magic and mystery contained within it. Rituals enabled a priest or elder to move beyond the mundane to the spirit world and reinforce learning, spiritual insight and understanding. Regular performance of the ritual reinforced its message.

Many of the rituals carried out by our ancestors have been passed down. Whilst we have lost much of the wisdom and knowledge of the ancients, rituals still hold some of the magic and power of the past. When conducted with clear intention, and in sacred space, honouring rituals have the power to transform and bring healing to our whole lives.

Through repetition, rituals empower us to embrace change. They support us in maintaining the universal laws of the world we live in. Rituals uphold ancient cultural traditions, and bring the sacred into the mundane.

The energy of ritual can take so many forms – from the simple act of lighting a candle to the making of marriage vows. It is the sacred energy, and repetition, which charge the ritual to go to work on our behalf. When the ancients performed rituals they knew they were channelling the healing powers of the divine.

Each ritual should have a clear intention and purpose. If the ritual is, for example, about learning to forgive it will probably involve letting go of old stuff or saying goodbye to the past. By strengthening your connection with a higher power you invoke the energy that will support you in moving to a place of forgiveness and greater understanding. Once the intention is clear, the repetition of the ritual over time helps to bring about the desired outcome.

But there is something even more magical about rituals. It is in the very act of performing the ritual that the sacred energy often descends and consumes you. So often, while performing a ritual, I am returned to my centre, connected to God, to the universal life force. In that moment I am one with the world. Rituals take us beyond time, as we know it, and remind us of who we truly are. When you perform a ritual, no matter how simple it may seem, you are openly calling in a higher presence. This presence, when honoured, will always go to work on your behalf. Rituals remind us of the work we must do to uncover the wounds, the hurt, the pain that keep us from the divine.

Treat your rituals as regular spiritual workouts that keep you on track. But also give them the utmost respect, for they are not to be played with.

Your rituals can include any or all of the following: chanting, meditating, being in silence, performing a symbolic act, carrying out specific tasks over a designated period of time, writing, burning papers, releasing energy. Plan and prepare the materials you will require for the ritual. If the ritual is written down, read it through to make sure you understand what you will need to do.

The next step is your inner preparation. This may involve fasting, meditating, being in solitude or some form of purification. Your inner preparation is the inner core (or sanctum) of the ritual. As the outer symbolic act is performed regularly, and in sacred space, you create the energy to manifest the change in your inner sanctum. We learn by doing, through the repetition of the ritual.

At a recent Christmas service at my daughter's school church, my daughter – along with most of the children present – made a symbolic candle-holder using an orange as the base. I watched as the children delighted in the simple ritual of lighting a candle, and placing it in the centre of the candle-holder. When the lights went dim the flickering light of all the candles made a wonderful sight. As we left the church I noticed the care with which my daughter held her candle in her arms.

I believe this simple but blessed ritual that removed them from the normality of their everyday activities had evoked a presence not only in my daughter Aida but in many of the children. It seemed to return them to a place in their souls which was familiar. On arriving home, my daughter lovingly placed her candle on my altar in the living room. Ten days later, when the orange had shrivelled up, she still wanted to keep it there. Only when I pointed out that she could replace the old dying orange with a fresh one was she prepared to move it.

The sacred energy had been captured in the poignant moments of its making. And the candle served as a reminder.

Ritual calls on us to remember, recapture, re-enact, reclaim and re-ignite the sacred traditions of the past. Our task now is to adapt and discover new rituals to take us into the future.

The rituals in *Soul Purpose* have been designed specifically to combat the stresses of modern life. Do not underestimate their power. Honour them, and treat them with respect, and they will serve you well.

THE SPIRIT OF SEVEN

Throughout *Soul Purpose* I use the number seven in breathing exercises, meditations and rituals. There are good reasons for this.

In many cultures and ancient traditions numbers carry their own spiritual energy. When I was young, I remember three being a lucky number. As my consciousness expanded, I became aware that there existed many different numerological systems derived from different spiritual teachings.

In 1995, during a one-year life mastery course led by Jasminder Kaur Love, I was introduced to a numerological system based on the numbers 1 to 11. On the first day of that course I randomly selected a seat in a circle of ten other chairs. The teacher explained that the seat we had each sat in reflected the energy we were seeking, or had to move through, over the next year.

According to Jasminder Kaur Love, each seat carried the following energy:

1 Reflects new beginnings, based on the fact that our life experiences are circular. It is also about starting something that will change your life.

2 Reflects a relationship issue, both your relationship with self and with others.

3 Carries the energy of communication – in terms of union with self, union with others and union with God.

4 Means overcoming transformable blocks, perhaps in the areas of money, relationships and family dynamics. These blocks represent major hurdles in our lives which need to be overcome.

5 Carries the energy of transforming negative to positive (once you have overcome the blocks).

6 Carries the energy of family dynamics, expressing a need to explore family relationships both past and present.

7 Was the seat I held. I held my breath as Jasminder talked us through this number. Seat 7 was about reaching spiritual fulfilment and spiritual happiness. It was the seat of happiness on all levels. I realised that this was what I had been searching for, for most of my life.

8   Naturally flows from spiritual happiness, in that it creates abundance on all levels, emotionally, financially, physically and spiritually.

9   Carries the energy of letting go, often in the form of a life test. Letting go is a testament to faith. It means removing all that no longer serves you; letting go so that you can receive.

10   Moves naturally into the state of leadership; making progress by taking a risk.

11   Moves beyond the confines of everyday blocks and barriers to a life of self-mastery and union with God.

So seven was the number I had been given. Connections began to strike me almost immediately. When I looked back I realised that several major turning points in my life had taken place in seven-year cycles. I was sexually abused when I was seven, and seriously assaulted by my boyfriend at the age of 21.

And, of course, seven is a significant number in life generally. There are seven days in a week. Sunday, the seventh day, has traditionally been considered a holy day, a day of worship and rest. In the West seven notes make up a musical scale. There are seven colours in a rainbow. There are seven sacred energy points on the body (called the chakras) and there are seven wonders of the world.

In 1996 I attended an empowerment workshop in Ohio, USA, led by empowerment specialist and spiritual life counsellor Iyanla Vanzant. During the workshop we each received a numerical profile based on our date of birth. Sure enough, my life lesson number, based on my birth date profile, was seven.

My numerical profile said, in part:

> You have come to life to learn how to use spiritual laws to acquire material gifts. Your challenge is to learn to trust the world of spirit and your own spiritual senses. This means you must learn to trust yourself, love yourself and be yourself. The major challenge for the seven person is developing a sense of worth.
>
> The seven is the metaphysician and must continually seek and increase spiritual knowledge. This is the sacred number. Spiritual revelations come in silence, to the quiet, trusting mind.
>
> The seven fears being shamed. Feelings, thoughts, instincts,

intuition are the foundation of the seven. They must learn to trust them. Difficulties early in life, emotional abandonment by loved ones, negative criticism by those who they trusted can throw the seven out of balance. You must learn to see the deeper meaning. The seven is always learning, always teaching, always serving, that is the nature of spirit.

According to the profile, orthodox religions don't offer sevens much spiritual satisfaction and substance. Yet those who do find themselves in the right religion will move into positions of great power.

To support his or her development, the seven must spend time in nature, the ocean, the mountains and the woods. If at all possible the seven should live in the country. The reading finished by saying, 'Because you flow in spirit, negative words flow against you. Do not gossip! It will destroy your mind. Pace yourself for the long haul. Get plenty of rest. Above all, learn to pray and do it often.'

I was also told that my colour was purple and my gemstone was an amethyst.

When I wrote this Introduction, I had not read my birth chart numerical profile for almost a year. Much of its content I had forgotten. What hit me, as I read through it, was how my life has gone on to reflect nearly every word.

This is why the number seven appears throughout this book. I use it because of its spiritual nature, its magical significance and its meaning in my life. Enjoy embracing the number seven in your exercises, rituals and mediations.

Thank you Lady Helen Hannon and Iyanla Vanzant (Inner Visions Spiritual Life Maintenance) for preparing my profile. May God continue to bless you both.

In God's name

Before I embarked on writing *Soul Purpose*, my Christian background had alienated me from the term 'God'. Instead, I had accepted and celebrated the wholeness of 'Goddess'. Words like Divine, Great Spirit and Creator had created a safe space for expression. I wanted to stay safe and distant but I kept finding myself using the term 'God'. Rather than resist it, I went with the flow.

As I explored my connection with the word, I realised that the God from my past was a punishing God, a God to be feared. Now I have discovered the feminine nature of God, I have come to know God as all loving. The word has a warm feeling as I utter it. It is no longer an embarrassment, no longer associated with an oppressive religious background. I can finally accept the female/male God inside me and love her/him.

This has been my experience. It may not be yours. I do not wish to alienate you from your own definition of spirit. As you read *Soul Purpose*, replace 'God' with your own personal word or term.

Words, like life, can be changed. Today it may be 'God', tomorrow you may prefer to use the term 'Great Spirit'. To help you find the right name, I have made a list of all the words I know to describe spirit. Go through the list and observe which names you identify with. This list is by no means complete, so you can add your own if you wish. Then, if you feel ready, decide which word or term best fits your personal definition of spirit.

God	Divine	All Powerful
Christ	Holy One	All Knowing
Jesus	Allah	Universal Intelligence
Jehovah	Holy Father	Messiah
Mother God	One God	Lord
Goddess	Supreme Being	Holy Ghost
Father God	Creator	Buddha
Infinite Being	Holy Spirit	Great Source
Most High	Mohammed	Holy Mother
Jah	Great Spirit	Mother Mary
Higher Power	Universal Source	

SELF-DISCOVERY EXERCISE
Finding Your Soul Purpose

ARE YOU HAVING difficulty identifying your Soul Purpose? Use this exercise to make contact with your hidden desires, then write your responses in your Soul Purpose Journal.

- List ten things you feel really passionate about. Do not stop to think about your answers, just keep writing.

- List ten things you would like to learn more about.

- Write down the names of two people you admire. Which of their qualities do you admire?

- What did you want to become when you were eight years old? If you can't remember, take a guess.

- If you could change your job or career tomorrow, what would you change it to?

- If you could change where you lived tomorrow, where would you live? What kind of house would you live in? Which area, which town and which country?

- Write down the name of someone in the public eye who does a job, or holds a position, which you believe you could do better.

- If someone was to write a book or make a film about your life what would the title be?

- Write down all the positive things that you love about your job, career or life work.

- Write down all the negative things you dislike about your job, career or life work.

- Now balance the scale. On a scale of 0–10 what would you say is your level of satisfaction in your job, present career or life work?

- Write down three thoughts that occur to you as a result of looking over these lists.

- Imagine that you could consciously choose your career or calling for your next life. What would it be?

- Name the thing you most regret not having yet done in your life.

- In a face-to-face conversation with God, what is the one question you would ask pertaining to your life right now?

- If you had the blessing of coming back to earth as an angel, who is the first person whose life you would touch and why?

- Write a letter to an unborn child telling them how to stay in touch with their Soul Purpose. What would you say in your letter?

- What single thing could you do at this very moment that would move you closer to your Soul Purpose?

- Do it.

- Take a deep breath and give yourself a big hug. You are one step closer.

- Trusting that you know the answer, write down your immediate response to the following question: What was God's divine intention for your Soul Purpose here on earth?

SELF-DISCOVERY EXERCISE
Creating Your Own Soul Purpose Prayer

- Prayers are our intimate conversations with God. Create your own prayer requesting your higher power's support in the manifestation of your Soul Purpose here on earth.

- You may wish to decorate your prayer, frame it, type it up or stick it onto card. You could even make yourself a set of prayer cards. I have a prayer I wrote whilst on a writers' retreat which always ignites my spirit. Imbue your prayers with the power and poignancy of your words and God will hear them. Let go of all attachment to the way in which your prayers are answered.

- Enter your prayer(s) in your Soul Purpose Journal.

SELF-DISCOVERY EXERCISE
Soul Purpose Cards

SOUL PURPOSE CARDS carry a powerful energy and are capable of providing insightful, intuitive answers to your questions. Use them to keep you focused and support you on your creative and spiritual journey. This exercise explains how to create your own deck of Soul Purpose cards.

- First, buy a packet of plain cards. My local stationer sells a packet of 100 small white cards for use as business cards. These are ideal. For this exercise you will require 40 cards.

- On the first ten cards write ten positive, healing affirmations.

- On the next ten cards write down ten spiritual quotes, phrases or sayings that inspire you.

- On the next ten cards write down ten spiritual principles that you wish to integrate into your everyday life. For example, you might wish to learn how to have more faith, how to trust, how to become more abundant, or how to connect more with your spirit. You can, if you wish, write down your understanding of the principles and the gifts they bring into your life.

- On the fourth set of cards write down ten prayers, or the words of a song that you find moving.

- On your 39th card write down the words 'I AM'.

- On the final card write down 'I [your full name] am a child of God' (or the name you use to describe a higher power in your life).

- Decorate each card.

- Place your cards in a special box or wrap them in a beautiful piece of fabric. I found a wonderful deep purple and orange velvet drawstring bag in my local supermarket in which I house my cards.

- Use your cards once a week or whenever you feel you need to connect with your Soul Purpose, your dreams, your inner self or God.

How to Use Your Soul Purpose Cards

- Begin by smudging your cards with incense or a smudge stick, an incense stick of cedar wood, sage or sweet grass herbs. Smudging is an ancient ritual of purification. Light your incense or smudge stick and fan the smoke all around the object, neutralising the energy as you do so. If none are available simply visualise encircling your cards with white light (see Chapter 14, Sacred Spaces).

- Find a quiet place. Centre yourself and enter sacred space.

- Light a candle as a way of acknowledging that you are requesting the spirit of the divine to assist you with your reading.

- Begin with an opening blessing (see page 18).

- Make your request.

- Shuffle the cards and select one card with your left hand. (Energetically, the left side of the body carries your receiving energy. The right side carries your giving energy.)

- Say aloud your question or request.

- Sit quietly for a few minutes and consider what the question means to you.

- Turn to your Soul Purpose Journal and write down the question and the answer on the card you picked.

- Write down any thoughts you have. Make a note of any action you may need to take.

- Stay focused on the card throughout the day. Write down any other thoughts that come to you.

- When you have finished, give thanks, or close with a prayer.

- Replace your cards in their box or bag.

- Use your Soul Purpose cards regularly before writing in your Soul Purpose Journal and at the end of the day before you go to sleep.

PART ONE

Exploring
Yourself

CHAPTER 1

Just As I Am

Life's CHALLENGE TO ME has always been to accept myself as I am. I mean really as I am. Not how I want others to see me, not based on my distorted perception of myself. But me, in my pure essence. I entered this world with a strong loving sense of myself. My inner core vibrated with love and light. Then darkness, in the form of the abuse, entered my life. It overshadowed the light, the inner core of my self-esteem shattered into a thousand pieces. My life journey has been a quest to find the pieces of that inner core and put them back together again.

Self-esteem

The loss of my self-esteem meant that I became unbalanced within myself and the world around me. It was as if I had been poisoned by the abuse. It tore at my values and beliefs. My sense of love turned instead into shame, humiliation and a deep conviction that I was ugly both inside and out. I internalised these feelings for many years. And they ate away at my core, leaving a deep internal wound.

We all bring our past beliefs, thoughts and feelings into the present to create our current realities. The past is no longer with us so we know we should let go of these beliefs. Instead, we hold on to the idea that we are ugly, or that we're not good enough, or that we will be rejected, and it becomes ingrained in our thought patterns and beliefs. But the human mind is truly amazing. We can program it to believe anything we want it to. And that belief will create a new reality. I know this because my negative beliefs about myself always brought about negative situations and experiences. And, in contrast, my positive thoughts always brought about a positive outcome.

Healthy self-esteem means approving of our whole selves, whilst acknowledging that there are parts of us which require development and change. Self-esteem is a deep honouring of ourselves.

When we lack a healthy sense of self-esteem we often end up pretending that things don't matter and we put on a hard, cold front. Or we may fall into the role of victim. We either try too hard to overcompensate for our low self-worth, or we don't try at all. Whichever one of these negative behaviour patterns we buy into, it is deeply rooted in our belief system from the past. Our beliefs keep us imprisoned. They stop us from fully experiencing life and fulfilling our potential.

We can only give up our negative beliefs when we really *want* to let them go, not because we feel we have to or we should. When we do things out of a sense of duty or obligation we place extra burdens, demands and expectations on ourselves. This is why we often turn and run, or feel resentful about letting go of negative beliefs.

REPLACING THE NEGATIVE WITH THE POSITIVE

Right now, be really honest with yourself. On a new page in your Soul Purpose Journal write down ten beliefs that you have about: relationships, money, career, health, spirituality, leadership, success. When you have finished take a look at your list. What are your thoughts? Are your beliefs mainly on the positive side or more on the negative? Are you surprised at what you find?

If you find that your beliefs are mainly negative, let's get to work. Make a new list under each heading and write down five positive beliefs you want to create for each of these areas. Once you have finished, read through your new list. How do you feel now? I bet it feels different from the first time.

Note your response in your journal. Read it over again and when you have finished close your eyes. Take a deep breath and relax.

Now focus on the first set of beliefs about relationships. Say to yourself:

*'I freely choose to let go of all my old beliefs about
relationships.'*

Visualise all the negative beliefs from your first list floating away into
the distance. Watch them as they slowly disappear. Now repeat:

'I freely and gracefully accept my new gifts and beliefs.'

Now see yourself being showered with all the new beliefs you choose
to accept into your life. Do the same for each of the different head-
ings.

Remember, our negative beliefs about ourselves are false images
that distract us from the truth of who we are. Your mission is to find
that truth. This is a possibility that is firmly within your reach.

LEARNING TO LOVE OURSELVES

Letting go of old beliefs makes room for us to really learn to love ourselves. I am not talking about loving ourselves in a selfish or arrogant
way, but in a gentle, healing way that enriches our connection with
the self.

Intellectually, many of us know the importance of loving and
valuing ourselves. These are the buzzwords on everyone's lips. We
attend workshops and seminars on these subjects, and we eagerly
read books on personal and spiritual development. The challenge
comes when we have to put into practice what we already know.
Speaking for myself, this has been by far my greatest lesson.

Even though when I was young I closed myself off from the world,
my spirit did not fully disconnect. It lay quiet within me, patiently
waiting.

On the face of things, I was an able student. I was popular and had
lots of friends, I was keen on sport, I went to the right school, the
right college and the right university. But I hid behind a false aura of
confidence. I learnt the right things to do, say and be. That was easy.
But it was all very much on the surface.

It didn't matter how many degrees, certificates or qualifications I
gained it didn't make me feel the slightest bit better about myself.
Any achievements would be quickly forgotten as I reverted back
to my previous negative self-beliefs. The emptiness I felt inside

remained with me for a long time. Looking back, I realise that being confident doesn't necessarily mean that you like yourself.

Over the last 14 years I have spent quality time getting to know who I really am. It has been a long process, sometimes fantastic and sometimes terrifying. But it has created a fantastic opportunity for me to participate in a truly meaningful relationship with myself. Looking back into my past has helped me heal my experiences of abuse and domestic violence. I realise now that, whilst those things did happen to me, they are not me. I am not the sexual abuse I experienced. I am Jackee. Now I choose to thrive rather than survive.

It was never ordained for any of us to simply survive. God's plan was always for each one of us to reach our highest potential. We all have choices about the way we lead our lives. When I saw myself as a victim, life presented me with victim experiences. When I chose to move into leadership, life presented me with leadership experiences. All the time we are choosing and responding to the beliefs we have about ourselves. Our lives simply reflect this.

I received so many mixed messages about who I was, as an African woman. On the one hand I was brought up to be ladylike and to know my place. On the other hand, society fed me so many negative stereotypical messages – a black woman was supposed to be as strong as an ox, highly sexed, only good enough to be a single mother living on welfare. Mixed messages about who we are often distort our views of ourselves. Our society makes so many assumptions based on culture and gender.

An incident when I was a 16-year-old college student went a long way towards reinforcing these negative messages. I was taking three A levels and I had the ability to pass all three easily. Yet one lecturer, my law lecturer, was extremely critical of my work and at times, I felt, very racist. Intuitively I knew something was wrong with his attitude and his approach. I started missing his lessons.

One afternoon he caught me walking along the corridor. My immediate thought was to turn and walk the other way but I didn't act quickly enough. I couldn't believe it when he started backing me up against the wall. I could feel his breath on my face. I could see the hatred in his eyes. I looked around for a way of escaping, praying that someone would walk by. But no one did. We stood staring at each other. I tried to be defiant but inside I was quivering. The words he spoke shattered me: 'Why don't you just go out and get pregnant like all you other girls do?' I was shaking when I entered the student common room. I didn't attend lectures for the rest of the day. I internalised his words as if they were my own.

There is a little girl inside every woman. When you were young, all she wanted was to express love, to feel safe in the world, to have fun and be free. Any negative experiences, thoughts or feelings you had impacted on her in a big way. If she was not taken care of, she would either hide away and only surface when things were really, really, really rough, or she would cause absolute havoc in your life in order to get attention.

What role has your little girl taken on in your adult life? Have you spoken to her today? Have you woken her up and told her how wonderful she is? Have you shared with her the progress you are making? Have you played and had fun?

She is a crucial link with your self-esteem. She is a constant reminder of the nurturing and care that we all need to give ourselves. When you neglect her, you neglect yourself. Talk to yourself the way you would wish a new lover to talk to you. Give yourself constant powerful messages. Feed this into your psyche until it becomes a habit.

AFFIRMING THE POSITIVE

So many of us become masters of negative self-talk; now it's time to become masters of the positive. You can do this by using affirmations. Affirmations work according to the universal law of give and receive. What you give, you get. An affirmation is a positive word or sentence that you say aloud or silently to yourself.

The purpose of the affirmation is to manifest that which we believe to be true or that which we want to create for ourselves. This could mean changing a belief, creating a change, or moving towards the manifestation of a physical object.

However, an affirmation will not work unless you also change your underlying belief system. This is one of the challenges with affirmations. We want to change the surface without digging deep down. Yet we must first go to our beliefs before the affirmation can really work. The affirmation breaks the illusion by declaring your desired outcome in the present:

'I am powerful. I am lovable. I am healthy and wise.'

The world is full of words and words are full of energy. Negative words are like swords battling through the universe, and returning to us, having created the same negative vibration with which they left us. The energy with which we feel our thoughts or say our words is the energy with which they will eventually come back to us. Positive words go to work on our behalf. They flow through the universe, return and make manifest that which we desire.

You can strengthen the power of your affirmations by changing your belief systems, repeating the affirmations regularly, writing them down, and acting as if they are already true and have been given to you.

For example, a painter won a prestigious art prize. When he arrived on the platform his words were: 'I'm stunned. I don't know what to say and where's my cheque?' I had no doubt about his ability but somewhere deep inside I wondered if this promising young man had really affirmed himself and his talents. I asked myself why that acceptance speech had not been ready to flow forth from him. Affirmations help you to be ready for that moment when opportunity knocks on your door.

When we constantly engage in negative self-talk we quickly come to believe it. Repetition of affirmations works in very much the same way. What you are doing is gradually replacing the old thoughts, the old beliefs, with a new script. By repeating the new lines over and over again you will eventually begin to believe the message.

So how do we go about maintaining a healthy sense of self-esteem? We have to be responsible, which means we need to nurture ourselves.

You don't have to have lots of money to do this. The simple things in life are often far more effective than the things we pay a lot for. The rest of this book is full of ideas for you to try. Find people in your life with whom you can be yourself with, where you're not in a role – as a manager at work, as a mum, big sister, wife, partner or daughter. Being with people with whom we can be ourselves is vital. They give us space to breathe and a chance to escape from the roles which limit the way we express ourselves to the world. And the more you come to accept yourself, the more you will express the real you in other areas of your life.

Fill up your time, and the empty well inside you, with activities that you feel passionate about. That empty space is calling you. Often the task or pursuit you fill it with is also part of your purpose, your mission here on earth.

Have a deep, sensual love affair with yourself. Yes, yourself. Don't wait to be in a relationship to experience love. Have it always there for yourself. Take the time to pamper yourself. Your self-esteem grows through your intimate connection with yourself and others.

Intimacy means more than simply being in a relationship and having sex. I realised that all my life what I had been searching for was intimacy: a close, deep, sensual relationship, full of respect, trust and passion, and not necessarily sexual. What I really needed was to find that intimate place inside me. Everyone needs a shoulder to cry on, a helping hand, to be shown affection and to be appreciated. Create sister circles with women you trust. Bring food, sit, talk, and share. Exchange skills, do whatever feels right. But just be there for yourself and each other.

As you travel through life, don't compare yourself to others. Comparing only undermines your self-esteem. You are a unique child of God. Uniqueness has no place in the corridors of comparison. Instead, pay attention to the distance you have travelled, the terrain you have covered, to reclaim that love of yourself. Feel your love expand, and your sense of yourself swell, as you live each day in the loving presence of your light. You are the best there is.

RITUAL
Self-Marriage Ceremony

THIS RITUAL IS a rite of passage, a ceremony affirming a significant change in your life. It is an opportunity to make a declaration to God, yourself and the universe, to make a deep commitment to your spirit and self.

♦ First cleanse your body by fasting (see pages 69–70). It is ideal if you fast for at least 24 hours before your self-marriage ceremony.

♦ Purchase a ring which you will use in your ceremony tomorrow.

♦ Have two photographs taken of you before your ceremony. Photographs from a photo booth will be fine.

- Stick your photographs onto a blank piece of paper and underneath write a goodbye letter to the old you. The night before your ceremony, just before you go to sleep, read your letter.

- Prepare a platter of sumptuous fruit the night before your ceremony. Lay the table with your finest cutlery and plates. Put a vase of flowers in the centre. Make sure you have a beautiful glass from which to drink your natural champagne water.

- To make your natural champagne water, purchase a bottle of good-quality mineral water. The night before, pour the water into a jug. Bless the water and pour several times between two jugs. Add four or five slices of lemon to the water. Cover and leave to stand overnight.

- Cleanse yourself by taking a salt bath the night before (see pages 237–238).

- Before the ceremony, record what you are saying goodbye to in your Soul Purpose Journal.

- The night before your ceremony write a letter to the woman you are now becoming. Tell her why you are so in love with her and why you will be committed to your marriage. Place the letter in an envelope with scented flower petals or spray the letter with your favourite perfume.

- Before the day of your ceremony you may feel called to cut your hair, dye your hair, give things away, do something different or drastic. Allow yourself to move with the energy you feel. This is a sign that you are ready to make the transition.

- Before you go to sleep, prepare the clothes you will wear to your ceremony. Choose a colour that you love.

On Awakening

1 Take seven deep cleansing breaths and say a prayer of thanks

2 Open a holy book, such as the Bible, the *Bhagavad-Gita* or the Koran, and read that page from left to right.

3 Run your bath and scent it with essential oils or deeply scented bath salts. Scatter flower petals into your bath and use them to cleanse your skin.

JUST AS I AM

4   Perform the skin-brushing ritual in Chapter 3 before you enter the water.

5   On completion of your bath, anoint your body lovingly with a favourite oil or cream.

6   Dress and beautify yourself.

7   Begin by burning the goodbye letter you wrote the night before.

8   If you are outside, bury the ash in the earth.

9   If inside, place the ash in a container and bury it in the earth later.

10   Read your letter aloud to the woman you have become. Say it with clear intention and meaning. Hold a rose quartz crystal in your left hand as you read your letter.

11   If you have a ring place it on your finger.

12   Say your commitment declaration out loud: 'I joyously declare that I [your name] will love myself totally and unconditionally all the days of my life.'

13   Dance to music that marks your transition. Read aloud a poem or piece of writing that moves you.

14   Write a celebration letter to yourself in your Soul Purpose Journal.

15   Drink a toast of natural champagne water to yourself.

16   Meditate on the new life that lies ahead of you.

17   Perform the self-blessing ritual in Chapter 3.

18   Make an offering to Mother Earth (such as burying a crystal in the earth beneath a particular tree).

19   Enjoy your wedding feast.

◆ This is simply a guide. As far as possible, follow the suggestions for your preparation rituals. You can then devise and create your own content for the ceremony itself.

◆ If performing outdoors, begin your ceremony at sunrise under a tree, or by the shores of the sea. If friends attend, have them take photographs of you and create your personal self-marriage photo album.

♦ Each year, if you wish, you can repledge and rewrite your vows with a special celebration with friends or on your own.

MEDITATION
I Am Woman

THIS MEDITATION CONNECTS you with the goddess within. She is the wise woman, the innocent child. As you embrace the voice of your goddess, the soul offers words of wisdom for your journey. 'I Am Woman' strengthens your sense of self.

♦ Take a deep breath and relax. Close your eyes and release the tension in your body.

♦ Enter sacred space.

♦ You find yourself in an enchanted forest. Birds are singing, flowers are blooming. The scents of the flowers create a blanket of delightful fragrance in the air. Breathe it in.

♦ You are barefoot. The grass under your feet feels warm and inviting. You find yourself skipping lightly through the forest. The forest grows thicker but not thick enough to block the rays of sunlight that shine through the tops of the tall trees. The rays of sun light the path. You walk easily through the forest. Your heart feels light. You are excited. Take a few seconds to enjoy your walk.

♦ Suddenly your pace quickens. In the distance you hear the voice of a woman calling. The voice sounds very familiar. As you move towards the voice, the words become clear: 'I AM . . . I AM . . . I AM . . . I AM . . .'

♦ Take a deep breath. You come to a clearing. The space has an air of magic about it. In the middle of the clearing are seven huge trees. As you approach them you see that these trees are not like trees you have seen before. Their trunks form the shape of a woman. Their branches are clearly two hands outstretched and they are all joined.

You feel the trees smiling at you, welcoming you. You smile back. You feel the energy. You know that you have met before. These are the standing people, your ancestors.

◆ Move slowly towards the trees, and in your own time sit with your back nestled into the trunk of a tree you feel comfortable with and relax. Pause for two minutes.

◆ Suddenly you are aware of a presence nearby. When you raise your head you see the body of a woman standing before you. You blink and look again so you can make sure that what you are seeing is correct. The woman who stands before you is an exact replica of yourself. Slowly explore the face of the woman who stands before you.

◆ Now enter her mind, hear her thoughts. Look into her heart and soul and ask her: 'Who am I . . .?' Open your heart as you receive the messages that are being sent to you. Be open to any images, symbols, people or colours that may come through as you listen.

◆ Pause for two minutes.

◆ Now you are ready to hear her words. Stretch out your arms towards her and take seven deep breaths.

◆ After each breath, as loud as you can, hear yourself shouting the words 'I AM', followed by any other words that intuitively come. Take a deep breath and repeat the words 'I AM'. The seventh time, say 'I AM' and finish with the following:

'I AM [your name] a divine creation of Mother/Father God, an earth angel who loves all that I AM. Thank you. Thank you. Thank you.'

◆ Pause for one minute.

◆ Now embrace your twin and, as you do, feel her melt into you. See her as a glowing little girl inside you, happy, and at peace with herself. Thank her.

◆ Pause for 30 seconds.

◆ Now it is time to make your way back. But, before you go, hug and thank each tree and listen to the message she whispers to you. The gift you receive from each tree will reflect a different level of your development, your spiritual and physical growth.

- Pause for seven minutes.

- Make your way back through the forest and return to the place where you began your journey. At the count of seven you will return back to the room:

'One, two, three, four, five, six, seven.'

- Open your eyes and, when you are ready, have a good stretch.

- Without talking to anyone pick up your Soul Purpose Journal and write down any messages that you received from the meditation.

- When you have finished writing, read through the messages and reflect on the spirit of what is being said to you.

- Now if you wish create a prayer, an affirmation, a poem or a piece of creative writing that captures the spirit of your messages.

- When you have finished take seven deep breaths.

SELF-DISCOVERY EXERCISE
Nurturing Festival

PLAN A CELEBRATORY one-week nurturing festival for yourself. Think about all the things you could treat yourself to that involve the minimum of cost. This exercise requires you to carry out at least one loving, nurturing act for yourself every day, for seven days. You can of course totally immerse yourself in the celebration. Enjoy.

Ideas for Your Nurturing Festival

- Treat yourself to a full body massage.

- Go for an hour-long walk in the park.

- Spend an hour in a flotation tank.

- Visit a free museum or art gallery.

- Spend the day at a spa.

- Go swimming/take a water aerobics class.

- Take a class in a subject you have never taken before.

- Plan a morning at home of nurturing yourself. Take a scented bath, wash your hair, treat yourself to a facial, have a relaxing foot bath, do a home pedicure and manicure, moisturise your skin with a rich cream or an aromatic massage and body oil.

- Go to see a film in the afternoon.

- Visit another town or city.

- Go for lunch/dinner by yourself.

- Cook a special meal for yourself where you are guest of honour.

- Go to the gym or sauna.

- Curl up in bed and read a favourite book.

- Spend 30 minutes sitting and listening to a favourite album.

- Write a letter of appreciation and encouragement to yourself and mail it.

SELF-DISCOVERY EXERCISE
Gratitude Journal

I BEGAN MY FIRST committed Gratitude Journal on 11 May 1998 which also marked my 36th birthday. Writing down five blessings on that first day was easy. It was the days that followed which proved more challenging. Just the thought of writing down five appreciations about your day or about life in general can cause most of us to stare blankly into space. Our minds immediately grasp for an example of something momentous, something big, that we think is worth mentioning to others. We believe that we should be grateful for the big successes in our lives: the degree we have achieved, the driving test we have passed, the promotion we have just earned at work.

Yet gratitude has its home in both the obvious, and the smaller, less obvious, miracles of life. You can begin right now by giving thanks for the greatest gift bestowed on any human being – the gift of breath. We take this essential element of our existence for granted. But without it we would not be here.

Whenever you get stuck use this as your first entry in your Gratitude Journal. What about the home you live in, the flowers you pass every day, the sun that provides heat and warmth, the rain that nourishes and blesses the earth? What about the bus that took you safely on your journey to work, the person who gave you a seat on the tube? Every day we go through a multitude of experiences for which we can express our gratitude.

To tell the truth, I found expressing my thanks awkward and cumbersome at first. It wasn't that easy to find things that I wanted to say thank you for. But the more I turned up to express my gratitude, the more the words of thanks flowed. Once, a near-miss accident in my car caused me to pull over and take a few precious moments to connect with how lucky I was. I pulled out my Gratitude Journal and began to write. I realised I had been going too fast. Writing my thanks made me realise how lucky I was to be alive.

After my near miss I began to take stock, taking time to notice the wonders and pleasures which surrounded me. This led me to move to a place where I was open to receiving from the universe. A morning sky radiant with clear blue touched my heart. The image of a father and son holding hands and running towards the child's school spoke of hope. A chance meeting with an old friend was followed by an intimate, bonding conversation.

When I express my gratitude I am reminded of the beauty that exists in life, the pleasures that one can receive. When I take the time to examine my day by giving thanks I am reminded of how the hand of grace and the hand of spirit have been at play not just today but every day.

What to Do

◆ For your Gratitude Journal you will require a blank notebook, preferably one with a hardback cover.

- Spend at least seven minutes writing in it each day.

- Write down seven things that you appreciate each day. It doesn't have to be long and drawn out, just keep it simple.

- By turning up on the page and sharing your thanks, you are making direct contact with God. This is your own personal book of blessings.

- Writing down your thanks will also impact on the way in which you show others your appreciation. By honouring that which you are grateful for, you will foster a much richer and more meaningful relationship with others. What you give will be mirrored back abundantly over time by what you receive.

SELF-DISCOVERY EXERCISE
Loving You Journal

EVERYONE, AT SOME point in their life, has received that special card. Perhaps it was on your birthday or at the start of a new relationship. You remember the feeling inside you when you opened it and read those words. What if you created a journal for yourself that evoked the same feelings but this time the words were being sent from you to you?

- Purchase a new blank book in which to create your Loving You Journal – a series of love letters to self.

- Each month write yourself a love letter using words and phrases that make you feel special and loved. Enhance the beauty and specialness of your Loving You Journal by adding letters of appreciation from others, thank-you notes, photos of people you love and who love you, meaningful cards, and anything that reminds you of your wonderful attributes.

SELF-DISCOVERY EXERCISE
Your Own Book of Affirmations

WHY NOT MAKE your own book of self-healing affirmations?

You will require up to eight sheets of coloured A4 paper, a stapler, scissors and some string or ribbon.

What to Do

◆ Fold the A4 paper in half. Punch two staples along the middle spine. Tie the string or ribbon down the centre and create a bow or knot on the outside.

◆ Design your front cover, making sure your name is written clearly on the front. You may wish to stick a photograph on the front and give your book a title.

◆ Fill the pages with healing affirmations for future inspiration and encouragement.

◆ You may wish to give your book an introduction, outlining the purpose of your affirmations, or you may wish to write a message to yourself at the end.

◆ Alternatively, you could create your own personal affirmation cards.

SELF-DISCOVERY EXERCISE
Success List

WHEN YOUR SELF-ESTEEM is low and it is difficult to find anything that you like about yourself, make a success list.

◆ List everything you are successful at, or have been successful at.

◆ Then affirm seven times:

'I am success.'

◆ Repeat this affirmation seven times a day, saying it seven times on each occasion.

SELF-DISCOVERY EXERCISE
Transformational Language

THE WAY IN WHICH WE use language has a massive impact on our thoughts, on our behaviour and on how we feel about ourselves. If we use negative language it has a negative effect on our thoughts. Positive language, repeated consistently, creates a positive vibration in our thought patterns. We all have the power to transform the language we use.

◆ Write down ten things you don't like about yourself.

◆ Now transform the negative words into positive ones by focusing on the positive qualities that lie hidden behind the negative beliefs. For example, if you think you are involved in too many different things in your life you can turn that around to mean that you have an abundance of creative ideas and you express yourself in many different ways.

◆ By writing down your negative thoughts you decrease the effect they have on you. By focusing on the positive you are training your mind to focus and find the positive in any challenging situation. Over time, this will affect the way you respond to situations you encounter in life.

MEDITATION
I Am Hilltop

HIGH POINTS ON Mother Earth have a way of lifting our spirits. 'I Am Hilltop' focuses on saying aloud two powerful words 'I AM' and sending their vibration out into the universe.

◆ Find a high spot or point on Mother Earth.

◆ Stand with your arms open wide.

◆ Take a deep breath and say aloud ten times: 'I AM'.

SELF-DISCOVERY EXERCISE
A Tribute to Yourself

DON'T WAIT UNTIL your funeral to have a glowing obituary read out about you. Have your life mission honoured while you are alive. Seize the moment now.

◆ Write your own celebration of life tribute. In it share your successes and the lessons you have learned. Talk about people who have touched your life, and reflect on the people whose lives you have touched. What obstacles have you overcome? What joys have you experienced in this lifetime?

SELF-DISCOVERY EXERCISE
Your Own Celebration of Life Party

THIS IS A WONDERFUL exercise to do on your birthday.

◆ Invite a group of trusted friends to your celebration of life party.

◆ Ask each friend to bless your party by making a special dish or bringing a handmade present. They may feel called to share with you a special poem or song which reminds them of you. At a recent celebration of life party friends offered services such as coming round to cook dinner one evening, paying for a hairdo or offering a few hours of cleaning.

◆ Buy yourself a beautiful blank book that you will treasure.

◆ At your party ask your friends to write a tribute (appreciation of your life) in your celebration of life book.

◆ During the gathering ask everyone to share their dish or gift and to say why they chose this gift or dish for you.

◆ Finish by asking each person to verbally share their tribute to you.

RITUAL
A Sisterhood Circle

I ORIGINALLY WROTE this ritual to be celebrated on 8 March, International Women's Day, but it can be performed at any time of year by any gathering of sisters. The ritual pays tribute to the millions of women who have have ever lived and gives thanks for those who have survived.

♦ First prepare the space where you will celebrate with an abundance of food, gifts, candles and incense. Make sure you have a large enough space for your circle of sisters to be seated comfortably on the floor, linking or holding hands. This can be in someone's home, or in an open space like a park or garden. If you choose an open space find a place where you will not be disturbed. Being in the open brings you closer to the elements and to Mother Nature and strengthens the power and magic of your circle.

♦ Ask each woman present to bring a meaningful gift which she will exchange with one other person at the close of your ritual. Encourage women to create their gifts themselves rather than purchase something.

♦ Start your ritual by entering sacred space and saying the opening blessing (see page 18). Have everyone imagine a huge circle of golden light surrounding the group.

♦ Pour a libation in honour of your ancestors who have paved the way for you to be here. (A libation is an ancient African tradition through which we honour Great Spirit and ancestral energies.) Ask the oldest member of the group to pour the libation. Use spring water, mineral water, gin or white rum, and pour it into a vessel that will be used only for this purpose.

♦ Before you pour the libation you may wish to say a prayer or have each woman in turn call out the name of her ancestors. As each woman calls out a name pour the liquid from the vessel directly onto the earth if you are outside, and onto the floor or onto a thriving plant if you are inside.

♦ Next, add prayer (which is our way of communicating directly with God). This can be done by each sister in turn, or by just one member of the circle. Have a moment of stillness and silence. Play a guided meditation tape or have a member of the group guide you through a meditation. Meditation stills the mind and helps restore balance. Keep reminding the group of your love for each other – as women and as sisters. Love is the driving force within your circle of sisterhood.

◆ Announce the circle now open but unbroken. You may wish to place an object of spiritual significance, such as a crystal, a fertility doll or a stone, in the middle of the circle. Ask every sister to pick up the sacred object before she shares her experiences over the last year. Outline the guidelines for sharing. For example, what have been your successes over the last 12 months? What lessons have you learned from your painful experiences? What are your visions and goals for the coming year? Whoever is sharing should not be interrupted. Allow each woman the space to be heard.

◆ During this sharing process keep appreciating each other. You can do this even if the women present have just met for the first time. Spirit will lead you to see behind the masks and the facades to the essence and light of each woman in the circle. By this time much of the fog that sometimes exists between people will have been removed.

◆ If you are familiar with each other you may wish to share aspects of each sister that you would like to see maintained and aspects that you would like to see changed. Give your feedback with love. Feedback given with love never wounds.

◆ Now is the time to exchange gifts. Give each gift with love and receive your gift with love.

◆ Declare the circle open to sharing of food, talking, dancing, sharing poetry, telling stories or peacefully sitting in the sanctuary of each other's love and energy. Invite sisters to openly share aspects of their lives with each other.

◆ Close the circle with words of encouragement and inspiration to each other for the year ahead. A meditation, guided visualisation or prayer will help to ground and focus each sister as she prepares to take leave and embark on her journey home.

◆ Your circle of sisterhood can last for a couple of hours or for the whole day. Hold it at sunrise, at sunset, at night or during the day.

Each time has its own unique power and magic. Our ancestors knew the power and the magic of sacred space. This was the secret of their survival. Women met in the kitchens, in the yards, in the fields, to support and nurture each other during times of happiness and times of suffering. Now a circle of sisterhood offers the space for us to celebrate our successes and strengths. All you need do is adapt the steps according to your members' own knowledge and level of spiritual understanding.

◆ Feel the power of sisterhood flow. Celebrate your priceless worth as women.

The Beauty of the Dancer in the Mirror Whose Eyes You Cannot See

We dance and hold each other through the night. She feels exactly as I want to feel. She has made it through whole and well. She is beautiful, strong and free. She is also me.

This poem is dedicated to all sisters who cannot see the beauty in her eyes

She lived inside my eyes,
Swirling, dancing, grooving.
She did not miss a beat.
Her eyes always smiling,
Loving, caressing, embracing.
She knew what love was.
She knew no fear, just dared to live
The way she was meant to
Her scent could fill a hundred fields,
Her beauty was overwhelming.
She lived inside me, deep in the forest.
I could not see her, could not feel
The rhythm of her pulse.
Yet every day she wished a thousand wishes for me.
She prayed for me,
She asked for my eyes to be opened.
And then one day, amazingly, I caught her face,
Glimpsed her reflection in the bathroom mirror.

I gasped, taking a deep breath,
Could not believe the face that stood before me.
She boldly stepped out from inside me,
Held my hand.
We kissed, embraced and danced together
She is beautiful.
She feels divine.
My feet are free.
I am free.
For she is all of me and I am she.

'The poem is the poet's prayer.'

CHAPTER 2

Relationships are Mirror Reflections of Ourselves

RELATIONSHIPS OPERATE like mirrors. Whatever thoughts we have about ourselves, whether they are positive or negative, we energetically pull people into our lives that reflect those beliefs right back to us. When I was 17 I fell desperately in love with a man six years my senior. He was everything I thought I wanted in a man. He was tall and good-looking and I felt so privileged that he had chosen to go out with me.

At that age my self-esteem was very low. From the moment he expressed an interest in me I was walking on air. It didn't matter that he was over two hours late for our first date, didn't have a job and hadn't worked full-time for years. The fact that he turned up was enough. He was the man of my dreams. Because I was so taken in by external appearances, I ignored all the warning signs and ended up getting into deep, deep water.

This was my first serious relationship and I was very, very needy. I believed that all my problems would disappear as soon as I found someone who would love me. I invested all my happiness in what another person could offer me.

As the relationship progressed, the early excitement soon began to wear off. Quickly the cracks began to show and my partner's undesirable qualities became apparent in his actions and attitude towards me.

My neediness stemmed from my low opinion of myself, and my belief that I was lucky to have anyone pay attention to me. I really didn't believe that I deserved love. Before long, these beliefs about myself were being reflected back in the harsh words and abuse that I experienced from my partner.

Imagine my horror when he repeatedly told me I was ugly, that other women dressed better than me and made love better than me. Even this treatment wasn't enough for me to let go of the relationship. I still clung on for dear life. I tried to dress and act in a way I believed would make him value me.

Even though I was a student at the time I gave him money when he needed it. I even felt it was my fault when I started to experience physical violence in the relationship. One day, in the view of an elderly black man who was walking towards us, my partner reached out his foot in an attempt to kick me. The man's words stayed with me for a long time: 'She's not a dog.'

Life has a harsh way of making us wake up to reality. No woman deserves to be hit, slapped, punched, kicked, thumped, prodded, pushed or shaken. No woman deserves it and no woman has to put up with it. I put up with it because, at the time, I really believed that was all I deserved. I felt very much a victim, particularly when it came to close, intimate relationships. Ever since my earlier abuse I had felt disempowered and lacking in confidence. This relationship (whilst I am in no way condoning the physical and emotional abuse I experienced) simply reinforced what I believed about myself.

But there were also times when I displayed a fierce warrior spirit. I defended myself against many of his physical and verbal attacks. When I look back on that period in my life I realise that the real battle was going on inside my head. The person I most needed to make peace with was myself.

WISDOM COMES TO THOSE WHO LISTEN

As strange as it may sound, I really believe I called my first partner into my life. Underneath all the hurt I experienced, I always had a deep desire to find out how to love and respect myself.

Our lessons about life and ourselves do not always come gift-wrapped. The pain I felt in our five years together finally pushed me to a place where I could find compassion for myself and accept compassion from others. Many good friends – let's call them Earth Angels – showed up to help along the way. Earth Angels live as human beings. They are our friends, family, or even strangers who at different points step out, and whether consciously or unconsciously, help us along our way. I am thankful to all my Earth Angels for the support they gave me at a time when I was confused and lost.

A couple of days before writing this piece these words came to me: 'Wisdom comes to those who listen.' I wrote it down and kept repeating it in my mind. When we listen, we learn and we act from a wiser place. From the moment I met my first boyfriend I knew he was a womaniser, I knew he was unreliable. He turned out to be all those things and more. I can remember clearly the first time he physically pushed me in public. The warning bells went off loud and clear in my head. I just chose to ignore them.

When we don't have boundaries for ourselves other people will walk all over us. My daughter is ten years old and we discuss what is okay and what is not okay for her in relation to her interaction with me, her father, her family and friends. My goal is to instil in my daughter a strong sense of herself; a clear view of the boundary between what is and what is not acceptable.

At the age of 17, I had no clear boundaries. Because of the earlier violation of my personal space I didn't feel it was even worth bothering to establish them. In any case, I had lost faith in my boundaries being respected. If you or anyone you know has experienced sexual abuse the issue of boundaries may be a painful one. When our boundaries have been violated we must heal the violation of our sacred selves.

But, even at 17, I knew I needed to take action. I knew the way I was being treated didn't feel right and wasn't anywhere near what I deserved. But I didn't believe in myself enough to act on it. The same may be true for you. For instance, if you are locked into a lifeless relationship you don't have to stay just because you have been together for years, or for the sake of the children. These excuses are simply a delaying tactic.

Admit right now that you are choosing to stay exactly where you are. Now make a decision to change your choice and choose again.

Five years into my first relationship, I woke up one day and set myself free from the prison I had locked myself into. I took a look at the person I was with and I realised I really didn't want to be there any more. Suddenly his words and threats had no power over me.

Now he was like a mouse. And I was the giant. I told him what I thought, and what I felt. He, for once in his life, listened. We spent a wonderful weekend together, the best weekend of our five years together. Then we said goodbye. No tears were shed. Our words remained unspoken, yet their meanings hung in the air. Unconsciously he begged forgiveness from me. I forgave myself. A part of me healed. I took a step forward and moved my life on.

I had two more long-term relationships after this one. My second relationship forced me to face up to my low self-esteem. But I also experienced being hit in this relationship. I still had a lot of work to do on myself. Still needy, I attended workshops, had therapy, and put myself through a long-term personal development programme.

Over the years I was able to release a lot of pain and hurt from my past experiences. The more I worked on myself, the more I began to see that, in order to have a relationship based on healthy love, I needed to love myself. No relationship would make me happy until I found happiness within.

RIDING THE ROLLER COASTER

So where does all this leave us? What are the issues that we need to address in relationships? Let's begin by taking a proper look at heartbreak. Sometimes I know I'm a bit of a drama queen when it comes to this one. Not only do the tears flow but also, because I have been so used to playing out the victim role, I put on a damn good performance.

In the past I believed that having my heart broken really was the end of the line. Heartbreak brought up my worst fears of rejection. I acted like a broken woman. As far as I was concerned, my significant other was totally and absolutely responsible for what I was feeling.

I mean, I was the one who had been mistreated. Surely I was entitled to cry for days, wallow in self-pity, become depressed and be the most miserable person on earth. The only time I would resurface was when there was a glimmer of hope, a possibility that we could get back together again. Then, almost immediately, I'd feel relieved and the pain in my heart would ease . . . until the next time.

If the relationship was rekindled we would revert – for a few weeks at least – to the honeymoon period. We would only have eyes for each other. Then that dreaded moment would come. My partner would do something I didn't like, we'd have an argument and then he'd drop the bombshell – he had to leave/he'd found someone else/she was expecting their child. Then came the heartbreak and the pain and we'd be off on the roller coaster again.

Sounds familiar? At this point, out comes the voice of the victim: 'Look what he or she has done to me.' Our worst fear materialises. Now we move into heavy judgement of the other person. We project all the blame onto him or her, refusing to ask ourselves: 'What was I doing there in the first place?' 'What did I ignore?' 'What could I learn from the situation?' and 'What was my responsibility?'

If you are anything like me, and your heart has been broken more than once, you next move swiftly into full-scale defence mode. On goes the armour, out come the weapons: 'Out of the way, I'm in control!'

When you move into control all the pain you have been feeling is temporarily frozen. With a bit of help from the ego, you decide that, from now on, you will run the show, you will decide when you see someone/sleep with them/do anything at all with them. You might be in a new relationship but you make sure your partner knows who is calling the shots.

To people looking in on your relationship from the outside, you may appear really together, when in fact you are operating very independently of each other. Your desire to operate independently has over-ridden your need for trust, commitment, integrity, honesty and forgiveness in the relationship. Rather than forgive, you go to battle, determined to take control, and be in charge. There's only one problem – your partner, not wanting to face defeat, goes into battle too.

Ever been there? Then you know what it feels like. Your words become as sharp as swords, or they are like stones dropping into a silent void. If asked, you quickly launch into why you can't stand your partner, and how you don't know what you saw in them in the first place. This is the sign that you've reached a no man's land in the relationship. A pattern of boredom has set in, where you no longer know what attracted you to your partner in the first place. Often, when we get stuck like this in a relationship, we also get stuck in our lives as a whole.

When this happened to me, I didn't want to let go and I didn't want to forgive. Me forgive? Why should I? After all, it was always the other person who was the problem. They were the ones in the wrong. They should be asking for forgiveness from me. My ego ran amok. Forgiveness was the only way out.

When you move to forgive, it releases the pain trapped in your heart, gently dissolves it and replaces it with love. Then you can begin to view the situation and the person with new eyes. Suddenly they seem different because you are different. The forgiveness has brought a sparkle to your eyes, sweetness to your voice, honey to your touch. Now you appear irresistible because, through your honesty, the other person finally gets to see your true essence. Now you can have a genuine heart-to-heart communication, created in a sanctuary of trust involving honesty and risk-taking. This is the time to recommit to yourself and to the relationship. Or it may be the time to say goodbye and move on.

TENDING THE GARDEN

Recommitment is not about returning to the old ways of being. It's a new level of partnership. To maintain this new state, both individuals must be committed to tending what I call the relationship garden. For instance, your garden will require regular watering – to keep the roots of your relationship alive. You will also need to keep it clear of weeds by ensuring that your channels of communication remain open. The weeds are the old patterns of behaviour – make sure they do not take root again. By being honest you create the fertiliser that will feed your garden and keep your flowers blooming.

Your relationship, like a garden, will also change according to the different seasons. But a good gardener knows that, even in the depths of winter, spring is always around the corner, bringing the promise of new growth. Make sure you nurture your relationship garden, even in the difficult times, and it will bring you moments of immense pleasure and joy.

From this place, the relationship can naturally move into a state of leadership. Now both individuals can start taking charge of their lives, taking the steps needed to bring their dreams into reality, moving them closer to their purpose. Through the bond you have created, you both support each other in your endeavours. You are not threatened by each other's successes; you naturally want the best for each other. When things get tough you are there for each other. You know when to give, and you know when to step back. You trust your intuition and act accordingly.

Once the relationship has moved into this state of leadership, your everyday life will be filled with grace, ease and spontaneity. Your goals will naturally manifest around you. Before you know it, you will be easily and effortlessly working on joint projects. You will begin to create a long-term vision of what you want individually and what you want together.

Without a vision for your relationship, what are you working towards? Take a look at the relationships around you. Are there any you could learn from? Do you know of any relationships that have reached a place of leadership and vision? Where do you keep on getting stuck in your own relationship cycle? If you are unhappy in your present relationship ask yourself why.

Relationships can bring us our greatest joy and our greatest pain. They also tell us so much about ourselves. We can use them as tools for honest self-reflection. They are our toughest training grounds.

SELF-DISCOVERY EXERCISE
Relationship Assessment

WE OFTEN MOVE through relationships without really assessing how fulfilling or unfulfilling they are. Use the following questions as a guide to uncover the state of your relationship:

◆ On a scale of 0–10, how would you rate your present or most recent relationship?

◆ What changes do you feel you need to make in the relationship?

◆ In your Soul Purpose Journal write down your intuitive responses to the following questions: What is the purpose of your involvement in this relationship? What are you in it to learn? What are you in it to teach?

SELF-DISCOVERY EXERCISE
Do You Have What You Desire?

DO YOU REALLY know what qualities you desire from a partner? And are you asking for qualities that you yourself possess?

◆ Make a list of all the qualities you look for in a partner.

- Now make a list of how many of those qualities you possess your-self (be honest).

- Next, compare the two lists. Where do the gaps exist? What qual-ities do you need to work on?

It is often a challenge for a relationship to work when we expect a partner to behave in ways we feel unable to, or we expect them to possess qualities absent in ourselves. Focus on developing more of these qualities for yourself. When you can be a loving mate to your-self you are more ready to be a soulmate to someone else.

SELF-DISCOVERY EXERCISE
Digging For Buried Treasure

THE SAYING GOES that everyone comes into our life for a reason regardless of the quality of the relationship we have with them. Sometimes it may take a while before we realise the reason; and even longer before we realise the benefit of the experience.

At the time I could see nothing good about being in an abusive relationship. Years later I can see that this relationship taught me to have compassion for myself. It gave me the passion and determina-tion to empower others and myself. It was the point at which my soul reawakened me to my life mission. Even though I would not want to relive that and other experiences, this relationship was where I learnt about my strengths and the potential that I had.

All our relationships, good, bad or indifferent, teach us valuable lessons about ourselves and our relationships with the world. They are our fertile training ground.

This exercise requires you to let go of blame and the role of victim. Looking for buried treasure in the midst of what looks like a rubbish heap can be challenging. This is a call for you to be accountable. On a deeper level your soul called this person into your life so you could learn and grow. When we don't dig deep we lose so much valuable knowledge and information about ourselves.

Make a list of all the things that past and present lovers and part-ners have taught you about yourself. It may be aspects of your self that the relationship brought out; or as a result of the relationship you may have realised what you really desired for yourself.

SELF-DISCOVERY EXERCISE
Fulfilling or Dead Relationships?

THIS EXERCISE WILL help you assess the quality of the relationships in your life at present.

◆ Draw four large circles, one inside of the other.

◆ In the centre circle write the names of the people in your life who mean the most to you at the present time. This might be your children, partner, parents or a close friend.

◆ In the second circle write the initials of the next group of people who are really important to you.

◆ Do the same for the third and final circles. These may include the names of people you see occasionally but who you really like. As you move towards the outer circle these names should represent those people who are less important to you than the people in the first and second circles.

◆ Go back to the first circle in the centre. Give each relationship a number from 1–10 based on how you would rate the relationship at present. Ten is very fulfilling. Three means the relationship needs some work.

◆ Next go through each name in each circle and write down how you would really like the relationship to be.

◆ Now make a list of ways in which you could take responsibility for improving the relationship. For example, could you spend more time with a loved one? Could you write a letter to a friend to clear up a disagreement? Or why not send a card to a friend who you have not seen for a long time?

◆ Be really honest as you work through the names. After your review you may be willing to acknowledge that there are relationships that you wish to let go of.

Relationships, like all things in life, require our attention. Like a garden they need to be cultivated, dug up and replanted.

By taking out quality time to review your relationships you have begun the process of change you consciously or subconsciously desire. Don't be surprised if some of the very people whose names you have listed get in touch with you.

SELF-DISCOVERY EXERCISE
Natural Water Releasing Ritual

THIS IS A RITUAL to release a past relationship or friendship. You will require the loving assistance of a trusted group of sister friends, spirit sisters, a spiritual teacher or guide. It is best performed on the shores or banks of natural water (ocean, river, sea), in a place where you will not be disturbed.

◆ Wear any clothes or items of jewellery which you still have in your possession which were given to you by the person you wish to release. Otherwise, wear old clothes for the first part of the ritual.

◆ Begin by grounding and centring yourself.

◆ Take seven deep cleansing breaths. Bring the image of the person to the forefront of your mind. Visualise their face and hold the image for a few seconds.

◆ Sit as close as you can to the sea. Pour your heart out to the sea and tell Yemoja (a Yoruba deity, Goddess of the Sea) who it is you want to release. Take as long as you like. When you have finished take seven deep cleansing breaths.

◆ Visualise in your mind the person you want to release standing before you. Imagine you are attached to each other by a cord. Visualise the cord slowly disappearing, bit by bit, until it has gone.

◆ With the cord gone, turn your attention back to the sea or river and begin to walk into it. As you do so, imagine the person walking away from you in the opposite direction, severing all ties between you.

- Have the sisters/friends who are with you accompany you into the water. Go in until the water reaches your waist. When you have gone this far, repeat the following chant seven times:

'I give thanks for the release. My attachment is gone. The water has washed it away. 'I am free.'

As you repeat the chant, discard your clothes and dip yourself fully into the water. Your guides or friends may wish to gently hold you as you dip your body into the water.

- Now visualise yourself free to move on to reach your higher good and to find true love and friendship.

- Walk back to the shore where your sister friends will be waiting for you with a new set of clothes. Do not look back into the sea. By the water's edge leave an offering of food or flowers, a small stone, crystal, silver or copper coin to Yemoja.

- As you dress ask the women to sing a song that embodies the beauty and freedom that your release will bring you.

- If the weather and location are right, light a small fire. Gather around the fire. Affirm a positive future for yourself. Thank the sisters who have taken part in your healing release.

- See the flames of the fire as the light of new life.

- Give thanks.

CHAPTER 3

Blessing Our Bodies

THE BODY IS TRULY the first wonder of the world. Take a minute to stop and think about the millions of functions your body performs. It is greater than any computer or living animal on this earth.

I have never felt so proud of my body as I did when I gave birth to my daughter Aida. Before my pregnancy I knew I did not truly honour and respect my body. Life has a way of moving you towards different understandings of yourself. Pregnancy was one of those miraculous movements.

For the first time, I was totally in tune with what my body needed and what was going on inside it. I told my body how beautiful it was, I pampered and nurtured it, and it showed. I blossomed like a flower through my pregnancy. People would stop me and tell me how wonderful I looked. I felt strong and healthy.

This was completely different from my previous experience. For most of my childhood and my teenage years I simply disconnected from my body. Everywhere I went, I was always one of the tallest girls. Back then, I wasn't comfortable about my height and it showed. Not only was I tall but I was very slim. My breasts were small. I had no backside and no curvy hips. Throughout my school years I was called 'Longers', 'Tall Girl' and 'Giraffe'. I really didn't see any need to appreciate my body. This was because I was carrying a lot of guilt and shame about it as a result of the sexual abuse. Instead of appreciating my body, I projected all my negative feelings onto it.

--- 66 ---

In addition, I grew up in an environment with hardly any positive images of black women. The few we saw were often stereotypical, aggressive and sexual. Or we were subjected to the downtrodden, mammy types in the old black and white films. There were few positive role models of black women feeling good about themselves. For all these reasons, my new relationship with my body during my pregnancy marked a turning point in how I felt about myself. I was 26 years old. Most people were really surprised when I told them of my pregnancy. They had seen me very much as a career woman who had no time for children. My relationship with Aida's father was very rocky. He was emotionally unavailable throughout the pregnancy. Yet this did not affect me in the way such things usually did. I felt as though I had accessed another part of myself. I was aware of the pain I should have been feeling but the energy just kept on pushing me to take care of myself and the child I was carrying. For nine months I loved my body with all my heart.

On the day I gave birth to my daughter, naturally, without any pain relief, it was as if heaven and earth moved inside me. It is hard to fully describe the surge of power and joy that took over the whole of my body. In that moment I made a decision to transform my life, to follow my dreams. I felt connected to God, to my daughter, and to the body I had been blessed with all my life.

OUR BODIES, OUR SELVES

If you were asked to sculpt your body as a work of art how would you portray it? Would it be a small flower? Or would it take the form of a sturdy tree, with branches outstretched, embracing the world? Your body is the heavenly sculpture you were sent to earth with. When you were a baby you loved every inch of that body. You had no guilt, no shame, and no feelings of inferiority. You loved your body exactly as it was. But then, somehow, something changed. Perhaps you were criticised, or compared to your brothers and sisters. Sooner or later this society forces us all – very, very early in our lives – to stop appreciating and loving our bodies and to start criticising them.

Women, in particular, have a very hard time with their bodies. Our bodies have been sexualised and exploited, and had all the sacredness and honour squeezed out of them. It is time for us to return to and reclaim the divinity of our bodies.

How do you bless your body? What do you say to it each day? If we say negative things, whether consciously or subconsciously, the subconscious mind accepts what we say and sets about putting into place exactly what we tell it to. Start to change your body conversations. Plant new seeds in the fertile soil of your mind. Cultivate a new, loving relationship with your body. Stand in front of a mirror each morning and repeat the affirmation ten times.

'I love my body.'

Your body requires more than food. You can bless your body by giving her adequate rest, by making quality time for her to relax, by treating her to sensual massages, by caressing her skin with aromatic baths and oils and by feeding her with life-sustaining foods. Take her on walks. Sit with her in sacred spaces on the earth. Feel the peace and tranquillity flow through her. When you bless your body you bless yourself. It doesn't take a great deal of money to bless your body.

Three years ago I decided to take up running. I hadn't run since I was 16 but I knew I had to do something. I was always tired and worn out. My energy levels were really low. It was one of the best decisions I've ever made. By pushing past my pain barrier and 'can't go any further' belief, I found that I had a natural affinity for running. Running put me firmly back in touch with nature, I released loads of toxins, and instantly felt energised. Running fuelled my creative ideas and my writing. It re-established my relationship with nature, through which I connected with the divine. Moving my body brought my spirit alive.

Any kind of exercise fights disease, and lowers cholesterol levels and blood pressure. It helps us fight cancer, it builds bones and promotes weight loss.

It is also a great reliever of stress and depression. Whenever I find my spirits sinking I know it is time to dance. Dancing is guaranteed to remove any tension or stress. Many mornings will find my daughter and me dancing and singing at the tops of our voices before we commence our day.

In Africa, dance has traditionally been seen as a healing ritual. The body was the vehicle through which the spirit or deities could be communicated with. Today, dance still holds a central place in African and black communities around the world. Many of the traditional dances of my ancestors have survived in different forms throughout the diaspora. To my parents' generation, having left their homes to live in Britain, and finding themselves in a strange environment, dance was a way of letting go of their emotions, and reconnecting with their rich cultural heritage. There have been times when I have found myself forgetting where I was, as I moved freely from the centre of my being and surrendered to the music. Dance can take you into a natural state of trance. You can literally dance your way through blocks and connect with a higher power.

Celebrate the magnificent temple of your body. Adore her, adorn her, and love her from the inside out. Take time out and be with her. Have fun with her, receive pleasure from her, feed her foods that please and nourish her. Wrap your arms tightly around her. Tell her you love her. Close your eyes. The ecstasy of your body awaits you.

THE JOY OF FASTING

In the same way as we cleanse our homes, we need to cleanse our bodies and our minds. Fasting puts you in tune with a different spiritual frequency. It makes you more open. Fasting is to the body what clearing out clutter is to the home. But remember: always seek professional advice from your doctor or holistic practitioner before fasting.

Three years ago I had volunteered to be a spiritual teacher's assistant on a one-year programme. In preparation for a weekend workshop, all staff members were instructed to fast 24 hours before we arrived. I decided that I wasn't having any of it. So I didn't do it.

When I arrived, the fact that I hadn't fasted was discussed. I didn't see why it was such a big deal. I was told I would have to fast during the weekend. My mouth dropped open. This particular retreat centre always prepared wonderful food. On top of that I was told that the universe would choose the number of hours I was to fast for. The numbers '24', '36' and '48' were written onto separate pieces of paper. I was asked to choose one at random. And yes, you guessed right. The one I selected was 48 hours. That meant I would be on a fast for almost the entire weekend.

I was depressed. For the first few hours I wallowed in self-pity. I scowled at everyone eating dinner until eventually I forced myself to retire to my room. But slowly, over the next 48 hours, I began to notice a shift. Gradually, the lack of food began to take a back seat.

Instead, I became more acutely aware of myself and my thought processes. In the workshop room I felt much more grounded and connected to the energy of the room and the people within it. I began to feel lighter. People started noticing a change in my face. I found myself getting totally immersed in a sacred ritual which allowed me to access an even deeper part of myself.

By the third day I was feeling on top of the world – energetic, at peace with myself and my surroundings. By fasting I had given my soul some spiritual food. The lesson was an invaluable one.

DETOXIFYING

We take in many toxins in the food we eat: sugary food, fatty food, food that is processed, chemically preserved and treated with all kinds of pesticides. Even the air we breathe is toxic. Walking through South London, where I live, toxic gases pour from the constantly flowing traffic. Physical toxicity tends to be reflected by emotional and spiritual toxicity.

The reality is that what goes in normally stays in. It may take years before you release the harmful effects of what you eat, and what you breathe. But, even if you can't see these toxins, take a moment to reflect on how you personally feel them in your life.

For example, after abstaining from alcohol for six months (during which time I didn't miss it and felt great), I started drinking again. But now I notice that after even one glass I immediately get depressed. My energy is sapped. I become very irritable and all I want to do is sleep. I feel pretty much the same with certain foods like dairy produce, spicy meals (which I love) and white rice.

This is where detoxifying comes in. When I go on a detox diet, drinking only water and eating fresh fruits or vegetables, I feel completely different. Over a short period of time my energy quadruples, I feel focused and alive. That's not to say that I don't experience mood swings and low energy periods. But I see that as a natural by-product of the cleansing process.

Detoxing or fasting is your declaration to the body that you are embarking on a programme to clean all its organs: the kidneys, the colon, the intestines, the bowels, and the bloodstream. You are clearing out the dead and diseased cells.

Fasting or detoxing also brings a host of other benefits. By clearing out your physical system, you open the door for the emotional system to get cleaned out too. The emotional system reflects the body and vice versa. You will find yourself more tuned in to what you need to let go of emotionally.

The fasting or detoxing process is a time of purification, a time of healing, and a time of change. It is a chance to create a new you. I once fasted for 72 hours and felt a closer connection to God as a result. The purification eradicated the toxins that prevented my alignment with God and the universe. My conversations with God, through prayer, became the food for my soul. I liked what I had become but lack of discipline meant that, once I stopped fasting, it would be some months before I was to return there.

But I knew the truth. The truth is that when I am filled with fear and self-doubt, when I have no other solutions to the challenges before me, fasting is one way in which I can take action to cleanse myself. Fasting helps me understand what I really need for myself – spiritually, emotionally and physically. Listen to the messages when you fast. They will guide you to the sacred place where you will discover what you really should be doing with your life.

YOUR CROWNING GLORY

As a young girl, I thought Rastafarians (who wore their hair in locks) were the bravest people on earth. They defied all the social norms, all the taboos, and allowed their hair to evolve organically to an undisciplined, untailored look. They were my heroes.

Secretly I longed to be like them. But to do this would have meant rebelling against my Christian upbringing. My mother disliked locks intensely and even more the people who wore them. The more she spoke out against locks, the more I admired them. The person who had locks had risked ostracism, criticism and even ridicule of who they were and what they stood for. To me, these were people with a strong sense of their own identity and a strong faith.

Locksing my hair remained a distant dream for many years. Instead I tried just about every hairstyle there was for a young black girl of my generation. By the time I got to secondary school I had graduated to two cornrow plaits down the side. My hair never grew long. Instead it was short, thick and curly – the opposite of what I desired. I wanted long hair, blowing in the wind.

There was nothing at all wrong with my hair. But I couldn't see that. I had been raised in a society that equated prettiness with long hair. By the time I was attending college I was going all out to lengthen it. Every Sunday my best friend Pauline would come over. We would light the gas stove, place the hot iron comb in the fire, heat it up and proceed to press my hair. Before long, my hair would appear silky and almost double in length. I happily endured the burning smell of the hair grease oozing down my temples, forehead and neck and the numerous burns to the ears. After this I had a straight perm, then a curly perm.

Next came the braids. It took several attempts before I got the right style. Each weekend, when I arrived home, back from university, my mum would shake her head in horror. A mass of black flowing horse's hair plaits entwined with gold braids certainly caught people's eye, but not always for the right reasons.

Then I really took the plunge and cut my hair off. It was a brave thing to do. I did everything to ensure that no one mistook me for a boy. This new style required plaiting and greasing at night and it had to be kept constantly trimmed, otherwise it would start to grow out and look messy. This I couldn't contend with, so back came the plaits.

The next phase saw me reverting to wearing headwraps. For almost a year after giving birth to my daughter I wore my hair in wraps. At last I didn't have to worry about what my hair looked like and I felt confident. I believe the headwrap is symbolic protection for the spirit. With a headwrap on, I felt regal and infused with the pride of my African ancestors. My favourite brown wrap was my grounding wrap. With that on, I felt safe and protected. When I wore my blue wrap I felt like having fun.

Then, a painful end to a five-year relationship marked a new phase. I decided that I would grow my hair and return it to its natural state. I felt like a little girl again. The washing, the drying, the greasing, the brushing and the combing became a healing ritual for me. I felt as if a part of me had been reborn. This was the most peaceful relationship I had had with my hair for a long time.

Then I gradually discovered new parts of myself, mourning the outgoing relationship whilst embracing the future. At this point I was wearing my hair naturally in twists and loving it. I was redefining myself as a black woman and exploring my sexuality. My hair reflected these changes. Then, in 1991, I took the next natural step and decided I was ready to locks my hair.

Locksing is as much an internal process as it is an external one. It marks a spiritual shift in consciousness. I had become increasingly interested in the spirit world and wanted to do more work on myself. I had also begun a new relationship and entered a new phase in my life. My hair accurately reflected these changes. It marked my transition to embracing my fearlessness and womanliness. I became proud of who I was and of the female body which I inhabited.

At work I was the warrior woman, daring to step into unknown territory, willing to break the rules and to do whatever was necessary to get the job done. At the same time I allowed my hair to breathe and develop its own rhythm. At first it was shy and slow to grow. But gradually the roots of my hair began to extend in the direction of the sun and the moonlight. In those days I did very little to my hair, apart from watch it grow. The locksing process taught me how to be patient and have faith. This was a process of surrender. Like growing a healthy garden, I knew I had to plant the seeds and wait.

I felt proud of my hair, proud that I had broken the taboo of what hairstyle a nice black girl should have. My uncultivated hair made me feel like a strong black woman who took pleasure in defining her own beauty. Looking back, this was the part of the locksing process that I most cherished.

The wildness of my hair, the not knowing how it would form, gave me a thrill, a sense of adventure, a ripple of excitement. My head felt special for the first time in my life. I felt that my locks were a blessing, a daily honouring of my head.

Now I have seven years' growth of locks. A lot has happened to me in those seven years. I like to think that, like my hair, I have grown too. I am at peace with the fact that, at some point, I will say goodbye to this crown on my head, to mark the closure of one phase of my life and to open the door to another.

To tell the truth I look forward to it, to a new beginning, new growth, and to the chance to develop a new, deeper, more meaningful relationship with the spirit of my head. But until then I will continue to honour this crown of glory, until it is time to release its energy and move on to new pastures.

Why not spend an hour or more indulging in your own special nurturing hair ritual? If you cannot get to a spa, set it up at home. Purchase your favourite shampoo and conditioner. Wash your hair and leave the conditioner in while you take a relaxing bath. Take a good look at your hair when it is wet. How different is it to when it is dry?

Towel-dry or blow-dry your hair, plait it, colour it, and try a new style. Enjoy spending quality time with your hair. Make it a regular ritual. This is not about spending a lot of money on a trip to an expensive hairdresser. This is cleansing time for you and your hair.

PURIFYING YOUR BODY THROUGH A SWEAT LODGE

The sweat lodge is an ancient Native American purification ceremony aimed at body, mind and spirit. In many ways the sauna is a modern equivalent of the traditional sweat lodge.

Modern day rituals based on ancient traditions are valuable as long as your intentions are pure and in keeping with the original tradition.

Understanding the traditions of the sweat lodge will help you in conducting your own personal purification ceremonies using the modern day technology of the spa. You will find a guide to preparing your purification ceremony on pages 78–80. Meanwhile here is a more detailed explanation of the sweat lodge ceremony and ritual.

Before Entering the Sweat Lodge

Traditionally, the sweat lodge was made from the branches and leaves of the willow tree. The willow tree carries the energy of love and is the tree to which we can bring our tears. The lodge was circular at the base and had no windows so that there was minimal light. The stones for the sweat lodge were heated on a fire and ceremoniously placed in a small pit in the centre of the lodge. Before entering a sweat lodge it was customary to be purified by fasting or by being smudged with sage or cedar smoke. You entered the sweat lodge by crawling through a small opening on your hands and knees. The Native American people believed that this was how we would keep in touch with all other life forms. Going on your hands and knees puts you in touch with the spirit of humility and humbleness.

Entering the sweat lodge, which is warm but dark, is rather like re-entering the womb. Women gathered and entered the sweat lodge in their natural state. As they sang and prayed they let go of pain, giving it back to Mother Earth. They might listen to the beautiful singing of a sister outside the lodge who was pregnant and unable to participate in the ceremony.

A visit to a steam room may invoke the release of negative energy through the sweating process. Why not plan to fast or eat only fresh or organic fruits and vegetables the day before. Commit to drinking 8 glasses of water 24 hours prior to your visit. Prepare yourself for your purification by smudging yourself with cedar or sage. Exfoliate or scrub your skin before and after entering the steam room. Sing a song that moves you. Say a prayer or repeat a mantra aloud. Give yourself over to the process. It is the energy of surrendering which will support the transformation and allow purification to take place. Your purification ceremony can be done time and time again. Anoint your skin lovingly with your favourite oil. Spend the rest of the day if possible with yourself. Do something creative or go for a walk in the park. Prepare yourself a candlelit dinner. Write in your Moon Journal. Sip a glass of hot or cold water with added slices of lemon as you curl up to read a favourite book. The more you clear internally the more you will shine in your own light.

SELF-DISCOVERY EXERCISE
Detoxification

ALWAYS SEEK PROFESSIONAL advice from your doctor or holistic practitioner before you start a detoxification diet or fast. Try, as far as possible, to eat organic produce.

Breakfast and Dinner

Have fresh fruit but try to avoid bananas and oranges (oops, I love them) because of their acidity. Have some hot water with a slice of lemon to start the day.

Lunch

Have a freshly made salad of raw vegetables (shredded greens and grated root vegetables dressed with a little lemon juice).

Drinks

Drink plenty of water – at least 6–8 glasses a day. Water is a great purifier. It helps to flush toxins from your system. Avoid sparkling/carbonated water, as this can interfere with the fasting and detox process. Drink as much herbal tea as you like.

SELF-DISCOVERY EXERCISE
The Spirit of Your Hair

YOUR HAIR COVERS the spirit centre of your head – the crown chakra. Women have a long-term relationship with their hair. Use the following questions to reflect on your relationship with your hair over the years:

- Write a piece in your Soul Purpose Journal that describes and explores your relationship with your hair over the years.

- Which hairstyles have you been happiest with?

- In what ways have your hairstyles reflected inner changes in you?

- If you could choose right now to change your hairstyle, what would you change it to?

- Rejuvenate your scalp and hair by using nourishing essential oils. Create an aromatic tonic for the scalp of four drops each of lavender, rosemary and jasmine. Mix together and massage gently into the scalp. The blend helps to moisturise, removes toxins and reduces dandruff.

RITUAL
Brushing Your Body with Love

YOUR SKIN, THE CLOAK of your body, eliminates huge amounts of toxins and negative energies which are stored beneath its surface. Removing these dead skin cells and toxins, as they rise to the surface of the skin, makes room for the production of new cells.

The ancient art/ritual of skin-brushing helps to cleanse and flush the lymphatic system. Skin-brushing works magic on the outside of your body. Through skin-brushing you are speeding up the process by which the skin cleanses itself. In much the same way as cats clean themselves, skin-brushing is your personal skin-cleansing body ritual.

- Use a natural fibre body brush or mitt.

- Begin by brushing the soles of your feet. Brush firmly, with love, in slow, circular motions. As you do so, be conscious of your breath. Reflect on the different journeys your feet take you on every day. Thank them for their reliability and their strength.

- Now work your way up your body, brushing the front and back of your legs, your calves, your knees, your thighs, your abdomen, your buttocks, your stomach.

- Place your breath consciously in the stomach region and think about the birthing process – either the birth of human life or the birth of new projects and ideas. Gently caress this area of the womb before you continue.

- Avoid the breast area when body-brushing. As you brush your body, bless each curve, each shallow dip, the flat regions, the full regions, the smooth and the rough surfaces of your skin. Give thanks for all the different regions of your body.

- Continue body-brushing your back, your neck, your shoulders and your arms. As you continue, imagine you are brushing away all the negative emotions that you have been holding onto.

- Imagine unblocking your pores and allowing past negative memories to drain away.

- Now visualise filling the pores of your skin with golden light, representing the new memories of your future.

- Take as much time as your body rightfully deserves. Take several deep breaths to mark the completion of your Brushing Your Body with Love ritual.

- Now give your body a big hug. Feel her tingle as she enjoys the refreshing feeling. Give her a loving body massage with a deep cleansing cream or aromatic body oil. As you anoint each part of your body, bless her with loving words.

- Give thanks and be ready for the start of a brand new day.

SELF-DISCOVERY EXERCISE
Revitalising Foot Spa

OUR FEET SUPPORT US every day. Often we forget they are there. But, like any other part of the body, they require nurturing and care.

According to the ancient healing practice of reflexology, there are areas or zones in the feet connected to all the major organ systems in the body. By stimulating and kneading these specific points the healer can detect and treat specific conditions.

By immersing your feet in the luxury of a foot spa, you will revitalise your whole body. Here are two foot spa recipes for you to try. Simply add the ingredients to a bowl of hot water, immerse your feet and relax.

Orange Geranium Foot Spa

> 2 drops geranium essential oil
> 2 drops orange essential oil
> 1 tablespoon citric acid

Dead Sea Salts Foot Spa

A wonderful remedy for hot and sweaty feet. Dead Sea salt is available at most chemists or natural health food stores.

> 1 tablespoon Dead Sea salt *or* 3 tablespoons natural sea salt
> 10 drops peppermint essential oil

RITUAL
Millennium Woman's Purification Ceremony

THIS PURIFICATION ritual works well when you are feeling overwhelmed, need to release negative thoughts, and have a desire to cleanse and purify your body. It is based on the Native American sweat lodge ceremony – an ancient purification tradition.

◆ Twenty-four hours before, commit to eating fresh/organic fruit and vegetables for the day. Otherwise, eat as healthily as possible.

◆ Aim to drink a glass of mineral water every hour or two throughout the day.

◆ Prepare the items that you will need for your purification ceremony:
  – Your Soul Purpose Journal
  – Spa equipment, including facial packs and shampoo
  – Body exfoliants
  – Towels
  – Favourite outfit

◆ On awakening, if possible, drink a glass of freshly squeezed fruit or vegetable juice. This contains concentrated nutrients and enzymes that rush through your system to restore stamina.

◆ Start the day with a warm bath and do the Brushing Your Body with Love ritual (see page 76).

◆ Make a list of your intentions for the day on one piece of paper. On another, write down what you want to release. Burn your list of what you want to release.

◆ Sit in silence for a few moments, or meditate, or perform something physical (like a dance). Smudge yourself using a smudge stick of sage or cedar or use a natural Indian incense before leaving the house.

◆ Arrive at the spa. If you have to go to work beforehand, try to stick to eating fresh, nourishing food throughout the day. Continue drinking a glass of water every one or two hours. Aim to enter the spa at least three hours after you have eaten.

◆ Remove your clothes in silence.

◆ Begin by taking a shower and scrubbing your body to remove the dead skin cells.

◆ Wash your hair, put on a face mask, use a body wash or body exfoliant, as you desire.

◆ Before you enter the steam room, visualise yourself being encircled by a protective circle of white light.

- Enter the steam room, gently get yourself into a comfortable position, and begin a gentle inhaling and exhaling rhythm.

- As you feel called, take seven cleansing breaths and stretch your body out as much as possible. Sing or say a prayer throughout your time. Surrender yourself to the heat. Do not go over the maximum time allowed in the steam room.

- Drink lots of water throughout. End by washing your hands and face and say:

'I am cleansed and purified.'

- End by repeating an affirmation three times aloud with feeling.

- If you have access to a pool, ceremoniously dip your whole body in. Embrace the water as you let your negative emotions slip away. Lie on your back and float or swim a few lengths but nothing too strenuous.

- Leave and take a shower. As you shower, feel your skin and see it as new skin that has been cleansed. Bless your body as you go along. If there is a full-length mirror take a good long look at your beautiful body and affirm her.

- Lovingly anoint your body with oil.

- Dress in your favourite outfit.

- Adorn your hair.

- Finish with a gentle nurturing ritual such as writing a loving letter to yourself in your journal to end your purification ceremony.

- Enjoy a relaxing mug of hot water with lemon as you curl up in bed and finish the day by writing in your Soul Purpose Journal.

- End with a closing ceremony (see page 18) as you lie in bed. Visualise yourself being showered with an abundance of symbols of gratitude that say thank you to you for taking quality, healing time for yourself.

- Look up at the sky, the moon (if it can be seen) or the stars before you go to sleep.

SELF-DISCOVERY EXERCISE
Buddha Belly

YOU CAN AFFIRM the different parts of your body by giving each one a different name. For example, the birth of my daughter left me with ripples of excess flab. Over the years I have added to this. I love this part of my body. I am so proud that this outer skin was the protective layer which shielded and protected my daughter for nine months. I love its elasticity, its flexibility. I can squeeze into clothes easily because it is so pliable. I had women in stitches on a workshop as I expressed how I felt about this part of my body.

The name I have blessed this area with is my 'Buddha Belly' – how appropriate. You can also have fun positively affirming and renaming different parts of your body. Pay special attention to the areas you are most critical of and bless them with a positive name.

By renaming these areas you are transforming your relationship with them. Here are some examples to get you started:

'I love my Buddha Belly.'
'I love my Mother Earth skin.'
'I love my bluebell eyes.'
'I love my enchanting forest of hair.'

SELF-DISCOVERY EXERCISE
Pamper Yourself Day at Home

GIVE YOURSELF a special treat and enjoy a day pampering yourself at home. The shops are full of reasonably priced beauty products – purchase all the items you need beforehand.

◆ Start by applying a face mask, perform the Brushing Your Body with Love ritual (see page 76), then take a relaxing bath.

◆ Give yourself a self-massage with a deep moisturising or aromatic oil.

◆ Treat yourself to a glass of natural fruit juice or spring water every one or two hours throughout the day.

◆ Switch off the phone, unplug the computer and relax.

MEDITATION
River Blessing

RIVER BLESSING CAN be performed either as a meditation or as a ritual on the banks of natural flowing water.

- Relax, deepen and enter sacred space. You find yourself at the edge of an enchanted forest. The trunks of the trees radiate the smiling faces of ancient people. You are not afraid. As you walk past the trees, the branches sway in the breeze, sprinkling you with blessings. Thank each tree in turn as you follow the path into the forest.

- You enter the forest, and then find yourself standing on a huge, open, green field. In the distance you can see a range of mountains. You begin your walk across the plain. It is a beautiful, sunny day. The gentle breeze cools you down. Enjoy your walk. Pause for one minute.

- You hear the sound of running water. You cannot see where the sound is coming from but you continue your walk.

- Suddenly the plain descends down a slope. As you carefully make your way down, you are greeted by the sight of a small river of silver water flowing fast, through the middle of the plain. The water shimmers as the sun's rays bounce off its surface. You arrive at the edge of the river. You kneel and say a prayer.

- The water is crystal clear. Looking into it, you see the most beautiful coloured fish and the most gorgeous shells. This is an enchanted river with magical powers. You are thirsty, you cup your hands and drink the water. You gaze at the crystal clear reflection of your face in the magic river. Pause for one minute.

- In your stillness, the fragrance of fresh lavender from a butterfly lavender plant nearby washes over you. It is now time for you to physically perform your river blessing.

- Cup your hands again, dip them into the water and pour the water over the top of your head, saying:

'Bless the spirit of my head so that it may guide and bless me each and every day.'

◆ Cup your hands together, dip them into the water and pour the water onto the region of your third eye (on your forehead, between your eyebrows), saying:

'Bless the wisdom of my third eye so that I will trust and act on my inner knowing and intuitive powers.'

◆ Cup your hands together, dip them into the water and pour the water over your eyelids, saying:

'Bless my eyes so that I may see more clearly.'

◆ Cup your hands together, dip them into the water and pour the water over both ears, saying:

'Bless my ears so that I will hear "all" that is said to me and understand the message behind the words.'

◆ Cup your hands together, dip them into the water and pour the water over your mouth, saying:

'Bless my mouth so that I may speak my truth.'

◆ Cup your hands together, dip them into the water and pour the water over your heart, saying:

'Bless my heart and fill it abundantly with love.'

◆ Cup your hands together, dip them into the water and pour the water over your womb, saying:

'Bless my womb as she gives birth to my creative powers.'

◆ Cup your hands together, dip them into the water and pour the water over the front area of your vagina, saying:

'Bless my sexual organs as I embrace my sensuality, the healing power of my sexual energy and my connection to Mother Earth.'

- Cup your hands together, dip them into the water and pour the water over your feet, saying:

'Bless my feet that I may find and walk the true path of my Soul Purpose.'

- Now that you have completed your river blessing, rub your hands together in the water saying:

'I give thanks to my hands and the service they give to me with every day.'

- End by pouring water over your face, your hair and the top of your head. Stand quietly by the edge of the river and reflect on the blessing you have performed and the words you have spoken.

- Feel yourself filled with a peaceful, loving energy for yourself and the universe.

You may adapt this ritual and perform in the bath.

CHAPTER 4

Busyness is a Disease

Breath creates balance and harmony in the body, mind and spirit. It brings a gentle breeze to the whirling rush of busyness. Breath is a wind of healing fragrance with which to slow things down.

I KNEW THINGS had got terribly out of balance when I missed my daughter's school prize-giving ceremony. As she stepped onto the podium, she looked in vain for the smiling face of her mother to confirm her achievement and to share her pride. Instead, I was on the other side of London, weighed down with deadlines. I was so busy – I actually forgot this important occasion. By the time I remembered, it was too late. I felt so bad.

Driving home that evening seemed to take forever. I imagined, over and over again, the scene that would greet me when I got home. I visualised my daughter's face. What would I say to her?

There was an eerie silence in the house when I entered. On seeing me, my daughter burst into tears. We held each other tight as we both released our pain and disappointment. This was a harsh lesson, a bitter realisation that my busyness had completely unbalanced my life.

MORE HASTE, LESS SPEED

In today's world, busyness is often seen as a measure of success. Modern technology has given us ever quicker ways of communicating. Mobile phones, faxes and the Internet have created expectations of instant response.

But whilst, at times, speed is okay, constant busyness can suck all the joy out of life, bringing tension, stress, pressure and worry. Busyness takes us out of the natural flow of life and makes us swim against the current. This consumption of our time is often a reflection of our inner 'dis-ease' with life itself. I have realised that I often use busyness as an excuse because, if I stop, I will discover that what I am doing is not what I really want to do or is unnecessary. It also means that I will have to face up to the truth about where I am at.

Intuitively, I know when a spell of busyness is approaching. I start forgetting things, and miss important personal engagements. I put off doing the smallest of tasks and get into a chronic pattern of lateness.

I find myself disconnecting from my feelings. There have been times when I have increased my intake of alcohol in the hope of feeling more relaxed after a busy and stressful day. But alcohol and drugs do not deal with the root of the problem. They simply create a false sense of security, eroding our anxieties for a short time.

During your busy spells the power of meditation – to still the mind and go within – is essential. Meditation, if built into your daily activities, is a healing tonic that will support you greatly at these times.

The first step is to address your busyness before it becomes established. Regular meditation is a preventative measure, rather than a cure. Energetically, busyness creates a masculine vibration, an ability to get things done. To create harmony and balance, the masculine vibration has to be balanced with the feminine. By connecting with your feminine energy you gain an opportunity to feel, to be intuitive, and to know when to take time out and let go.

If our lives are always filled with busyness, how will we hear the voice of God? By connecting with my spirit, I have been able to inspire and re-energise myself throughout busy periods. What I do is to simply stop, take the time and space to sit quietly in silence, and meditate.

Silent meditation allow us to give up our desire to be in control. It opens us up to limitless possibilities, which – if we remain open – feed our intuition and spirit.

Simply through stopping, I have created new solutions to existing problems. I have approached tasks in a gentler and more graceful manner. I have connected with any negative feelings, released them and cleared the way to move on.

PUTTING OFF TILL TOMORROW . . .

Being busy does not increase your self-esteem. In fact it does the opposite. It erodes self-esteem. In the past my apparent busyness has been a cover for my tendency to procrastinate.

I used to procrastinate on just about everything – from writing a report to avoiding someone I believed I had let down. In both my professional and personal life, I would leave tasks until the 11th hour. Then I'd have to pull out all the stops, stressing myself out in the process, in order to get the job done.

I have learnt some painful lessons from operating in this way. Hard work went unappreciated because I failed to complete a needed report in time. I used to produce work below my capabilities simply because I did not give myself enough time. I often felt bad and guilt-stricken because I had missed important deadlines.

It's hard to believe but I once even missed a friend's wedding because on the day I had to rush out to the shops to get an item I had put off purchasing during the week. Another time, the night before flying out to Barbados on holiday, I was frantically typing up a tender application for a training consultancy I knew I would have been brilliant at. End result – the computer crashed, losing most of the pages I had typed. I was at the end of my tether and decided to call it a day. Procrastination stops you fulfilling your potential and kills your self-esteem. I often used to feel guilty because of my tendency to procrastinate. But guilt is simply blame projected inwards. Rather than taking responsibility for my actions, I just felt bad and fed on the victim role. But feeling bad and being a victim does nothing to alleviate the problem of pro-crastination. The only way to bring about change is by making the decision to act.

TAKING ACTION

By taking action we respond physically. This is the opposite of what we do when we procrastinate, i.e. nothing. So many times, by completing a task immediately, rather than procrastinating, I have significantly increased my self-esteem and self-confidence.

Taking action is a real motivator. It is a necessary requirement for those who are successful. Apparent failure does not stop the successful person; it actually motivates them to continue until they get it right. In pursuit of our true purpose, we all have experiences that cause us to doubt ourselves. Fear of what we might achieve and fear of failing are both strong reasons to procrastinate.

I was once asked which I feared most – success or failure? I realised I feared both. And my busyness was a way of avoiding the things I really needed to do in order to embrace my true purpose. Even while writing this book I procrastinated about getting it completed. My excuse was always the same – there were so many other things I had to do. In the end, even *I* got fed up with the worn-out record.

Yet, once I decided to take control and enjoy the evolution of *Soul Purpose*, the writing process itself lifted my spirits. I acknowledged what I needed to do in order to connect with the quiet space inside me. Now my self-esteem no longer relies on an external appearance of busyness, and I increase my confidence by being realistic about deadlines. I commit to saying 'No' even when I am feeling pressurised to say 'Yes'. And I have transformed the energy on the word 'deadlines' by referring to them as 'lifeline dates'.

Through internal reflection I was able to acknowledge that my busyness was making me disconnect from my spirit. It was a way of blocking out the blessings that flow when I stay connected to my source. Praying and meditating are essential, especially during hectic periods. These activities help me to stay grounded and connected to the well of power and inspiration that flows through me. As a result I become an open vessel, no longer blocked by busyness. When it all gets too much, I simply let go, move out of the way, and open the door for spirit to come in.

SELF-DISCOVERY EXERCISE
Take a Break from Busyness

TAKING TIME OUT of a busy period provides you with space to listen to the voice of your higher power. In peace and stillness, you will be able to move beyond the limitations and negative energies that the disease of busyness brings.

When you find yourself going through a busy spell, try the following exercise:

◆ Give yourself permission to stop whatever task you are involved in, and go for a walk. Or, if you are able to take some quiet time at your desk, simply sit still and do nothing for ten minutes. If all else fails, excuse yourself and go and sit on the toilet. This is the one place where you are guaranteed uninterrupted privacy.

◆ Firstly, connect with your breathing. Your breath is a stream of vibrant light energy that feeds your spirit, thoughts and actions. Breath is the source of life. Many of us are cheating on our life source through incorrect breathing.

◆ Take a deep breath and inhale through your nostrils to a count of four. Feel the air you inhale move down past your chest to the pit of your stomach. The air should push your stomach muscles outwards.

◆ As you inhale, visualise yourself completing or letting go of this busy spell. See yourself somewhere, doing something that you love. Keep this image at the forefront of your mind each time you inhale.

◆ Now exhale slowly, to the count of four, visualising all the things you want to let go of right now in your life. See all the negative energy dissolving through the release of breath.

◆ Continue inhaling and exhaling, and spend some quiet time reflecting on your current state of busyness. Listen to the voice of your intuition, the voice of truth within you. When we're too busy we drown this voice out.

SELF-DISCOVERY EXERCISE
Beat the Busyness Blues with a Soothing Bath

BATHING IS A wonderful way to beat the busyness blues. When I was young, taking a bath was something the whole household did every morning. I would rise early so I could savour my time in the bath and also guarantee myself the luxury of enough hot water.

Bathing is about privacy, renewal and the joy of maintaining a healthy body, mind and spirit. It also has an element of ritual. At the Pentecostal church I attended with my parents, water was treated as holy and sacred and used for spiritual cleansing, for baptisms and for the christenings of babies.

The ancient Khemetians (my ancestors from Egypt) were masters of holy baths and soothing aromas. I named one of my ranges of bath salts after the Khemetian queen Cleopatra (which was also the name of one of my grandmothers). Cleopatra knew all about the healing properties of bathing and became famous for her baths of asses' milk.

Water is the heart of the bath; salts, fragrances, essential oils and flowers give us the scent. Scents – sweet, strong, pungent or subtle – can move, stir, tantalise and almost hypnotise. Our ancestors used fragrance in sacred rituals as well as in their daily lives. So we are bringing sacred energies into our baths when we use scent in this way. When we use a healing combination of oils to restore our body, mind and spirit, we return to the element of water, which was home to us all before we were born.

For me, bathtime has helped bring harmony to what I can only describe as a very hectic lifestyle. I use my bath as a retreat in the early morning, in order to replenish my energy in readiness for the day ahead. The physical action of lying down is healing and restorative in itself. When you are busy it is easy to treat bathtime as just another activity that needs to be quickly completed. Why not relax and savour it in order to get the full benefit.

If you think the only time for a soothing bath is before bed or as soon as you get up, think again. Sometimes I complete all my morning chores, get my daughter off to school, and then take great pleasure in preparing my bath. Other times I take my bath an hour before she is due home.

For those who work full-time, a bath immediately after arriving home makes a nice bridge between the hectic work day and the domestic front. I find it calms me down and gives me new energy to cook dinner and engage in meaningful conversation with my daughter.

If you have trouble sleeping, a late-night bath will soothe frazzled nerves and slow you down, relaxing your body in preparation for sleep.

When you have your bath, close your eyes and listen to the sound of the water. Feel its vibrations. Silence is healing. Embrace it. Enjoy it. Place slices of cucumber on your eyelids to cool your face and soothe strained eyes.

Keep tensions and pressures under control by enjoying a quiet bath any time. The following healing, aromatic baths will help soothe the busyness blues.

Oshun Sunrise Orange Bath

Orange is my favourite essential oil, perhaps because according to the Nigerian Yoruba tradition my deity is the goddess Oshun. She is the African Aphrodite, Goddess of Beauty, Love and Sensuality. Orange is the colour associated with Oshun who heals with cool water. Her voice is carried in the rivers, lakes, waterfalls and streams.

  3–4 drops orange essential oil
  1.5 litres (1 gallon) distilled water
  600 ml (1 pint) semi-skimmed or organic milk
  2–3 tablespoons honey

- Mix together the orange oil and distilled water.

- Add the semi-skimmed or organic milk, a natural moisturiser for the skin.

- Now add the honey and pour liberally into bath water for a fragrant morning soak. Sprinkle the bath water with orange blossom flowers.

- Sip some orange juice along with this bath. On a special day you can add champagne to the bath or to your juice.

Camomile Flower Bath

For a restful sleep when you are overtired and need to relax. Preparing the flowers is part of the relaxation process.

  75–100 g (3–4 oz) dried camomile flowers
  600 ml (1 pint) water

- Steep the flowers in boiling water for 1 hour, strain and add to warm bath water.

- Fill a vase with your favourite summer flowers and place so that you can see them whilst you are in the bath.

- Put on your favourite music, lie back and relax.

Lemon Mint Bath

This is one of the most refreshing baths you can indulge in on a hot summer's afternoon.

> 1 tablespoon fresh mint leaves, crushed
> 1 cup fresh lemon juice
> 2 teaspoons almond oil

- Steep the crushed mint leaves in the lemon juice overnight in the fridge.

- Strain the next day and add the almond oil.

- Pour under fast-running water for a delightful and cleansing bath.

- If you like, add 1–2 teaspoons of lemon mint juice to a glass of iced water and sip it while you soak.

Lavender and Basil Bath

> 4 drops lavender essential oil
> 4 drops basil essential oil
> 4 drops cinnamon essential oil

- Add all the essential oils as you run your bath.

- Swish the water with your hand before you enter. Enjoy.

Elderflower Milk Bath

This bath has a gentle, sweet scent, which will revive your spirit and refresh your skin.

> 1 tablespoon elderflowers
> 600 ml (1 pint) milk

- Soak the flowers in the milk for 3 hours. Then warm gently, strain and add to bath water.

◆ Rose petals (or 2–4 drops rose essential oil) may be added to the milk if a more fragrant bath is desired. (Pure rose essential oil is expensive – you can substitute rose geranium essential oil if you like.)

Tonic Bran Bath

This is a soothing and wonderfully aromatic bath. It is warming and very good for the skin.

225 g (8 oz) wheat bran
225 g (8 oz) rye bran
600 ml water

◆ Combine all the ingredients in a large saucepan and bring to the boil.

◆ Steep for 10–15 minutes, strain and add to warm bath water.

Buttermilk Bath

This makes a wonderfully soothing and moisturising bath for chilly autumn days.

125 ml (½ cup) buttermilk
60 ml (¼ cup) orangeflower water
2 teaspoons almond oil

◆ Combine all the ingredients in a pan, heat gently and pour under fast-running bath water.

Hot Ginger Friction Rub

A great way to warm up quickly on a cold autumn day, this rub stimulates the circulation and softens the skin.

15 g (½ oz) fresh grated ginger or dried ground ginger
250 ml (1 cup) water
3 teaspoons almond oil
2 teaspoons witch hazel

◆ Steep the ginger in boiling water for 20 minutes.

◆ Then mix 3–4 teaspoons of the ginger water with the almond oil and witch hazel.

- Massage directly onto wet skin while in the bath, using a loofah, brush or coarse cloth to rub briskly.

- The remainder of the ginger mixture may be added to the bath if desired.

Fragrant Oatmeal Bath

This is a really soothing bath for the skin.

8–10 tablespoons of ground oats
2 tablespoons of dried lavender flowers
2 tablespoons of sweet almond oil

- Combine all the ingredients in a mortar and pestle and grind until the mixture has the consistency of coarse powder.

- Tie the powder in a small bag of muslin cloth and suspend under fast-running bath water.

- Along with this warming bath, sip a cup of warm herbal tea, with some cloves or cinnamon or even a shot of brandy added. A warm drink in a warm bath will promote healthy sleep. Be sure to bath in a heated room, and your relaxation will be complete.

Simple Rosemary Bath

Rosemary is a fragrant and stimulating herb when infused in bath water. This will warm you up after a long, frosty winter's day.

50 g (2 oz) fresh rosemary
500 ml (2 cups) water

- Put the rosemary and water in a pan and bring to the boil.

- Steep for 15 minutes and add to bath water.

- Add 1–2 teaspoons of bath oil if your skin is feeling dry.

Ginger Tea Bath

This is a wonderfully fragrant bath. It is good to breathe in the steam of this bath to ease tightness in the chest if you suffer from asthma.

25–50 g (1–2 oz) fresh grated ginger
2 teaspoons lemon juice
500 ml (2 cups) water

◆ Put all the ingredients in a saucepan and bring to the boil.

◆ Steep for 15 minutes and add to warm bath water.

◆ Add 1–2 teaspoons of bath oil if your skin is feeling dry.

SELF-DISCOVERY EXERCISE
Say No to the World and Plug Yourself Into Peace

WHEN THINGS GET on top of you, simply say 'No' to the world.

◆ Close your front door, unplug the phone and switch off the telly.

◆ Instead, plug yourself into inner peace and solitude. Solitude provides inner guidance and energy. If your private space is invaded, remember:

'No' is a complete sentence.

SELF-DISCOVERY EXERCISE
Combat Busyness at Work – Sanctify Your Workplace

HAVING A SACRED SPACE at work, however small, can keep you calm and centred even when you're under pressure.

◆ Create a special place on your desk, or maybe on a windowsill. It doesn't matter how big or small it is.

◆ Arrange some flowers, a plant, a stone, a crystal or a small item or object that you treasure in your designated space.

◆ When things are hectic take time out to meditate on your space, object or image. Take a few minutes for yourself, focus on your breathing and quietly say a prayer or ask for guidance.

◆ Don't wait until things are on top of you before you focus on your space. Get into the habit of saying prayers and blessings throughout the day.

SELF-DISCOVERY EXERCISE
Learn to Use the Time You Have

LIKE MOST PEOPLE, I constantly need more time but I have finally realised that I had better get used to effectively using the time I have. If we had all the time in the world we would still complain about there not being enough. The trick is to learn how to master time, rather than letting time be your master.

Remember, nothing is so important that it can't wait a little longer. If you stop for a while, everything will still be there tomorrow. By using time to serve you, you will be better equipped to deal with those things in the future.

Try this simple approach to time-managing your daily tasks.

◆ First thing in the morning, write down all the tasks you have to complete during the day.

◆ Next to each one, write down how long it will realistically take to complete.

◆ Mark each item with a 'P' for Priority or a 'CW' for Can Wait.

◆ Begin your day by focusing on getting the priority items out of the way. Decide how much time you will allocate to tackling them. Get used to sticking to that time and using it for that purpose only. Once you have completed a task on your list, cross it off. Make a new list every day.

◆ Next, write a list of things you would like to do for yourself – let's say an activity that you enjoy, but you tell yourself that you simply haven't got the time to do. Make a list of four or five things.

◆ Next to each activity, write how long it will take to do.

◆ Choose one item from your 'I would love to, but simply haven't got the time to' list. Decide how much time you can realistically spend on this activity at least once a week. Even five minutes is fine, although allocating more time would be better. For instance, I find that I love to do creative things, like sticking an image in my pocket book of dreams (see Chapter 12) or writing a letter to a friend. Five minutes allocated to an activity like this could be just what you need to get that letter finished. It's worth taking that time. It will leave you feeling energised, with a sense of personal fulfilment.

♦ Schedule at least 20 minutes walking time into your week, even if it only means walking around the shops. (Running frantically around the shops in your lunch hour is not real walking time.) Walking through a park or an open space is ideal. And being out in the open will give you the energy you need to get your tasks completed.

SELF-DISCOVERY EXERCISE
Where Does Your Day Go?

DO YOU OFTEN SPEND your whole day running from one appointment to another? Sometimes the day goes so fast that every-thing you've done merges into one. Part of cultivating the life you want means examining the way you live. Begin by examining what you do in a day, then you can start making the day work for you.

You will need at least an hour, your diary (if you have one), your Soul Purpose Journal and a pen.

♦ One evening, make a list of all the activities you have completed during the day. Include every task or activity (such as taking a bath, washing the dishes, going to the post office, popping into your child's school, writing a letter).

♦ Read over your list. What are your thoughts? Are you surprised at the amount you have actually done? Or are you horrified by how little you've achieved? Can you see any patterns? Are there things that you could cut down on? How many activities in your day were unplanned?

♦ In all the day's comings and goings, how much of the activity was for you? Break this down into hours and minutes. Give yourself a score based on the total number of hours you were awake (between getting up and going to sleep). Say you woke up at 7am and went to sleep at 10pm. Your total hours awake would be 13. Now look back over your list and see how much time you had for yourself. You might find that you had only 15 minutes before going to bed that was just for you.

When I first created this exercise I tried it out on myself. But I had to stop – I couldn't bear to continue writing out my list. There was so much in my day that was about other people. It made me feel really tired. If you get this feeling it's a sure sign that you need to slow down and create activities in your daily life that harmonise your mind, body and spirit. If you don't get this feeling . . . great. Just keep putting more of what you love doing into your daily routine.

SELF-DISCOVERY EXERCISE
Create Your Own Self-Healing Ritual

WHEN I SLOW DOWN I have noticed that time slows down too, and there seems to be more of it. Suddenly I am able to achieve much more than when I was moving at the speed of light.

This exercise enables you to incorporate more time for yourself into your week. Creating a self-healing ritual, based on a daily or weekly routine activity or task, also helps to bring balance, spiritual focus and positive energy into your everyday life.

You will need your Soul Purpose Journal and a pen.

◆ Begin by grounding and centring yourself. Imagine that you are creating a self-healing ritual for yourself to perform daily or weekly that will strengthen your spirit and sense of well-being. This may be a normal everyday activity. Your goal will be to add your own special dimension to this task. Your personal touch announces to your spirit that you intend to honour the activity in a sacred way. Your ritual should last for at least ten minutes.

◆ Write down three ideas, tasks or activities that you perform regularly which may be suitable for turning into a ritual. The three ideas I came up with were: taking a bath, writing in my journal and going for a run.

- Next, decide which activity you will base your ritual on. Take a few minutes to think about how you can make it more meaningful, make it feel special or add a new dimension to it.

- Start to write down your activity as if it were a sacred ritual that was being presented to you. Go beyond the activity or task itself and allow the spirit within to guide you and bring to life the sacredness in the activity. As an example, here is the first part of the self-healing ritual that I wrote for taking a bath (if you don't like writing, you can record your self-healing ritual on tape):

We were born into a baptism of water. We spent nine months of absolute bliss in an abyss of black magic, inside our mother's womb. There we lay safe and secure, connected to the soul of our mother, fed through the sacred passage of the umbilical cord.

As I reflect on my first relationship with water, I prepare a warm bath with scented essential oils and aromatic bath salts. A pouring of creamy organic milk and two lavish heaps of smooth-running honey are added to my sensual bath water.

I light a candle and an incense stick. The scents of my favourite oils burn slowly in the background. I turn off the lights. For a few minutes I breathe in the darkness. I am not afraid. I know this is a good place for things to come forth.

I take another deep breath and ceremoniously remove my clothes. Now I am naked, just like a newborn baby. I step into my bath. The smells from the water fill me up. I lie back, close my eyes and return to that dark abyss of black magic that was once home. Here I am safe. Safe to think and safe to be. I can savour the sweetness of life and release the bitterness of my thoughts through breath.

I surrender my body to the water. She holds me lovingly in her stillness. In the background the silence of the morning is music to my ears. Now I am open to the voice of God speaking to me.

Some days I am quietly still; other days tears merge with the water in my bath; other days I am moved to sing or pray.

The sweet-smelling oils and fragrances anoint my skin. The honey creates sweetness for the coming day. I smell and feel like a princess. I give thanks, step out of the bath and give myself a bear hug as I dry my skin.

When it is time to finish I cleanse my skin, enjoying the aromas of the oils and salts. I say a blessing and smile at myself in the mirror. What a wonderful way to start my day.

♦ Give yourself as much time as you need to create your ritual. Your goal is to make a seemingly ordinary task or activity special and meaningful.

♦ You may wish to write your ritual onto index cards and create a ritual box to keep them in (adding new rituals whenever you wish). Keep your ritual box on your altar or in a special place.

CHAPTER 5

Leadership is Action

IN MY EARLY YEARS I had an 'on-off relationship' with leadership. In some parts of my life I was a natural leader. In others I would seize up at the mention of it, only to curl up with frustration when others took it on. My annoyance was really with myself.

A recent conversation with a dear friend, during which I was being unduly hard on myself, prompted me to re-examine my relationship with leadership. Her words at the beginning of our conversation were: 'You have always lived life on the edge.'

I suppose being so tall has always given me an edge. I was always noticed at school and college, and my height gave me an air of authority. At primary school I distinctly remember telling the whole class to be quiet when my teacher had left the room for a few moments and being praised for my impromptu action. It was natural for me to take the responsibility of keeping the class under control when my teacher was out of the room.

This role followed me through most of my years at school where I was always given positions of importance and responsibility. I don't remember being afraid. Being a leader gave me an inner confidence. It was very much the same at home. I loved initiating projects, dreaming up wild schemes and being the centre of attention.

Leaving secondary school and attending college I found myself moving further away from my centre. College was full of new faces, unexplored friendships and unclear expectations. My natural talent for putting myself forward dwindled as I tried to make sense of myself in a new environment.

My first leadership test had in fact been the sexual abuse I had experienced as a young girl aged seven. My abuse offered a tremendous opportunity for inter-generation healing within my family. But I had not realised that I was to be the vehicle for this healing. My test was to either face the challenge head on or choose to ignore it and become a victim. I chose the latter. Subsequently, when faced with other experiences which brought up similar feelings and emotions, I would withdraw rather than face the leadership challenge which was being presented to me.

For years I told myself that leadership was for others and not for me. I really did not want to face up to the fact that I had the power and the potential to change my life. At the same time I was always being given opportunities to lead. However, I only needed to experience one small failure and I would berate myself and doubt my leadership potential.

At work, in my personal relationships, in my social circle, I had a big presence, which radiated out and drew others in. Yet these relationships weren't always plain sailing. The truth was that leadership created havoc within me. Being uncomfortable with myself, I was uncomfortable with most aspects of leadership in my life.

WHAT IS LEADERSHIP?

True leadership requires 100% commitment. It requires you to turn up and keep going despite the obstacles and challenges. This means that, inevitably, you have to surrender yourself to the possibility of success and the possibility of failure – yes FAILURE.

Let's spell it out, spit it out, say it out loud: FAILURE is something that many of us are afraid of. The sound of that word sends us running for cover! It has stalled the most brilliant of minds. It is the red stop sign that holds you back from your dreams and keeps you from leadership.

It requires a huge dose of courage not to deem your experiences failures. Courage to stay on course, to breathe through the pain and the challenges. I have yet to meet anyone who, deep down inside, enjoys criticism. And the faintest sign of failure always invites criticism – not only from others but, more importantly, from ourselves.

To bring leadership into your life, you need to keep moving despite the setbacks. You need to quieten the voice of negative self-talk by just taking action. Those around us, those who have gone before us, and those we admire and look up to, have all failed at some point in their lives. Have you not been inspired by their tenacity, their willingness to accept and demonstrate to the world their shortcomings? Have their tears not moved you and subsequently moved the world? The truth is that their influence is magical, uplifting and awesome. It is better to have tried and failed than not to have tried at all.

This is why it is so important to study the leaders around you. Not in order to belittle them but as a gentle reminder that they too had bridges to cross, doubts to overcome, demons to face, and failures to make peace with. Focus on the skills, abilities and spiritual principles they drew on to see them through. Leaders, above all, have to weather the storm. They stay clear and focused on their vision or goal, especially when they are under attack.

BRAVING THE SLINGS AND ARROWS

Whether you are taking on leadership in your own life by being true to yourself, or you are in a leadership role in your community, career or the wider world, you cannot avoid being attacked.

All great leaders faced attack – Jesus, Gandhi, Malcolm X, Martin Luther King, to name but a few. Attacks go with the territory. They strengthen your conviction and courage, and give you the opportunity to face fear and master it.

But it is the *fear* of attack which is the greatest cause of millions leading mediocre lives. We would rather do nothing to rock the boat than face the uncertainty and responsibility of leadership. It takes courage to get up and speak when others are silent. It takes courage to stay committed to a project even though you know people are talking behind your back. But facing the attack helps you discover an untapped inner strength.

Some years back, I was invited to conduct a live interview with civil rights African American activist Angela Davis in front of an audience of about 700 people. I admired her greatly and felt very honoured to be asked. Totally unaware of the storm that was brewing up behind the scenes, I stayed at home, focused on my research and prepared myself for the big day. As the date of the interview drew closer, unpleasant rumours began to reach my ears. And one notable black newspaper carried an off-the-cuff derogatory remark about the unknown Jackee Holder interviewing Angela Davis. Still undeterred, I stayed focused on the task ahead.

On the day of the interview itself there were a few hiccups. Angela arrived late. The audience was eager and at the same time agitated. I scanned the crowd, looking for friendly faces. Some were there to support me but others were just hungry for blood. After the interview, I was criticised left, right and centre; my questions were not good enough; I was not a trained journalist; why wasn't a prominent person in the black media asked to interview her? Nothing I had done was acceptable.

When your centre is not stable you are easily rocked. I was too reliant on other people's approval and not on my own. I also learnt my first harsh lesson about being in the public eye: never give your full attention to the criticism. I did. I gave myself over to all the negativity. I allowed myself to sink lower and lower into an abyss of self-blame and self-criticism. Even though I received cards from friends sharing their appreciation of what I had done, I could not balance the praise against the criticism.

The last straw was when, a few days after the interview, a close friend called round to see me. I felt glad to see her after all the pressure I had been under. But it turned out that she had a completely different agenda. My friend's intention was to criticise every aspect of my interview. I sat there speechless. Her words sliced through the air like poisoned arrows aimed at my heart. I let them in.

Her strategy worked. I retreated from the world, wounded. I vowed not to venture out again into the public arena. My confidence knocked, my self-belief shaky, I would not be a visible target for attack.

Fortunately, this decision to stay in hiding lasted only a short while. I was blessed in having supportive, loving friends and a very caring partner. Eventually my spirit moved me to take responsibility for my life and my subsequent healing.

TRUE LEADERSHIP

I share this experience because I believe that many people are in some way fearful of what others may say or indeed what they think about them and what they stand for. Leadership is about staying true to your Soul Purpose, no matter what.

True leaders survive despite attacks, despite setbacks and despite failures. However this does not mean that leaders should not be open to feedback. What it means is that we should act with integrity, and, in the midst of criticism, respond to the truth of what is being said and abandon the rest.

When you have a strong sense of self, what others say or think does not matter. In the past I have measured my success by the way other people have seen me. But leaders see themselves clearly. They have a vision of who they are. They know where they are heading and they keep on moving. Leaders may be afraid sometimes but they do not let their fears stop them.

Leaders stand strong and secure in the presence of others who feel strong about themselves. They are not shaken by other people's power. In fact, they welcome it. I have witnessed this in the black women I have come into contact with through the Face to Face empowerment workshops. I have worked with women who do many things better than me, be it public speaking, writing or organising. I take great pride in honouring the strengths of others.

What excites and inspires me is how our lights can shine brightly together, creating even greater light. My purpose is to empower. When I see women out there transforming their lives, taking charge of the world, my soul is happy, because I know I'm on track and that the work is being done. It doesn't matter if others become more successful than you, what is more important is that you define and value your own personal vision of success.

My vision is of a world where we each work from our true centres, where we live a life of spirit. A world where we can join together to pursue our collective dreams and desires.

Great leaders give others the grace and inspiration to do what they have to do. They guide individuals to be where they want to be. Leadership requires you to keep your own counsel, to stay connected to your spirit and to be true to your Soul Purpose. Your goal, right now, is to find the leader in you and embrace her with all your heart.

SELF-DISCOVERY EXERCISE
Mentor's Spirit

I ONCE WENT TO a two-day workshop focused on achieving your goals in the business world. The Scottish motivational speaker, Jack Black, who was leading the workshop, was taking us through a guided meditation. We had just visualised ourselves entering a room where we were to meet our assigned Board of Life Directors – our mentors. We had to visualise our Board members.

I had no idea who my Board of Life Directors would be, so when Maya Angelou walked into my meditation I was caught by surprise. In my early 20s Maya Angelou had been a great inspiration to me. Her book *I Know Why the Caged Bird Sings*, and all the volumes that followed, really spoke to me. I believed I had long since replaced her with other inspirational mentors, but her presence brought to life the blessings she had given me in the past. During my meditation she recited the following poem to me:

> You may write me down in history
> With your bitter, twisted lies,
> You may tread me in the very dirt
> But still, like dust, I rise.

Sitting in my chair, I began to shake as the words anointed me. In the distance, to the sound of drums, I could hear the healing baritone of her voice getting ready to caress me with another of her poems – *Phenomenal Woman*. I surrendered to the power of her spirit, presence and influence in my life. She stood there before me. I could not stop the tears.

Next to enter was Nelson Mandela. I had not counted on a man sitting on my Board of Life, but his gentle presence totally overwhelmed me as I connected with the courage etched in his very being. We stood gazing at each other. Somewhere in the back of my mind the face of Marianne Williamson (spiritual teacher and author) started to form but it was Nelson who spoke the words. A year before, I had written out this same piece, inserting my name whenever the words 'your' or 'you' were used, in order to make it more personal. Nelson Mandela spoke these words to me during my meditation:

Jackee, your deepest fear is not that you are inadequate.

Jackee, your deepest fear is that you are powerful beyond measure.

It is your light, Jackee, not your darkness that frightens you.

Ask yourself, who are you not to be brilliant, gorgeous, talented and fabulous?

Actually, Jackee, who are you not to be?

You, Jackee, are a child of God.

Your playing small does not serve the world.

There's nothing enlightened about shrinking so that other people won't feel insecure around you.

Jackee, you were born to make manifest the glory of God that is within you.

It is not just in some of us; it is in everyone.

And as you, Jackee, let your own light shine, you unconsciously give other people the right to do the same.

As you, Jackee, are liberated from your own fear, your presence automatically liberates others.

The tears continued. I surrendered to the potency and sheer brilliance of these words. By now I was completely open. Even though I was in a room with 400 people I felt alone. As Alice Walker walked into the room I simply surrendered to the spirit of this Earth Angel. She did not speak. She just soothed me with her eyes. Her healing presence was more than enough.

Last to enter was Oprah Winfrey. She stood regal before me, reminding me that courage faces fear and thereby masters it. Some months later I was to read an article by her entitled *The Courage to Dream*. With her by my side, what more could I want?

A week later, I was clearing clutter from a desk drawer and happened to come across a postcard of Nelson Mandela. I had read about creating a Life Board of Directors collage and had already collected images of writers for a creativity altar I was planning to make. I decided that I would create a collage dedicated to the mentor's spirit. It would include members of my Life Board of Directors and writers that I have been inspired by. My collage was entitled *The Mentor's Spirit*. Here's what you have to do to create your own.

◆ Collect together images of your mentors, role models and people you would like to have on your Board of Life.

- Create a collage on a large poster-size sheet of paper.

- Write a thank-you note to one or more of your mentors, and add your thank-you note to your collage.

- Place your collage in a part of your home where you can see it every day.

I have placed my mentor's spirit collage on my bedroom door so that I can view it from my bed. I often stand before it in silence and meditate on the abundance and richness of my mentors. For all that is within them is also within me. This is also true for you. When things get on top of you, simply call on the spirit of your mentors.

SELF-DISCOVERY EXERCISE
How to Untap the Leader Within

DO YOU FEEL BLOCKED in terms of your leadership abilities? Use the following as a guide to unearth your leadership potential:

- Identify someone you admire who is a leader in your family, work or community environment.

- What skills/qualities do they demonstrate as they go about their daily lives?

- Which of these skills do you possess?

- Which skills do you need to develop?

- What steps will you take towards developing these skills over the next month?

- Follow the lives of people you admire, observe them in the media, read their autobiographies/biographies or write to them.

- Send a thank-you letter to someone you admire. Tell them how you look up to them.

SELF-DISCOVERY EXERCISE
What Makes the Great Great?

ASK YOURSELF THE FOLLOWING questions in order to discover more about your own relationship with leadership:

- What is it about the people you admire, the leaders you look up to, that makes them who they are?

- What specific qualities or skills do they have that you believe the vast majority of us do not possess?

- What percentage of our society has the potential to be remembered as heroes in the halls of fame?

- What makes you a hero in your ordinary life?

There are Martin Luther Kings, Mary Seacoles, Sojourner Truths, in every community. The universe is waiting for you to rise up and take your rightful place. What are you waiting for?

SELF-DISCOVERY EXERCISE
Leadership Acceptance Speech

OPPORTUNITIES APPEAR from nowhere. Don't be caught off guard and unprepared. Treat each day as if this was the day for you to give your finest speech. Leaders must always act like leaders rising to the occasion when a leadership opportunity occurs.

- Write your own acceptance speech for a leadership award.

- Stand up and read it aloud, imagining that you are reading it in front of a large audience.

CHAPTER 6

Empowerment

T HE WORD 'POWER' has been debased by the patri-
archal systems of our society – they have used it for oppression.
Many women have denied themselves the right to fully connect
with their power. My work has been all about reuniting women
(including myself) with the powerful women that we really are.

POWER WARRIORS

Put simply, empowerment is a state of being, of living, based on
sound principles. Principles that affirm who we are from the inside
out.

Empowerment is about commitment to our lives and our spiritual
growth, and determination to live out our Soul Purpose. It means
that we are focused and working towards our highest good.
Empowerment means realising who we are, as defined by our soul. It
is about taking firm action to move our lives in the direction of healing and recovery. It is about acknowledging that, to connect with
our inner power, we have to do our inner work, our soul work. Only
when we open up to our soul can the spirit move in. From this place,
we can empower our lives in so many ways.

Empowerment has no room for procrastination. When procrastination rears its ugly head we know that we have simply chosen not
to act. We have chosen to 'dis-empower' ourselves. I know this only
too well. When I procrastinate I am simply in fear. Fear of what?

Often it is a fear of success – I don't do my best because it might just mean that I get what I want. Or it may be a fear of failure – I fear failing, based on how I will view myself as a result, and how I believe others will perceive me. Lack of action moves us away from taking charge and away from our power.

When I take action my self-esteem flourishes. It has a ripple effect on other areas in my life. Taking action in my career encourages me to take action in my relationships, it pushes me to write to that creditor, it forces me to do my annual accounts. Living an empowered life means bringing back order, focusing on the things we really want to change.

LEAVING THE COMFORT ZONE

So many people moan about wanting a better life, yet they are afraid to do the work. I started empowering my life the day I faced up to what I really wanted for myself; when I faced the mess my life was in and took charge. When we avoid the messes and run away from our fears we are not living an empowered life.

So much of our time seems to be spent responding to urgent demands placed upon us by other people. Busyness takes us away from our power centre, depletes our energy and wears us down. When we are empowered we can invest in quality time with ourselves because we know we are worth it. We know that spending time outdoors, in nature, provides us with the energy and the inspiration to get that report completed, to get that idea off the ground, to make that call.

The comfort zone is a place where we are comfortable with the predictability of our lives and our relationships, even though we know inside that we are not really fulfilled. We stay in the relationship, even though we know the love has gone. We moan and groan about our jobs but make no effort to leave. The comfort zone saps our energy, creating a false reality that makes us believe that this is where we really want to be.

Leaving the comfort zone requires movement. Movement mobilises you to take action. It is movement that unleashes the power warrior inside you. And your inner power warrior can help you understand how to move through life in an empowered way without having to go to war.

When you act, without waiting for things to happen, you put the ball in your own court. When you decide that you will no longer be the victim, then you become a true warrior. The true warrior has faced her fears and has set about cleaning up the different areas of her life. Because she is being proactive, rather than reactive, life opens doors to her, doors that she would have been afraid to enter when she was operating from a place of fear.

Let me give you another example. When I know that I cannot pay a bill I can do one of two things. Firstly, I can contact my creditors and let them know that my payment will be late. Or, secondly, I can ignore the letter when it comes and hope that it will go away. Which is the most empowering action? Which one will leave me feeling powerless? The point is that avoiding problems usually gives us increased stress, when we could be energising ourselves by taking charge. We cannot avoid the challenges that life sends us. None of us is protected from these experiences. But, whilst we don't have control over what happens to us, we *do* have control over our responses to those events.

When we tune into our internal power we realise that it is ours, and no one else's. Because the heart of our power is located in our souls, its true essence can never be taken away from us. This is the power of our highest good.

Think of a time in your life when you have acted according to your heart and your intuition. Now think about the effect that action had on people around you. Try not to focus on the short-term effects. What about the long term? This kind of action almost always liberates those involved and creates less pain and hurt for everyone in the long run. This is the essence of our power. We are most powerful when we act from a place of inner knowing.

You block your power when you have unhealthy, negative beliefs about yourself. Your mind is your most powerful tool, and it is deeply affected by the beliefs you feed it with.

For instance, make a list of ten goals that you have. Then write down what you really believe your chances of achieving each goal to be. What do you notice? Are there some negative beliefs holding you back from fulfilling them?

Bringing your negative beliefs to the surface can be a way of killing them off. Negative beliefs prefer to stay underground, in the dark, poisoning your life. Shine a light on them and they begin to shrink. By taking action you immediately decrease their power. Now you can start believing and embracing the positive.

CIRCLES OF POWER

When I run workshops and seminars on empowerment I often use an exercise called 'the power circle'. Each woman shares a time in her life where she felt she acted powerfully. The examples bring home the truth of how amazing we are: stories of women saving other women's lives, transforming their lives against great odds, standing up for themselves, taking huge risks, acting on their intuition, the list is endless. These are not necessarily company directors, these are Earth Angels, spiritual beings, ordinary women like you and me. So often, it is acting on the sixth sense of intuition which lies at the heart of these women's stories.

When we empower our lives we grow like trees. Our power is the root of the tree. The leaves represent our courage, the abundance that awaits us, our limitless creativity, intuitiveness and resourcefulness. We are natural born leaders. When we are in touch with our power we move through the world with greater ease, confidence and sense of our own worth.

When we come together as powerful women our energy vibrates and touches other women around us. By holding hands in sacred circles we share our power collectively. When we strip away our masks we can be ourselves and move beyond our self-imposed limitations.

Living an empowered life is your divine inheritance; it is a sanctified gift from God, through which you can manifest your Soul Purpose here on earth.

SELF-DISCOVERY EXERCISE
Energy Words

THIS EXERCISE WILL HELP develop and focus your sense of strength and power.

◆ Make a list of 21 things that you love about yourself. Begin the sentence with, 'What I really love about myself is that I am ...'

◆ Don't hurry, but take this time to really connect with all that is precious about you.

- Next circle all the words that vibrate with energy and jump out at you. These words often point out your power points. I call them energy words. Choose 21 words from your list.

- Using the 21 words create an affirming poem.

SELF-DISCOVERY EXERCISE
Asking for What You Desire

IF YOU DON'T KNOW what you desire, how are you going to get it, find it and claim it as yours?

For years I felt guilty about asking for what I desired and having my needs met. You might have a similar story.

- Make a list of all the things you really desire for yourself. Is it a change of life, more passion and joy? Maybe you long to go on retreat, or be in a relationship with a loving partner. Once you can name it then you can claim it. You are now one step closer to achieving your desires. Use the word 'desire' instead of 'want'. The root of the word 'want' is 'lack of'.

SELF-DISCOVERY EXERCISE
Roots of Your Power

AT THE ROOT OF your personal power lie your belief systems. When your belief systems are rooted in healthy self-esteem, your personal power will flourish. If your belief systems are toxic they create a stranglehold on your power base. An empowered life includes assessing your belief systems, turfing out negative beliefs and laying healthy new foundations.

- Make a list of areas in your life that you find challenging.

- Next write down a sentence that accurately describes what you believe about each area or issue. Make sure these are your authentic feelings. Is it your truth?

- Read through your list. What does your list tell you about your authentic beliefs? Your authentic beliefs are the foundation upon which you have built your life. These are the laws by which you are living.

- Are you ready to make a change? Right, let's go. Take a blank sheet of paper and make a new list of positive and self-affirming beliefs. You cannot change what you don't acknowledge. You are rebuilding your foundations.

- Be sure to go back as far as you can. Sankofa, an African bird symbol whose body faces forward, while its head faces backwards, reminds us to go back to our roots, heal ourselves, and then move forward.

SELF-DISCOVERY EXERCISE
Hour of Power

NEGATIVE WORDS ARE like swords; they hurt when used. Positive, affirming words revive our hearts, soul and spirit. This exercise focuses on positive affirmations combined with a period of silence to create an hour of power. It requires a commitment of one hour each day for seven days.

- Each morning on rising open your Soul Purpose Journal and make a list of nurturing affirmations for seven minutes.

- For the next 53 minutes remain silent. This may mean rising an hour early each day to avoid interruptions.

Talking and doing things clutters our mind. Having a period of silence allows you to be more aware of and in touch with the other senses. In silence you give your mind permission to enter a process of inner meditation. Your hour of power creates a space each day for you to detoxify your thoughts.

Repeat your affirmations throughout the day. You may wish to create a list of different affirmations every day or work with the same affirmations for seven days.

Here is a list of affirmations that you may use to get started:

- As I allow my natural, authentic power to radiate I automatically fill the world around me with light.

- All risks, challenges and obstacles that I face are simply healing gifts sent to awaken my courageous heart.

- My humility is my vulnerability, the crystal in the rock, cradling my strength.

- I embrace the dynamic, creative power within me.

- I accept and appreciate the wisdom, knowledge and healing that makes me the woman that I am.

- My soul has no limits; there are no boundaries on the possibilities, opportunities and gifts that life holds for me.

SELF-DISCOVERY EXERCISE
Confession is Good for the Soul

GUILT, BLAME AND SHAME all erode your power. When you confess, you pull the plug on these toxic emotions. You create the space for your power to re-emerge. Confession cleanses the heart and is good for the soul. It relieves the burden the soul is carrying.

You will need a blank sheet of paper. In your mind go back as far as you can remember and make a list of all the unkind acts, harsh words, thoughts and deeds that you have committed towards others and yourself. Remember whatever you are confessing right now is between God and yourself. God does not judge us. We judge ourselves.

When you have finished, centre yourself and relax. You may wish to perform or visualise the next stage of the ritual.

- Light a small fire in a fireplace indoors or outdoors.

- Hold the sheet of paper in front of you.

- Read through each confession one by one. Pay attention to your breathing. Keep going until you have breathed your way through all your confessions.

- Fold the page in half and then quarters. Centre yourself and in your mind ask for assistance in releasing these burdens and toxic emotions into the fire.

- Light the papers or place them into the fire. As the papers burn repeat these words in your mind if you are visualising and aloud if you are performing the ritual:

> My heart is lighter
> My soul is free
> My spirit soars
> I am now free to be me.

- Close by offering a few words of personal thanks. If you have performed the ritual outside sprinkle some sage into the fire and onto the surrounding earth. Continue repeating the words above as you do so.

- If you are visualising after you have repeated your words of thanks in your mind bring yourself slowly back into the room. Have a stretch.

- Turn immediately to your Soul Purpose Journal. Write down how you are feeling. Confession is the soul food for your spirit.

SELF-DISCOVERY EXERCISE
Storytelling is Medicine for the Future

IT IS IMPORTANT to keep your history and stories alive. Story-telling was one of the ways in which the ancients kept their sacred traditions and wisdoms alive. As future ancestors we are the gate-keepers of the oral and written tradition which can be passed onto future generations. So what are our stories?

Modern living has deadened many of us to the magic and mystery of life but I believe a piece of magic happens every day of our lives. By recounting your own stories you get to place another piece of the jigsaw puzzle of life together. You get to bring to life a piece of the past which has meaning.

Dare to encourage storytelling at family gatherings. Invite friends over for an evening of sharing. Breathe the life back into this ancient tradition that is probably as old as time itself.

♦ Think back to an incident or experience in your life when you displayed your courage, your determination, or acted on your intuition. These are the things authentic power is made of.

♦ In your Soul Purpose Journal write an account of the story as if you were telling the story to a group of strangers. To get you started try writing the story as if you were speaking it.

♦ When you have finished, light a white candle, centre yourself and read the story aloud. Feel empowered as you take in the strength and the power that resides inside your words and inside you.

♦ Create a storytelling circle in your home. All you need is a candle to create a storytelling atmosphere (remember traditionally stories were told around camp fires), some good food and a circle of friends.

♦ Prepare a list of topics to encourage the storytelling. For example, something really special that has happened to you in the last six months, the most extraordinary thing that has happened to you, a time when a stranger that you have never seen again came to your rescue.

Stories stay with us, and the power points in the story can be with us for a lifetime.

SELF-DISCOVERY EXERCISE
Power Places

YOU ARE TOTALLY responsible for your personal empowerment. Connecting with Mother Earth and the four elements – earth, water, fire and air – can help you manifest your power. Finding your own place of power on the face of Mother Earth will enable you to access this energy.

Throughout history, people have sought places of spiritual solace and peace. Moses went to the top of the mountains. Jesus sought sanctuary in a host of power places: the desert, the garden and the sea. Buddha went to the Bodhi tree. Joan of Arc went to a shrine on a hill.

Maybe you have visited Goree Island, in the harbour of Senegal's capital city Dakar? It was from here that millions of African slaves were shipped to the Americas, to England and the Caribbean. Or maybe you have visited the Sphinx or the Pyramids in Egypt? A power place is any individual space that you are moved by on the earth. One person's power place may not necessarily be another's.

In your power place you feel a strong connection to Mother Earth. When I am standing in a power place I can feel the energy in my body. When people make comments about 'feeling moved', or say 'isn't this place beautiful' or 'doesn't this place have a funny feel', they are probably in a power place.

We can invoke the energy of a power place through various forms of ritual, like singing, drumming and dancing. And we can bless such a place on Mother Earth by praying there.

To find an individual power place, walk the land until you feel drawn or called to a place, or spot. The feeling of knowing is different for everyone. To decide if this is your power place, sit or stand at the chosen spot and feel the energy and vibrations of your surroundings. You will know if it's your place from the way you feel.

By connecting with your power place you align yourself with the four elements. And when you are totally connected with the power place of your choice you can bring about healing. You become full of energy, able to complete your goals and to use your natural talents, gifts and abilities.

Connecting with Mother Earth through your places of power is a natural way of recharging your batteries. Mother Earth is abundant with warmth, love and joy, willing to assist you in making the connection of knowing who you are and your true potential.

Seek your places of power and let them give you the energy you need to create and fulfil your dreams. Use the energy you receive from Mother Earth to assist you.

♦ Find a power place.

♦ Bless her and thank her.

- Give thanks to the four elements – earth, water, fire and air.

- Say aloud or write down your ten greatest desires.

- Close with a prayer of thanks.

SELF-DISCOVERY EXERCISE
Today is a Brand New Day

EMPOWERMENT MEANS making the most of every day.

- Imagine that you have only six months left to live.

- Make a list of all the things you really want to do.

- What are the things you want to say to people in your life that you haven't yet said?

- Death is nothing to be afraid of. It is a natural process and a part of our evolution; the one thing in life that we are sure of. Don't live to regret not doing or saying what you really want to. Say it and do it now.

SELF-DISCOVERY EXERCISE
Your Birthday Wish List

CREATE A WISH LIST of nurturing gifts for your birthday.

- Write your list several months in advance. Include some (extravagant) items, like the wonderful scented soap that drives you wild but you just can't afford at present.

- Include the names of shops that stock the items. Add the telephone numbers and addresses of the shops to make it easier.

- This list will remind you of things that you can splash out on when you do have the cash or when friends ask you what you really desire. It can also be used when you want to give yourself a gift or treat to show yourself some appreciation.

CHAPTER 7

The Healing Power
of Prayer

My PARENTS WERE devoted Pentecostal Christians and our whole life centred round attending church and praying. My Christian upbringing made a lasting impression on me – the restrictions of my faith, no make-up, women not being allowed to wear trousers, and a strong moral code all fuelled my rebellion. I did not feel that the church could offer me what I needed. I also found it difficult to reconcile the abuse I had suffered when I was seven with a god who was supposed to love and care for me. Feeling abandoned, I turned my back on God. This seriously affected my relationship with prayer.

As I got older, I prayed less. When I did, it was usually when I felt sad and frightened. It was in these moments, in the depths of my despair, that I would pour my heart out to God.

The only other time that I communicated with God through prayer was when I had something to confess. My confessions ranged from having negative thoughts about myself to doing wrong or having bad thoughts about others.

Growing up in the black Pentecostal church meant that I had a strong affinity with prayer. Prayer was the life force of our church – its very heartbeat. But there were times when I believed that I simply wasn't good enough to pray.

PRAYER IN ITS DIFFERENT GUISES

In our church prayer took many different forms. There were prayers of blessings, prayers for specific people, and prayers that focused on manifesting material goods and/or bringing about particular outcomes. There were prayers for saving someone's soul, and prayers for redeeming someone who had strayed from the path. At church you could pray for just about anything.

Other forms of praying including singing. Singing, to me, is a musical prayer. Pay close attention to the words of hymns and you will see what I mean. Just think about a song that moves you. Often it is a combination of the music and the words that creates the energy for your heart to open. It is your connection with the spirit of the message that brings the tears or the feelings that well up inside.

Earlier on in *Soul Purpose*, I said that the poem is the poet's prayer. This thought only came to me recently whilst I was reading a poem and reflecting on its content. When I was in a desolate place, when my spirit was at sea, it was poetry that guided me back to the shores of my soul. Through the poem I made contact with my inner world. I spoke about and wrote about the things I felt and the things that mattered to me. Who was I talking to? Not only was I talking to myself but I was also talking to God.

At church, prayer was often accompanied by the laying-on of hands, through which the power of the Holy Spirit would be called, to bring about a healing. There were loud prayers, singing prayers, prayers that had people dancing and hopping all over the place. There were deeply moving prayers, prayers of happiness and prayers of sadness. Prayers were a way of communicating your feelings directly to God.

Testimonies are another form of prayer, and the testimony sharing was my favourite part of the church service. I loved to hear the stories of how people's lives had been touched by God. Anyone could stand up and share their testimony. There would be stories of dreams which had helped someone make a decision, of overcoming a problem at work, or of having no money and then finding ten pounds on the floor. They were all testimonies about God intervening at crucial points in their lives. Before the testimony was even shared, the person would salute and give thanks to God or Jesus. Testimonies would begin and end with praise.

Our lives are living testimonies of the lessons we have been given.

You don't have to be in a church to testify. All you need is a quiet talk with God. Through prayer, you can testify to your heart's desire.

A GIFT FROM GOD

At church, I witnessed the cleansing effect prayer had. When people went up to the altar and prayed, they would return to their seats refreshed from the release, feeling and looking lighter. Prayer had a place outside the church too. Prayer meetings were held in the homes of church members who would come together every week to pray.

When my nephew Dwayne was paralysed in a hit-and-run accident it was prayer that brought the whole family through. People everywhere prayed for Dwayne. He had been airlifted from the scene of the accident and the doctors prepared us for the inevitable. The first-born of all the nieces and nephews, Dwayne held a very special place in our hearts.

Standing over his hospital bed, his head almost twice its normal size, I knew his spirit was hovering somewhere between this world and the next. He'd had three major brain operations and he was on a life-support machine, yet I could not comprehend that Dwayne might not make it through. One evening after arriving back from the hospital it all became too much. I threw myself on the floor and hollered into the carpet. I prayed with all my heart for God to allow Dwayne to stay in this world.

Our prayers were answered. Dwayne is still here with us, having made a remarkable recovery.

When I fast, prayer replaces food; it becomes my spiritual food. Once, when I completed an all-night ritual out in the open, it was prayer that moved me past my fears. And it was prayer that held my hand as I made contact with my soul. As the night stretched on, my prayers brought home my closeness to God and the earth. I emerged from the ritual peaceful, thanks to the healing power of prayer.

Prayer is a very personal experience. It is your own direct communion with God. Many people believe that you have to be religious to pray. You don't have to be. This is man's prerequisite, not God's. I believe prayer was and is a gift from God, a gift bestowed upon us all. Prayer gives each of us our own channel, a clear frequency, linking us directly to God. No one else can take over your frequency. The line is never engaged; it is always open, ready to receive your messages.

PRAYING WITH INTENTION

Your prayer does not have to be said or delivered in a particular way. You can pray any time and anywhere. You can use your words and say your prayer in your own style. Or you can use the prayers you have been taught, or recite a prayer from a book. It really doesn't matter. Only God and you know your intention.

One of the most famous prayers in the world is the Lord's Prayer. I grew up saying the Lord's Prayer – it is in my bones. But if you know that the Lord's Prayer doesn't sit well with you, find a prayer that does. The Serenity Prayer is one of those that does it for me:

'God grant me the serenity to accept the things I cannot change, courage to change the things I can, and wisdom to know the difference.'

But your own words can be just as powerful and effective as a prayer that passes the lips of millions. What is most important is that, when you pray, you pray with intention.

There have been many times in my life when I have prayed with doubt, fear and little faith at the forefront of my mind. Then I would get frustrated when the things I asked for did not happen.

But your intention and belief have a huge effect on the outcome of your prayer. This is why the saying 'everything in God's time' is so true. You will not be given anything in your life until you are ready for it.

You are cheating yourself when you pray from this place of not believing. What you are doing is, in effect, cancelling out your requests as soon as they are spoken. The power of saying aloud our praises and thanks to God should not be underestimated. Prayers are healing affirmations and mantras that we send out into the universe. The energy of these words will come back to us.

My most effective prayers are the ones that come from my heart. These prayers are often prayers of confession. From this place everything I say and feel is the truth, devoid of ego and pretence.

When I pray like this I am often praying for forgiveness. With my heart open, I am able to remember my true self – I feel cleansed and healed as my spirit and soul move into alignment. My body feels as if it has just come through a major overhaul.

These confessions and requests for forgiveness are often accompanied by a profound shift in my consciousness, as if I am being prepared to move to another level. Because I have been accountable for my own actions, I am able to see more clearly. And, because of the alignment that has taken place, I can listen to and respond to my intuitive powers, all because I have trusted and communicated with God.

Prayer like this is a powerful tool for our spiritual development. What is also wonderful about prayer is that it gives you an intimate, private relationship with God. Looking back over my life, I believe it was prayer which often kept my spirit alive as I tried to make sense of my experiences.

Expressing our gratitude is an important aspect of prayer; we should always begin and end our prayers with thanks. Throughout *Soul Purpose*, we give thanks and blessings at the beginning and end of any ritual or meditation. When we say thank you we are indicating to the universe that we are grateful, that our hearts are now open, and we are ready to receive more grace in our lives. Gratitude is a wonderful energy, helping us align with the soul as we move into the divine state of grace. From this place we know that all our desires will be fulfilled in God's own time. The requests we make through prayer will be taken care of; we only need to have faith. It is a state of inner knowing. Always end your prayers with thanks.

CREATING YOUR OWN PRAYER

Over the last few years I have written many prayers. As we assemble the tools to assist us on our life journey, we must learn to trust our own inner wisdom and knowledge. Remember, even the prayers that have moved generations were written by an ordinary person like you. Often, we are the best creators of exactly what we need.

I realised this when I read aloud a prayer that I wrote whilst on a writers' retreat. Entitled *How Blessed Thou Art* (see page 129), this prayer came forth from my soul and it touches me whenever I read it. Often I don't get past the first three lines before the tears start to come. Other times I start to tingle as I say the words. I always have to read it slowly so that I can drink in the meaning of each sentence. I wrote this prayer as a thank-you to God. And each time I read it, I feel the presence of God descend upon me.

Right now, before you read any further, grab your Soul Purpose Journal, take a deep breath and begin by saying a prayer of thanks.

When you have finished sit quietly for a few more minutes. You are now going to write your own personal prayer. Don't move, just sit and wait until the words come. Don't force it. If only one word or a few words come, write them down. Over time, if your intention is clear, your prayer will develop its own form.

Creating your own prayer will increase the power with which you communicate with God. Write out your prayer in your Soul Purpose Journal. Memorise it if you wish. Practise saying your prayer aloud and feeling the words in your body as you speak. Say your prayer in your mother tongue. Remember, your prayer has the power not only to heal yourself but also to heal others.

If you really don't feel able to write your own prayer (and of course you know that you are choosing this) you may find the prayers at the end of this chapter useful.

Prayer allows us to breathe in the holy spirit of life. When we give of ourselves to God, we open ourselves up to receive the goodness and miracles that await us. Don't worry about how and when your request will be fulfilled. Have faith, and allow God to take care of the rest.

PRAYING THROUGH CLEANING

*'There are hundreds of ways to kneel
and kiss the ground.'*

RUMI, PERSIAN POET

I didn't think that cleaning my kitchen floor could really bring about a spiritual realisation, but it did. I connected with the divine presence which exists in cleaning floors.

My mother's mother and her mother's mother had all been domestics. From doing the equivalent work of men in the fields, they had moved on to working in the homes of the rich and hotels. Cleaning was a means of survival for generations of my family. Funnily enough, as a child I loved cleaning, so it was no surprise that I lovingly gave myself to my floor at 8am on the first day of the New Year.

Within seconds, I was fully immersed in scrubbing, spraying and wiping the floor with the mop. I felt good. As my hands worked, my thoughts were free to wander. I allowed myself to think about how much I resembled the floor I was scrubbing. The very thought made me chuckle, for I had vivid memories of days when I had operated in a haze of fog and I had been very like my dirty floor. On these days it had been difficult for me to see clearly, as there was so much that got in the way.

Had my own life not been a testament to constant cleaning and repeated removal of the fog in order to see more clearly? Before I knew it, my thoughts had moved on to the lives of my grand-mothers, and their mothers and grandmothers before them. The thought hit me that we had all found ourselves in this position, down on our knees cleaning floors, often floors that weren't our own. What thoughts had passed through my ancestors' minds as they scrubbed away? What plans had they hatched? What dreams had they dreamt?

Did they ever feel, as I did right now, that the ground represented an altar at which I could pray? Here, on my knees, I could go wher-ever I wanted to. No one could control my thoughts. I was free to roam the universe of my mind. From this place I could close my eyes and imagine myself in a temple, in a church, kneeling before God. I could imagine the future. There were no limits to where I could go. There were indeed a hundred ways to kneel and kiss the ground.

From this humble place slaves made great escapes, outwitted their masters, and hatched creative schemes to survive. Maybe it was whilst on her knees that my mother dreamt of leaving the island of her birth, or raising a family and becoming a nurse. How many women, whilst on their knees cleaning, prayed for deliverance or sang a prayer of thanks? How many simply used the time to refocus and recharge their batteries? The possibilities are endless.

I was humbled by this simple revelation as it reminded me that the greatest acts are not necessarily carried out by those who stand and shout. It may often be overlooked in the grand scheme of things but the humble act of going down on one's knees enables us to easily and effortlessly connect the mundane with the divine. I am beautifully reminded that it is the simple, almost meaningless tasks that resonate and bring the sacred elements back into our lives. As Ganilla Norris said in her book, *Being Home*,

'Prayer and housekeeping – they go together.'

The Cleaning Woman's Prayer

As I kneel, or clean, hear my prayers; prayers of thanks, prayers of forgiveness, prayers of transformation.

As I clean, clear my thoughts, my mind, making room for positive and clear-sighted thinking.

As I scrub, cleanse my body of negative emotions and energy that may be trapped within.

As I wipe, wipe my tears so I can see and embrace the present moment and envision future possibilities, whatever my circumstances.

As I rise, rise with me, give me courage, give me faith, give me trust, fill my cup with love.

Trust Prayer

I wrote the Trust Prayer when I was at a very low ebb. It's words remind me that even when I believe my trust has been broken I know that God's trust in me never fails.

In my darkest hour you held my hand and stayed with me.
As I walked in fear you gave me courage to be.
When I could not speak you spoke through me.
When I could not sing you sang to me.
When I could not go on you waited for me.
When I would not forgive, you opened your heart even wider for me.
When I turned my back you still supported me.
When I doubted you, you increased your faith in me.
When I refused to follow my purpose you were patient with me.
When I forgot to give thanks you said thank you for me.
When I was tired you made my bed and you rested with me.
When I could not see my way you created light for me.
When I had no more to give you gave to me.
When I did not pray you prayed for me.
Dear Father God/Mother God, through your eternal love I place my trust in thee.

How Blessed Thou Art

This prayer has became the equivalent of my Lord's Prayer. Its words almost always move me to tears. It is a prayer of blessings, salutations and forgiveness. Use it to start and end your day.

Father/Mother God, smiling from the heavens,
Hear our prayer.
Your sun-kissed air breathed life into our lungs,
Opening our hearts, freeing our spirits.
Hallowed be thy name.
We call your name in praise and adulation for the wondrous
    things you've given.
Crystal blessings of heaven on earth.
How blessed thou art.
Thy will be done as we make manifest the glory of our divine
    purpose,
That which you ordained in each of us the right to give birth to.
Our souls rejoice with the glory of your words.
Your deeds sow seeds of joy as we witness the abundance of
    miracles you make in our lives.
We shout your name in praise.
Help us to forgive not only those who we believe have done
    wrong to us, but to forgive ourselves.
Let light, not darkness, shine over us.
As we dissolve our anger we allow the light in everyone to shine.
Your power has patience that intensifies and loves us even when
    we do wrong.
Judgement has no place in your heart.
Restore us to our rightful place.
Life giving, life infinite and life merciful,
We bow our heads in reverence to your name.
Amen [repeated seven times] *or*
Ache [repeated seven times] – Yoruba word of supplication mean-
    ing 'And so it is'.

Breathe in on the 'Ah' and exhale on 'men'.
Breathe in on the 'Ash' and exhale on 'sha'.

Prayer of St Francis

This prayer is very simple but moving.

Lord, make me an instrument of your peace.
Where there is hatred let me sow love,
Where there is injury, pardon,
Where there is doubt, faith,
Where there is darkness, light,
And where there is sadness, joy.

ST FRANCIS OF ASSISI

PART TWO

Crossing the Bridge

CROSSING THE BRIDGE – THE ROLE OF THE SHAMAN

At different points in our lives we all have to cross a bridge, come face to face with a crossroads, confront our deepest fears, as we change – often unconsciously – and move our lives on.

Crossing the bridge usually happens at a point of transformation – what some people refer to as a turning point. These turning points may be dark and gloomy at first but they bring with them new beginnings. They are often the result of a challenge or test of our inner strength.

The path I have walked has been one of constant evolution. From the age of 21 I spent time working on myself and trying to make sense of the world I lived in. I pushed myself through countless tests in my work where I really didn't trust my abilities, and in my relationships where I really didn't believe in myself. Yet all my striving for success was only on the surface. Underneath, I was very unfulfilled. During these years I paid little attention to my spiritual self. Although I was committed to my personal development I had very little spiritual stamina. For me, crossing the bridge really began when I became aware of the huge spiritual void that existed in my life.

In 1995 I had a major spiritual breakthrough. The previous year I had spent six months in therapy. These six months brought me back to my centre, and began to open my eyes to the existence of my spiritual self. As a seeker, I was assigned an African American therapist who was a spiritual teacher and guide. Her name was Namonyah Siopan. She gently assisted me in removing the veil from my eyes. At the time I believed I was an empty vessel. She made me aware of so much. I grasped what she gave me with great enthusiasm. It really felt as if I was being reawakened.

When our work was done, I moved on. However, I was increasingly feeling that something wasn't right. I was still working at the BBC, directing a mentoring programme for black students. But I was getting more and more disillusioned with the management style, the conformity and the lack of spirit in the organisation.

After two years I resigned. Following my resignation, I experienced a couple of situations where my work as a consultant and trainer was criticised. I was becoming more and more frustrated with my work and, underneath this, with myself. Deep down inside, I knew how I wanted to work – more dynamically, with more heart, with more spirit and with a creative edge – but I was really afraid. Other experiences, like the interview with Angela Davis, had made me very cautious about stepping out into the limelight. I struggled on, wishing for a teacher, a guide, to take me to the next level.

Finally the teacher appeared. I remember clearly the evening it happened. I was visiting a friend and she gave me a package outlining a course she had been invited to attend. From the moment I read the first line I knew this was what I had been waiting for. As I read the information I got more and more excited. Entitled 'The Mastery', it was described as a course for trainers and facilitators who wanted to train from a place of excellence. I was hooked. I had no idea where I would get the £3,000 to pay for the year-long programme but I knew I had to do the course. I had committed myself to a path of love and mastery.

During the course, every aspect of my being was challenged and my ego fought to take control. As a student, I had moments when I really battled with the teachings. In fact I was at war with myself. When the course came to an end I committed to a year (in service) as an assistant student and staff member.

I learnt even more from this role, and eventually I experienced what I call a breakthrough. I could no longer go on. Suddenly I stopped accepting training work. I had no energy left. Finally I found myself signing on the dole. I felt as if my life was just one big, black hole. I had entered what many spiritual paths refer to as the 'void'. I could no longer pretend that everything was okay. I couldn't continue performing in my professional capacity. I had no idea where I was going or what was going to become of me. All I knew was that everything had to stop. I was facing a major crisis – a challenge to my endurance and my faith, a test of my ultimate being.

Letting go of my role, returning to a place where I was unsure, feeling like a child again, was scary. By deliberately becoming unemployed I was consciously acknowledging the death of my old self. The challenge I faced was to transform the negative experience into a positive one. On the spiritual path this is known as a shamanic test.

The healer whose purpose is to assist you through this dark passage into the light is known as a shaman.

A shamanic test faces you with the possibility of moving to a higher level of awareness, understanding and consciousness. In other words, a great lesson will be learnt. We have all known people who have experienced devastation, only to bounce back and go on to bigger and better things. Through the challenges they have faced, they have grown wiser and stronger and more in tune with self. The shamanic test, which often takes the form of a seemingly negative experience, gives us the opportunity to let go, to say goodbye to our old selves, old beliefs and old habits. For me, giving up working (which felt right for me at the time) planted the seed of the life I really wanted to live. In truth, it was a big blessing in disguise.

By undergoing a shamanic test, we take a journey from the dark to the light. By facing the darkness, rather than running away from it, we eventually get to the light.

The role of the shaman originated in ancient times. Shamans were ancient healers in Africa, and amongst the indigenous peoples and first nation peoples of Australia. They were the medicine men and women in North America, the yogis and holy men in India, the witches and wizards in Europe. In Korea all shamans were women. Traditionally, shamans used herbal medicine and cleansing rituals to assist those experiencing darkness in their lives. The traditional shaman had the gift of telling the future, interpreting dreams, and warding off evil spirits.

Today shamans still exist. They are healers, people who are willing to confront their greatest fears and their shadow selves (or dark side). While a healer traditionally uses the positive power of medicine to bring about healing, shamans (because of their ability to travel into other realms) can successfully deal with the forces of darkness in order to help the seeker reach the light.

Having faced not only external darkness in their lives, but also the internal darkness which can take on so many different forms (such as public humiliation, fear of madness, loss of role and ego, near-death experience), the shaman can bring compassion to others as they experience the death of their old selves. The experience of getting through their own internal nightmares makes it easier for shamans to assist others.

The shaman's role is not for the inexperienced. Check out the credentials of all those who call themselves shamans. A true shaman does not go around loudly proclaiming that this is what they do. Those who need to know who they are and where to find them will be given that information if they are true seekers. Often shamans can be found existing in the everyday world, whilst carrying out their sacred healing work outside it. Always trust your intuition. It is easy for some shamans to lose themselves in the forces of darkness. However, there is great learning to be had from a true shaman who has experienced the death of his or her old self and can help you do the same. As you say goodbye to the old self you make room for the creation of the new.

CHAPTER 8

Forgiveness Sets You Free

Forgiveness is the great escape,
It is the underground railway to our hearts,
It is the love train,
Dissolving all the blocks along its way.
It is the greatest surrender, a show of courage and humility,
An act of self-love, as you hold your hand and journey on the
  freedom highway.

IF YOU DON'T FORGIVE, how will you forget? Forgiveness dissolves the memories and the energies attached to our negative experiences. I call forgiveness the underground railway of the spiritual world. It is impossible to move from one point of your life journey to another unless you forgive. Once you forgive, your heart opens and you surrender to the power of your spirit working its magic and weaving its spell in your life.

WHO NEEDS FORGIVENESS?

For years I believed I didn't need to forgive. After all, I was the one who had had a hard time and been taken advantage of. I was the victim and I was quite content playing that role. Indeed, I was too busy being the victim to even notice the possible benefits that forgiving might bring. Even though I believed I was a very open person, my heart was as hard as stone. I had cemented its doors shut by hanging onto the resentment, bad feelings and blame.

But forgiveness forces the heart to let go, to pour love into a situation that requires healing. Forgiving requires you to be present and to make yourself accountable by acknowledging the part you have played in the negative experiences in your life.

Here's an example from my own life. I was emotionally involved with someone and I didn't feel good about my involvement. As a result, I wasn't totally honest with my best friend about the situation. My friend therefore didn't have a clear understanding of my true feelings. I stood by and watched as she began a friendship with him too.

Eventually things came to head. Through no fault of her own, my friend had stepped over the line. As far as I was concerned, she had violated the mental boundaries I had created about what friends are and are not allowed to do.

The situation blew up out of all proportion. She had simply pushed the wrong buttons, unaware that she was releasing a whole host of buried toxic emotions. I remembered all the times when I had felt let down, had broken up with a best friend, or experienced rejection from a lover. Now I was really seething. Every day I brooded on what had happened. I did not speak to my friend for two years. The atmosphere between us became ugly and intense. When she tried to speak to me, to give her side of the story, I wasn't prepared to listen. I totally closed myself off from her.

My anger was all-consuming – I literally saw red. A few days after our falling out, my friend was offered a new post in the organisation where we both worked. I believe spirit arranged for this to happen. She moved offices the next week, going on to a higher-paid position with better prospects. I stayed put for several months afterwards, still stewing in my anger.

By not forgiving, I closed off from seeking clarification about what had really happened. I had chosen to back the fear, rather than face the truth. I had allowed my assumptions to run wild.

For months I went around bad-mouthing my friend. I believed I was entitled to do this – it was my justice and her penance. At the time I did not fully understand that spirit does not respond to negativity. Spirit would in no way harm my friend, even though that was what I believed should happen.

The reaction of friends was interesting. A few joined me in my negative spiral. Others, rightly, out of respect for us both, refused to discuss the situation at all. And I'm sure that many tried to talk sense to me but I was so busy being angry I just couldn't hear.

It took a long time before it dawned on me that the problem wasn't my friend. The problem was me. Not only did I need to forgive my friend and all the other parties involved, I also desperately needed to forgive myself. As long as I was putting out bad feelings about my friend, I was doing the same to myself. In addition, my life was spiritually dysfunctional. I was carrying a load of guilt about the same man I'd fallen out with my friend over.

Guilt is a toxic emotion that often signals when we are out of harmony with ourselves. If the guilt is unacknowledged it becomes a heavy burden that we hide in the dark recesses of our innermost selves. This guilt I carried needed some light shone on it. The light would expose the lesson I was being taught which, in turn, would help to strengthen my spiritual practice. Instead I used my anger to mask my own internal feelings and did an excellent job of projecting how I really felt about myself onto others.

Not surprisingly, all the bad-mouthing and attacking did nothing to make me feel better about myself. In fact it made me feel progressively worse. Years later, I was retelling the story to a spiritual teacher whom I greatly admired. Even then, despite the spiritual knowledge I had gained, I was still looking for some kind of confirmation that my friend had done me a great wrong and that I was justified in my actions. I still believed that she, not I, needed to sort her life out.

I was not prepared for the response. My teacher's reply was: 'What was your lesson in all of this?' I felt myself crumble as I finally realised that the person who really needed the healing was myself. My friend had been the vehicle through which I would learn this important lesson. She had in fact been an Earth Angel in disguise. My heart burst, bringing forth a flood of tears. And I realised that I had been waging a long, weary war with myself and no one else. I realised how little I thought of myself. I had been living in a place devoid of spiritual nourishment. I was afraid of intimacy, afraid of sharing my deepest thoughts, afraid of showing who I really was. And I had chosen to attack my friend, rather than face the truth about how I really felt about myself. I did feel hurt by her actions but she was not the cause of my pain. I was simply looking for love in the wrong place.

ESCAPING FROM THE PRISON

Forgiving my friend and forgiving myself created a new energy and vibration around our friendship and my life. I felt released from the emotionally toxic prison I had been confined in for many years. By examining my lessons I was able to do some deep soul searching and begin work on loving myself and cultivating a deeper spiritual faith. Forgiving marked a turning point, when I started clearing out my spiritual and emotional clutter.

Surrender is a crucial element in forgiving. Indeed, the two are deeply inter-related. Surrender requires internal action which produces external results. Forgiveness, on the other hand, requires an external action which produces far-reaching internal results. They are both required for change to happen.

By surrendering, you give up your need to be right, and your desire (whether conscious or subconscious) for bad things to happen to the other person. Once the surrender happens, it brings about a release. When you forgive, you move closer to seeking the good in the experience. When you forgive, you take off the blinkers which previously gave you only a distorted view of the situation. Now you can regain your perspective.

A question I am commonly asked, when running workshops, is: How can women be expected to forgive their abusers? Over the years, I have come to understand that forgiving is not the same as condoning the actions of the abuser. What you are doing, by forgiving, is releasing yourself from the anger that has tied you to the energy of the experience. By forgiving, you are giving up the role of victim. You are redefining the relationship between yourself and the abuser. You are taking back your power. You are saying you no longer need to be controlled by the experience. You are releasing your fear and moving on. In many cases you will also be releasing your abusers from the internal conflict, guilt and negative feelings they too may have carried about the experience.

I spent many years working on the sexual abuse I experienced. I relived it, time and time again, in group sessions, one-to-one sessions and therapy sessions. I travelled abroad, and went to workshops and seminars trying to rid myself of this experience. I cried as many tears as I could cry, until one day I had simply cried enough and the tears stopped coming. My well had run dry. I needed to refill it with something else. I accepted that it was time for me to get on with my life.

A workshop in California marked this important transition. We were high in the mountains, far away from the rest of the world. Maybe it was this heavenly location that triggered the shift, but something moved that week. Even the air I breathed felt different. We talked, counselled each other, and held each other, so much that by the end of the week I felt emotionally, physically and mentally lighter. It was this workshop that finally made me realise that I was bored with being a victim. Suddenly the feelings of resentment that I had had towards my abusers were disappearing, and being replaced by a strong desire for us all to live.

A GIFT TO OURSELVES

Two years later, in what I can only describe as a miracle of healing, I found myself making peace with both the perpetrators of my abuse. I did not initiate the contacts or the discussions that took place. In each case the abuser asked for my forgiveness. I am thankful that God had allowed my heart to be healed sufficiently so that I was able and ready to truly forgive.

In that moment the frightened seven-year-old returned to the original truth of her being. I connected with my beauty, my power and my enormous capacity to love. From there my life really did change. Yes, I still had a lot of work to do but I now had the foundation upon which that work could take place. God, in His/Her infinite wisdom, had shown me that, when we do the work and forgive, this foundation will be there for us. I thank God for that day when I was finally set free.

Forgiveness returns us to the memory of who we are. It is a true gift to ourselves. It allows each of us, from a state of grace and humility, to choose beauty before ugliness, to choose love before fear or hate. It reminds us of the enormous abundance of love we have within us, not only for ourselves but for those around us.

Forgiveness is the miraculous rain of love, washing us clean of anger and guilt, healing our wounded hearts and setting us free.

RITUAL
Forgiveness Cleansing Bath

FOR THIS FORGIVENESS release ritual you will require either a rose quartz or an amethyst crystal. One or two small crystals will be ideal.

Rose quartz heals the heart. It calms and soothes, thereby opening the heart chakra and allowing forgiveness to perform its healing magic. It opens you up to the divine emotion of love and helps you see your experiences more clearly. Rose quartz brings the gift of compassion for yourself and for others. The amethyst brings the healing energy of balance and forgiveness.

- Run a hot bath and place your crystals in the bath. Light some candles and some incense. Display a vase of flowers where you can easily see them whilst sitting in the bath.

- Before you enter your bath, bless it by saying a prayer and gently swishing your hands through the water.

- Sit silently in the bath for a couple of minutes.

- Say out loud: 'I [and the names of all whom you wish to forgive] seek forgiveness for [and say what it is].'

- Drench your body, including your hair, from head to toe with your bath water.

- Place one of the crystals on your 'third eye' (the region between your eyebrows). Give thanks aloud for the release forgiveness will bring. Say: 'I am now free to move on.'

- Leave your bath and wrap yourself in a towel. Clean the bath immediately. The dirt which will have accumulated is a physical representation of the negative energies and emotions you have just released.

- Wash your crystals in running spring water (pour directly over the sink or bath). Alternatively, smudge with incense, or place in a mild solution of salt water for 15 minutes. Place your crystal on your altar.

You may wish to deepen this ritual (before fully immersing yourself in your bath water) by activating the seven chakra energy points on your body. The following is a brief introduction to the chakras, for those who may not be familiar with them. For more detail on the chakras, read Caroline Shola Arewa's *Opening to Spirit*.

The seven chakras are located from the top of the head (the crown chakra), the region between the eyebrows (the third eye), the throat area (the throat chakra), the heart area (the heart chakra), the region around the womb (the solar plexus chakra), the region below the navel (the sacral chakra), and the base of the spine (the root chakra).

The energy of each chakra is invisible but can be visualised as a spinning wheel or swirling vortex. Indian tradition describes the chakra as a lotus, with each chakra or lotus having a different number of petals.

Each chakra draws in a different energy and each one has a separate colour, which it is identified with. The crown chakra draws in a violet ray; the third eye chakra draws in an indigo ray; the throat chakra draws in a blue ray; the heart chakra draws in a green ray; the solar plexus chakra draws in a yellow ray; the sacral chakra draws in an orange ray; and the base or root chakra draws in a red ray. The chakras need to be balanced with each other, and they can become blocked by unexpressed emotions, beliefs, feelings or hurts. Your forgiveness ritual will be enhanced by cleansing and ensuring that the seven energy centres, particularly the crown chakra, the third eye, the throat and heart chakras, are kept in balance to aid in the healing process of forgiveness.

- ◆ Relax and deepen yourself. Now visualise your chakras, one at a time, starting with your root chakra, and notice what may be blocking them. Dip your hand into your bath and pour seven handfuls of water onto each of the chakra regions. As you do this, visualise the water washing away all the blockages.

- ◆ Alternatively, place one crystal on each chakra point. Visualise the colour of that chakra swirling around the chakra region and washing away all blocks.

- ◆ Once you have finished, starting from the root chakra, fill each chakra – one by one – with a golden light. Nature does not like a vacuum. In spiritual cleansing all spaces must be filled, or protected, otherwise they are more than likely to attract exactly what you don't want.

- ◆ Give thanks.

SELF-DISCOVERY EXERCISE
Forgiveness Quest

- Make a list of all the reasons why you believe you shouldn't forgive.

- Make another list of all the benefits you could gain by forgiving.

- Read through your two lists. Which list keeps you connected to the flow of life? Which list makes you feel free?

SELF-DISCOVERY EXERCISE
Forgiveness Letter to Myself

SOMETIMES WE FORGET that, as well as forgiving others, we need to forgive ourselves.

- Write a letter to yourself asking for your own forgiveness. You may wish to ask to be released from all the times you have blamed yourself, disliked yourself, or felt guilty.

- Date the letter and sign it.

- When you have finished writing the letter, fold it up and keep it in a safe place (your altar is an ideal place), ensuring that it stays folded.

- Keep the letter for 40 days. You now have a task to complete for each of the 40 days.

- Each day, either in the morning or before you go to sleep, write yourself a love letter. The letters can be short and sweet or long and passionate. Write the things you would love a lover to say to you. Fill your love letters with appreciation, compliments, praise about yourself. You must write a different letter every day for 40 days.

- On the 40th day, set aside some time to complete the ritual. I suggest rising early and taking a warm sensuous bath. The day before, treat yourself to a bunch of flowers and place them either in your bathroom or on your altar.

- Centre yourself and read aloud your forgiveness letter. Keep breathing deeply throughout. Take seven deep breaths at the end to mark the completion of your reading.

- Now you are going to burn your self-forgiveness letter and release the energy back into the universe.

- Burn your self-forgiveness letter in a clay or metal vessel, preferably outside.

- Once you have released your self-forgiveness letter, you are ready to replace it with your love letters.

- One by one, read your love letters aloud. Drink in the healing tones of your loving words to yourself. After a while you should feel soft and warm inside, as you sink into the beauty of your love affirmations to yourself.

- Afterwards, write up your love letters on a large sheet of paper or keep them in a special book, or, even better, mount them on your bathroom mirror wall.

You can repeat this writing ritual throughout the year. A good time to do it is 40 days before your birthday. It's a wonderful birthday gift to yourself.

RITUAL
The Forgiveness Ritual

THE FORGIVENESS RITUAL is a seven-day ritual to release yourself and others by forgiving. You will require a brand-new spiral bound notebook.

- Each morning, before 12 noon, take a new page and write out the following sentence 40 times (Numerologically, the number 40 represents moving through blocks which is what forgiveness is all about. It is also a significant number in the Bible. Moses fasted for 40 days and 40 nights in the presence of God when he received the instructions for writing the Ten Commandments. Jesus also fasted for 40 days in the wilderness. It takes at least 40 repetitions before a shift begins to take place in our minds):

'I [your name] willingly forgive [the name of the person]. We are both free to move on.'

◆ Intuitively write down the names that come into your head even if they don't seem to make sense. If a name comes to you, and you intuitively know that this is someone that you don't want to forgive, write the name down in the space and move on. This ritual is a real test of your resistance, and will show you clearly when you are censoring who you believe you should or shouldn't forgive. By doing the ritual in silence, you allow the power of your intuition, your sixth sense, to go to work on your behaviour. Move your ego out of the way and simply write what comes.

◆ In the evening, before 12 midnight, write the following sentence 40 times, but this time in the space write your name:

'I forgive [your name] completely and unconditionally. I am free to move on.'

◆ In order to really intensify the energy on forgiving yourself, write down your full name. If you have changed your name, intuitively use the name you feel is right. You will know.

◆ If you miss a day and you are more than halfway through the ritual simply continue and add on the missing day or days at the end.

I have completed an older version of this ritual three times. My second time of doing the forgiveness ritual, on the second to last day I was on the phone talking to a friend. I finished the call just after midnight. It was only then that I realised that I had not completed my sentences. I was gutted, believing that I would have to start all over again. And I gave myself a hard time for this.

The reason I share this story is because *this is not the way to do it.* If you miss a day this is not an opportunity to be angry with yourself. Instead, make note of what your distractions were and what the possible message might be. What I soon realised was that the friend I was talking to was someone with whom I really needed to do a lot of forgiving. But, more than anything, I needed to relieve myself of a lot of the guilt that I carried about our friendship. Our conversation that evening simply alerted me to the work that I still needed to do. So, if you are more than halfway through and you miss a morning or evening, keep going, take your lesson and complete the ritual with grace and ease.

- On the evening of the seventh day or on the eighth day, gather together all your papers and go to an open space. Ideally, the burning of your forgiveness papers should be done outside. If this is not possible, burning your pages inside will be fine.

- Before you begin, centre yourself, then say a prayer and start burning the pages. If you are outside and there is a wind blowing, burn the pages in the centre of a nest of leaves. It may take a while, so stay focused on the ritual. Some pages will burn quickly and easily, whilst others may take longer and be more resistant to burning. On a deeper level this signifies the extent of your resistance or your willingness to let go. How your paper burns gives you some indication of how much work you may still need to do.

- When you have finished dispose of the ashes by giving them back to the earth or flushing them down the toilet. Sprinkle sage or rosemary onto Mother Earth.

- Now you are ready to say your Forgiveness Prayer:

> I am released from fear,
> I let go of bad feelings and resentments about others and
>   myself.
> I return to love myself and those who inhabit the world I live
>   in.
> I am free to explore and reach my highest good.
> I am free to remember I am me,
> A beautiful child of God.

- On the eighth day write out the following sentence 40 times once before noon and again before 12pm.

'I am willing to [fill this space with what you are now willing to do].'

Write down intuitively whatever comes into your mind. This is a way of spirit showing you whether you have truly completed your work on forgiveness. Keep writing these sentences until you feel complete.

SELF-DISCOVERY EXERCISE
Forgiveness Cards

WHEN I HAVE REACHED a place in my heart where I feel ready to forgive someone, I am often moved to make contact with that person in some way. Because I love to write, I frequently send them a card. In it I write a few words that reflect the release on my part. The intention of the card is not necessarily for a new friendship to begin, or a meeting to take place. By sending the card I am laying to rest the past and opening my arms to the future. A few simple, meaningful words may be all it takes to heal a wound in the heart.

◆ Send a card, using phrases like:

> *'Blessings to you.'*
> *'May your future be bright.'*
> *'I'm sorry.'*
> *'I was wrong in saying what I said*
> *or doing what I did.'*
> *'Thank you for allowing me to learn a*
> *precious lesson from my mistake.'*

◆ If you wish, you can go one step further, and add rose petals or dried lavender to your forgiveness card. Stationers also sell packets of gold and silver angels and I love to put a few in with a card. The scent of the rose petals or lavender buds alone will often melt the heart of the receiver.

◆ Do not expect a reply. Let providence do its work.

◆ Send yourself a forgiveness card to remind yourself of the forgiveness that is there for you too.

SELF-DISCOVERY EXERCISE
Forgiveness Visualisation of Self and Others

USE THE FOLLOWING exercises and visualisation to open your heart to forgive:

♦ Choose someone you wish to forgive and bring his or her face to the forefront of your mind.

♦ Make a list of all the resentments you have towards him or her. Write down as many as you possibly can.

♦ Read through your list.

♦ Go through each item, one by one, and ask yourself this question:

'Have I been guilty of doing the same?'

♦ Now agree to release all the negative energy you have towards this person. The following visualisation will assist you with your release:

> Take a few breaths and relax. Bring to mind the image of the person you wish to forgive. Take a few seconds as you make contact with their face. Aim to focus on connecting with them through the eyes. Take your attention to your heart. Feel your heart expanding as it fills up with a deep golden light. There is so much of this light wanting to come through that it begins to pour from your heart to the exterior of your body. Feel the golden heat of the light as it pushes through.

> Now turn your attention to the person you wish to forgive. See them standing before you. As you look towards them, feel your heart melting. The golden light zooms towards them, breaking through the layers of skin and pouring directly into their heart. As it does, it feels as if your body is being emptied of a heavy weight.

> The golden light creates a golden aura around the outside of your bodies. You stand before each other, smiling as you drink in the feeling of peace and well-being. Let your energy stand

in the gentle flow of your joining. In your own time say your goodbyes and watch as the person walks away and finally disappears into the distance.

◆ Open your eyes and return to the room feeling refreshed. Have a big stretch.

SELF-DISCOVERY EXERCISE
Forgiveness Mantra

MANTRAS ARE WORDS or sounds whose rhythm can change your state of consciousness, easing open the doorway to your heart.

◆ Whenever you are aware of feeling resentful or annoyed, practise saying the following mantra aloud or in your head:

'Forgiveness is my function as the light of the world – I would fulfil my function so that I may be happy.'

You may of course wish to write your own mantra.

CHAPTER 9

Your Creative Spirit

I BELIEVE IT IS GOD'S WILL for us all to be truly creative. Unlocking my creative talents has been the key to tapping into my Soul Purpose. So, what is your creative spirit? It is the treasure chest that lies within your spirit. It is filled with unique gifts that only *you* can express to the world.

WHAT IS CREATIVITY?

Creativity is by no means limited to professional artists. Creativity stretches beyond art, reaching into all areas of life. It is the thoughts that flow as your pen caresses the paper. It is in your hands as you arrange a vase of flowers. It is the smell of the bread you have just baked. It is your joy when you find the item you wanted to give a dear friend as a present. It is the words you write in a card that touch a friend's heart.

Creativity is born of inspiration. And inspiration is the fuel that lights the creative fire. When I am inspired, my creative mind speeds up. Ideas and answers flow, as I am inspired to take action. Planning becomes secondary when I am blessed with the grace of inspiration. I am transported from the mundane to a higher level. It is as if an invisible force moves my creative spirit into action on my behalf.

Creativity is an enormous power that has been given to us all. Your challenge is to choose how to channel and allow your creative gifts to make an impact on the different areas of your life.

A RIPPLE IN THE UNIVERSE

Creative expression is a permanent companion on your journey to realising your Soul Purpose. No matter what challenges you have to confront, God will always back you in the use of your creative gifts. Once you start expressing your creativity, a ripple begins in the universe. All manner of things start to happen. God goes to work on your behalf.

For instance, a few years ago I was unemployed, confused and frustrated. Frustrated because I knew I was avoiding following my heart's desire. More than anything, I wanted to write and I wanted to run workshops for black women which were spiritually healing and empowering.

Whilst I was on top of things I always put this desire off. I talked myself out of it with comments like, 'I'm not qualified enough' or 'Someone else will be far better than me' or 'What if it all goes wrong?' But when I hit my low point, my spirit would let me stall no longer. I plucked up my courage, designed my leaflet, produced a training pack and said to the universe 'I'm ready.' The universe moved straight into action on my behalf. A discussion with a friend who was the director of a black mental health project resulted in me being offered a wonderful venue for a whole weekend free of charge. Since that first weekend workshop in April 1995, which 14 women attended, I have facilitated over 30 workshops and retreats.

I began breathing again. I opened myself to the full expression of my creative talent. My workshops became my stage. I intuitively developed new exercises; I played and had fun as I trusted my creative self to be free.

This is not to say that the development of the workshops has been easy. I have been personally attacked, talked about and undervalued. But, unfortunately, this goes with the territory. Expressing your creative self is no guarantee of acceptance or acknowledgement. What you must always ask yourself is whether this experience brings you joy. These workshops have brought me great joy and fulfilment. If the answer is yes, keep going. As we have seen, your failures are the stepping stones to your success.

The other way in which I constantly evaluate if I am on the right creative track is the state of my mind. When I'm not being creative I am very irritable and frustrated. This often leads to me retreating

deeper into myself and getting depressed because I am not expressing myself from the inside out. Creativity allows our talents and
skills the space to flow outwards. Once I make the decision to do
something – write, tidy up my bedroom, paint some cards or make a
collage – my mood suddenly lifts. Surrendering to my creativity is so
much more graceful and pleasurable than resisting it.

TIME AND CREATIVITY

A question I am often asked is: how can you get in touch with your
creativity when there are so many other things to do? I always smile
at this because it is a problem I know so well. Our busyness shuts us
off from our creativity. But we all need to be really firm and set aside
some regular time to nurture ourselves, which will in turn nurture
our creative spirit.

Something magical happens when you do this. Your energy
increases because of the investment in your creative spirit, which
provides that extra energy to complete all the other tasks that await
you. This is also about changing your belief patterns. Your creative
time doesn't have to be hours or days. It can be 15 minutes, as long
as it's good-quality time. You could stick some more images into your
pocket book of dreams (see Chapter 12), gather together sacred items
for your altar, or sit in silence for a few moments and reflect on the
words of a song, a poem, or the short story you are writing. Linear
time disappears when you plug into your creativity; it makes you feel
as if time is on hold.

THE JOY OF CREATIVITY

It was running through the park in the early morning, back in 1996,
that enabled me to create this book. I was really unfit when I started
but I kept going. Within a few weeks, that commitment saw me running a distance non-stop from my house that I had never contem-
plated being able to do. I fell into a rhythm, which each morning
seemed to take me physically further and further.

On another level, something else was happening. I stopped focusing on the running – my body took care of that. Instead, I began to
explore the world around me: the trees, the grass, the colours of the
changing leaves. At times I would break into song; at others times
the words of a power affirmation would form in my head. When I

got back I would race to the computer, eager not to forget anything. The running was where the ideas started. It was where the magic took place.

Eventually I started carrying a pen and notebook with me, and finally a dictaphone. As I ran I would speak the thought in my head into the tape. Many mornings, after finishing my run, I would sit and meditate under a tree. On one particular morning, as I sat peacefully against the trunk of an oak, a river of words burst forth. As I spoke the words of a poem into the dictaphone, one particular line – about the birds above my head – was acknowledged. A group of crows crowed loudly at the same moment.

The ecstasy and joy that I feel at such moments is almost indescribable. I had no need for food; my spirit was free to soar. I was ready to give birth to my creation. All I had to do was to be ready. I was not in a church but I felt close to God. I realised that God was not only in me, He/She was in the trees, the grass, the flowers, the sky, the clouds, the earth, the sun and the moon.

By nurturing yourself in this way you give life to your creative self, which eagerly awaits its release. If running is not for you, walking can give the same results. Take time to drink in the sights around you. Really explore the village, town or city you live in, as you walk down the street that you normally walk down every day. Ask yourself: 'What have I been missing?' Maybe it's the colour of the brickwork, or the small detail on a building that you've been taking for granted. Walking is an excellent cure for all sorts of challenges. As your feet take care of moving your body, your mind is free to go to work and find solutions.

Some days, making contact with your creativity will seem slow and difficult. It may feel as if you are searching for it in darkness. Like all good things, your creativity will go through murky, scary, challenging times. But just keep going. Ideas need time to mature. They need time to incubate before they are presented to the world. Surrender to this, have faith and trust. One day the raindrops of your ideas will become a shower of creative beauty.

Some African artists (who are considered shamans) used to bury the chess pieces they created in the earth for one year. The purpose was to fill the pieces with the healing energy of Mother Earth and to give each piece a magical power of its own. They also knew that in the pursuit of creativity time becomes irrelevant. It is the magic of what the piece is transformed into that inspires the world.

POURING SPIRIT INTO YOUR ART

Whether you are a creative artist, a healer, an accountant, an engineer, a mother or unemployed, when your spirit ignites your creative talents it touches whatever you do in a very deep way. It gives you a sense of well-being and what you do is noticed and valued by others.

When I was a child no one could make sandwiches the way my mum did. When she packed our suitcases for a trip abroad, we could instantly tell that my mother's hands had been at work. It was as if only her hands had the magic of healing and soothing away our childhood ailments.

Whether it is the simplest of everyday activities or a complicated creation, when we let our creativity flow we put our personal stamp on whatever we are doing. Even a simple vase of flowers can inspire others just by the way the flowers have been individually arranged.

To the creative artist, the sacred act of opening up to the creative spirit brings the work alive. Art is the sensory form of the creative self. Through art, we can tell stories, and bring messages of hope, healing and inspiration. Through art, we can touch, not only others' lives, but also our own. Art is often the way in which artists speak to their deeper selves.

In 1998 a friend of mine, Mel Jennings, held an art exhibition. It reminded me of the fact that, when our art comes from a deep, untapped and forgotten place inside ourselves, we move others to respond to the feeling or energy that we express. When we move past our fears and our judgements, and share our work with the world, we can inspire and touch the lives of others.

One of my friend's many paintings, entitled *Affirmations*, totally mesmerised me. My requests, along with several others, to purchase the painting were denied because of the painting's personal significance to the artist. A few months later she told me the story of how the painting came about. I share it with you now to illustrate the importance of staying true to our passions, and to show that when we connect with our soul self we bring inspiration to the world.

Mel's painting shows us that art is a vessel through which we can make peace with unresolved emotions, a ship that takes us on a journey from the dark to the light. Here is the story, in her own words:

At the end of 1997 I created a picture called *Affirmations*. It's a long thin piece of work, almost as tall as I am, full of bright yellows and greens and positive affirmations about my life. The affirmations remind me of what I want for myself. 'I am connected to my desires,' 'It's okay for me to relax and have fun,' 'I enjoy my work.' Making the work was an important statement for me in many ways. It was created as the culmination of a personal development course called 'The Samurai', run by the Institute of Creativity. I had spent ten weeks getting up at 5am twice a week to go and share my dreams and fears with a group of 12 people. At the end of the course we were encouraged to present our plans for 1998 in a way which reflected our deepest desires. I knew straight away that I wanted to express myself through art.

I had suppressed my true creativity for a long time and the course had brought back my passion with a vengeance. Over the Christmas break I worked on *Affirmations*, using the kitchen table at a friend's hideaway on the coast. The inspiration came from many areas. Self-help books, good advice from friends and relatives over the years, dreams in the flotation tank, the general creative flow of the universe (as always) and the course itself. The course helped me to see so many things about myself. At the time of creating the work I felt down, as I was feeling ill, still grieving the death of my father, and the impending end of a relationship. However, I persevered, wanting to do justice to what I had learned and shared on the course.

Over the ten weeks we had cried, then got angry, felt hopeless, as well as feeling inspired. It was hard writing certain affirmations like 'I am a brilliant artist' or 'I am good enough' when I didn't believe it. I felt like I was boasting. But the course had taught me that unless I could tap into my deepest desires and own them I would not move forward in my life. It was up to me if I wanted to share my dreams but if I wanted to take myself seriously as an artist I would have to be open to displaying my subconscious to visual form sooner or later.

I wrote the affirmations on cotton using fabric pens and lost myself in creating intricate patterning for several hours. I felt fear again when I displayed *Affirmations* at my exhibition in 1998. I didn't plan on showing this piece but needed one extra piece of work to make the show complete. I deliberated for ages. I had stayed up half the night painting a new picture but I still needed an extra piece of work to show. Would people think how arrogant I was affirming this and that about myself? Or, worse, would they laugh?

In the end I showed it anyway. To my surprise, many people reacted to it in a very positive and even emotional way. I was surprised that such a personal piece of work could touch people in this way. The other painting I had stayed up to do and had allowed full creative flow on was also one of the favourites. I was amazed that people not only wanted to buy my work, but often the one piece that I felt the most scared to show.

This experience taught me to begin to let go of the fear of sharing my creative experiences of life with other people. I still look at my affirmations and still have to work on many of them, but it's good to remind myself that 'I love success'.

SELF-DISCOVERY EXERCISE
Setting Up Your Artist's Altar

WHEN YOU RELEASE your creative spirit you ignite the artist shaman in you. Just as we travel through life in pursuit of our Soul Purpose, the creative self must travel through the tunnel of darkness before it is fulfilled. There will be times when you believe that your purpose is totally out of reach, that you do not have the skill, or the ability, to reach your highest potential. This is when you need to feed yourself with spiritual sustenance.

To help keep you balanced and on track, the creation of a visible focus in your home can assist you in taking care of your artist self. An artist's altar can provide you with the energy of spirit, and an abundance of faith and trust, to sustain you on the long, dark journey to fulfil your purpose.

Use your altar as a place to draw strength, to refuel, to find peace. It is a place where you can nurture your creativity, a growing place, a healing space, where your ideas can incubate and mature, before they take flight. It is a place where you can dust yourself off in the event of what may appear to be failure or disappointment. Your artist's altar is a sacred space where you can heal your wounds, dismantle blocks and rebuild the wounded artist from within.

- Create an artist's altar that is separate from any other sacred spaces in your home.

- Follow the instructions for setting up an altar in your home in Chapter 14 ('Sacred Spaces').

- Declare to the universe that you intend to have a healing space where your purpose will be refuelled and the spirit of your creative artist will be fed.

- Your artist's altar is your acknowledgement that it is the loving hands of God that touch your hands, type on the computer keyboard, or send the pen across the page. It is through God that our creative selves unfold. It is creativity that fuels our Soul Purpose.

- You can connect with all five senses, and also the sixth sense of intuition, through your artist's altar. God is in everything: the rocks, the trees, the leaves, the flickering light of the candle, the smell of burning sage and lemon grass, the healing sounds of drum music. Fill your artist's altar with objects that reflect all your different senses. Bring your idea of God into your artist's altar: feel God, hear God, touch God, smell God.

◆ Create your own image of God – the Creator, the Goddess, the Divine – and place the image on your altar.

◆ Make time to visit your artist's altar. God will always be waiting there for you.

SELF-DISCOVERY EXERCISE
One-Day Creativity Retreat to Advance

THIS IS A RETREAT THAT I often perform when things have got on top of me. I call it a 'retreat to advance' because that is exactly what it is. You retreat from the world so that you can advance when you emerge.

Being a single mum means that my working day sometimes only lasts from 9am to 3.30pm when I have to collect my daughter from school. If this is the case for you too, don't despair. The hours between 9am and 3pm are more than enough for your one-day creativity retreat. You have six quality hours in which to immerse yourself in creative play to feed your mind, body and spirit.

If you have pre-school children, why not arrange childcare? Swap with another mum and then do the same for her so that she can also indulge in her own creativity retreat.

For this exercise you will need to prepare a clear space and make sure you have no interruptions. It includes seven different creative self-discovery exercises.

1 Personal Dream Collage

The creation of a collage is a very powerful tool. As the saying goes, 'A picture tells a thousand words.' Words can sometimes confuse us and keep us from the truth of what we are feeling. Many people are also put off writing for a variety of reasons. The wonderful thing about creating a collage is that it breaks down the division between artists and non-artists. Anyone can do a collage.

A collage allows your creative mind to flow, freeing you from the limitations you place on yourself. The images and colours of collages work powerfully and have a deep impact on your subconscious mind. Sometimes it is much easier to connect what we feel with an image rather than a piece of writing.

Collages can teach you a lot about where you are in your life. For example, on a course three years ago, I created a collage of successful-looking business women. I believed that these women represented the image of the success I wanted for myself. But when I presented it to the course the feedback was muted. I knew why. This collage did not truly reflect me, and my experiences over the next three years were to confirm this. I now know that I am an earth woman. I love the land. I love connecting with people's spirits. I love to be free. The business world is not where I want to be.

Allow your own collage to give you the answers or insights that will assist you in changing and transforming your life.

Creating collages is very exciting. I am never sure what images I will come across. Be sure to collect a variety of magazines, especially ones that you don't normally read. Starting with a blank canvas, tearing out images and coming up with the final creation can be both therapeutic and exhilarating.

You will need a pile of old magazines (as opposed to newspapers). Magazines tend to carry more positive images than newspapers. Also, colour images work much better on the subconscious mind. You will also need glue and a large sheet of poster paper so that you can make your personal dream collage as large as possible. Too many of us keep our dreams small and keep them to ourselves.

- Put a nicely coloured note on your door saying 'Creativity Retreat to Advance in session – please do not disturb'. Turn off all radios and televisions. Minimise your contact with the outside world for the day.

- Ground yourself and the space you are going to use. You can do this by lighting an incense stick or burning some aromatic oils. It may also be helpful to put on some soothing meditation music.

- Start with a mediatation or visualisation such as I Am Women (page 42) to get you focused. Light a candle – any colour will do – and state your intention, by declaring it out loud.

- The purpose of your dream collage is to create a picture that depicts strong vibrant images of what you desire for yourself in the different areas of your life. For example, you may choose a stunning image of a sunset because this is a place you would like to be. Or you may have an image of the type of home you would like to live in, or a person doing just what you would love to do.

- I suggest including eight main areas in your dream collage: spiritual, family, health, finances, career or life purpose, relationships, housing and environment.

- Tear images from the magazines and take your time as you allow your mind to open up to all the possibilities. You just never know what images you are going to come across, so enjoy the adventure and the discovery.

- In the middle of your collage, place a happy, smiling photograph or image of yourself.

- Put an image that represents the god/goddess/higher power of your heart in your collage.

- Halfway through, cook yourself a nice lunch or have the ingredients prepared the night before. Make sure it is a meal that doesn't take long to prepare. Do take a break. Go for a walk in a nearby park or walk around the block to flex your creative muscles.

- Place your collage in a space in your home where you can see it every day.

I am always amazed at the power and brilliance of this exercise – I have used it with everyone from unemployed women to senior managers. The last group I used it with created a fantastic array of beautiful, vibrant images. I suggested that they each placed their collage in a large clip frame and kept it in a space in their home that they were sure to see it every day.

2 Blockbuster

♦ Write down what you stand to gain by *not* painting, setting up your own business, writing, singing, getting fit, or whatever it is that you are avoiding doing.

♦ Now write down what you *do* stand to gain by painting, setting up your own business, writing, singing or getting fit.

3 Wish Upon a Star

I always loved that song by the 70s soul group, Rose Royce.

♦ Wishing connects us to our dreams and desires. Write down your top ten wishes for your life as quickly as possible. Suspend all judgements as you write.

4 Creative Review

♦ Write a review of one of your artistic creations in your Soul Purpose Journal. This can be anything from a great meal you cooked to a room you transformed in your home.

♦ Next to it, place a photograph of yourself.

♦ Sign and date your entry.

5 Do What You Love and the Money Will Follow

♦ Write down ten things you would love to spend the rest of your life doing.

♦ Choose one item from the list.

♦ Now make a list of ten different ways you could make a living by doing that one thing.

6 Treasure Chest for Your Creative Ideas

My creative ideas come to me at all different times of the day; when I'm having a bath, sitting on the toilet, driving, giving a workshop. When they come, we must be ready to catch them. Always have paper or post-it notes close at hand to write them down. Sometimes the ideas that come are for projects that I intend to work on in the future. So I have created a treasure chest in which I place all my creative ideas.

All you need is an old shoe box, some nice wrapping paper, and an image to go on the lid of the box.

◆ Cover your box in the wrapping paper and glue the image on top. (I have an image of a dancer on my treasure chest. I have also added scented paper to the bottom of the box. Each time I open it the aroma rises up to me.)

◆ Place your ideas in your treasure chest where they will incubate and become the jewels of your creative dreams.

7 Make Your Own Creativity Totem or Creativity Arrow

Create your own creativity totem using plasticine. Your creativity totem is your mind's own image of a god/goddess figure through whom you can access your creative spirit. Have fun making your totem and place it on your artist's altar.

SELF-DISCOVERY EXERCISE
Treasure Tree

THE PURPOSE OF THE treasure tree is to put you in touch with your creative abilities by sending special healing messages to yourself. The messages on its branches are your treasures.

◆ Go for a walk in your local park and gather together a collection of twisted tree branches. Ask permission from the tree before you break off a branch. Ideally, seek branches lying on the ground which the tree has already given to the earth.

- Willow branches are ideal for your treasure tree. They have spiral branches which carry a wonderful energy.

- You may wish to leave the branches of your treasure tree natural or you could spray them with gold or silver paint. For best results when spraying, work outside. Stand the branches in the drainage holes of an upturned flowerpot so you can walk around them easily as you spray. Allow the branches to dry. (Flower shops often have a good supply of willow branches, especially around Christmas.)

- Have your creative materials ready. Use crystals, seashells, or cowrie shells from Africa to decorate your treasure tree. Cowrie shells are white with a distinctive brownish jagged edge that runs the length of the shell. They were traditionally used as currency and for sacred purposes. Treat your cowrie shells with the same reverence as you would a crystal. Collecting your own shells will give your treasure tree deeper meaning.

- Drill a tiny hole in the top of each shell, thread it with ribbon and tie onto the branches of your treasure tree. Purchase crystals that already have holes.

- Purchase 14 tiny art envelopes. If these are difficult to find, make your own. Use handmade paper, wallpaper or wrapping paper. To get the shape correct, unglue an old envelope, copy a smaller version of the shape on to the paper you are using, and glue together. Punch a hole in the centre of the envelope along the top and fasten with ribbon or string. Cut a small piece of card or paper small enough to fit into each envelope.

- Date the outside of each envelope with the day you completed your treasure tree but using a different month on each one, e.g. '12 January', '12 February'. . . .

- Label the two remaining envelopes, one with the date of your next birthday, and one with '1 January' of the approaching year.

- Ground yourself and enter sacred space. On each card write yourself a special message. This could be an affirmation, a prayer, a healing message, or an appreciation. Place one card in an envelope for each month. Do the same for your birthday message and the message to yourself for 1 January of the approaching year.

- Tie your 14 envelopes onto the branches of your treasure tree.

◆ Open your envelopes on the designated day of each month. This is your monthly gift to yourself, a reminder of your divine goodness. You may wish to add to your treasure tree.

◆ Stand your treasure tree in a beautiful vase or pot. Find a special place for it in your home and enjoy the special meaning it will add to your life.

CHAPTER 10

Soul Food

SOUL FOODS ARE foods which originate from our ancestral roots, foods that have been passed down through different generations of the same family.

THE FAMILY THAT EATS TOGETHER . . .

In our family, food was always at the heart of our activities. We enjoyed lavish meals, which we all ate together gathered around the dining room table. The food was cooked with love and eaten with gusto.

I could tell the days of the week by what we ate. On Sundays we had the biggest meal of the week. It was huge – the dining table abundant with an assortment of dishes: roast chicken, roast potatoes, gunga peas and rice, macaroni cheese baked in the oven, a jug full of gravy, and apple crumble to finish. On Wednesdays it was corned beef and rice fried up with onions and tomatoes. On Thursdays it was fried fish, served with split peas and rice.

On Fridays we children were treated to fish and chips from the local chip shop or my mother's thick, home-cooked chips with fat Wall's sausages and Bird's Eye beef burgers. If it rained we would tuck into a sumptuous bowl of West Indian soup – laden with my favourite dumplings, sweet potatoes, English potatoes, pumpkin and neck of lamb or beef.

Saturday was Bajan day – my father's favourite. My mother would make a big pot of coo-coo, a national dish from Barbados, a blend of okra and corn meal, served with fish. On Saturday morning one of us would be sent over to collect the weekly dish of black pudding and souse, a combination of pig's liver and pickled pig's trotters. Awful as it sounds, it was a delicious dish, a real Bajan delicacy.

On Bonfire night, 5 November, Mum would make conkies from cornmeal, wrapped in foil and gently boiled. In October we would grind the fruit mix of sultanas, raisins and orange peel which would then be soaked in sherry in preparation for the Christmas cake which would be baked in early December. Just before Christmas day the house would be filled with the aromas of baked sponge cakes and sweet bread made with coconut.

FOOD THAT TAKES YOU BACK

On special occasions we would be treated to the soul food that I and all my siblings loved – bakes. These were delicious small pieces of dough made from self-raising flour, sugar and a pinch of salt, blended together with water or milk, and then fried in oil in small mounds. Bakes are my daughter's favourite. When she stays overnight at her grandmother's she is overjoyed when she has them for breakfast.

Aida often begs me to make bakes for her. I resist most of the time, saying I'm too busy. But now I realise I must show her how to make them. This is one soul food recipe that I have the power, right now, to pass on to future generations. I must teach her because I have never measured out the ingredients I use. Like my mother, and her mother before her, I just 'know' the right amount.

It is also true that some of our ancestral foods may not be particularly healthy. However, wherever appropriate, I believe it is important for us to eat foods that take us back to our roots and our culture. Use your own internal wisdom to decide which foods are best for you.

Right now, how about making contact with the soul food legacy of your own past? Which soul foods did your family enjoy? Was it authentic pizzas from your Italian upbringing? Tasty omelettes from your Spanish past? Or the roast beef and Yorkshire pudding of your English ancestry? Or maybe it was ackee and salt fish from your Jamaican roots? Whatever it was, write down the dishes in your Soul Purpose Journal and plan to include a soul food dish in your weekly menu.

Soul food can be nourishing to the spirit and the soul. For example, my friend Jacqui gave me a gift of pineapple punch. She told me how excited she was, about finally learning how to make her favourite punch. It took me back to my days of making Guinness punches – a blend of the canned drink Nutriment, egg, condensed milk and vanilla essence. Or the sweet, bitter drink of Mawby barks, a speciality of Barbados that my parents love. Or the red enticing taste of sorrel, made from sorrel leaves. Add a list of soul food drinks to your soul food menu.

By getting in touch with the history of my own soul food, I am reminded of the sheer brilliance of my ancestors who created good, hearty food even from the scraps they were forced to make do with. I applaud their creativity and originality, their skill in being able to cook without clocks or measuring equipment. They drew on their intuitive skills and their instincts to get the right taste and texture. They knew how to feed the five thousand with just five loaves and two fishes. When I eat soul food I am dipping into the rich memories of my ancestral past.

Why not plan an evening where you enjoy your favourite soul food? For example, I use the same type of pyrex dish that my mother used and still uses to bake macaroni cheese. The very act of grating the cheese puts me in touch with the Sunday meals of the past. Use a favourite dish to transport yourself back to your own past. Enjoy each mouthful, as you relish the flavour and texture of what you are eating.

If you can't cook a particular dish, find a cookbook of your cultural heritage and start practising. Or, better still, find someone who can cook it and get them to show you how. We must endeavour, at all costs, to keep the history of our ancestry alive in the food we eat.

SELF-DISCOVERY EXERCISE
Daily Recipe Menu Cards

'MUM, WE EAT THE same meals every week – pasta and chicken. Don't get me wrong Mum, they taste good, but I'm getting bored of them.' Thank God for Aida. Growing up, my mum's meals were never considered boring, except fish, which we children didn't really like. However, as soon as I heard my daughter's comment I knew that what she said was true.

I had made the kitchen my war zone. I resented having to step into it, even though I am a great cook, and used to love cooking. I viewed my kitchen as the place that stole my precious time. It was always needing to be cleaned and wasn't big enough for me to be creative. I was always waiting for the day when I would get the kitchen of my dreams. Well, seven years on, I still haven't got the kitchen of my dreams, so I'm learning to love and work with what I've got. I have finally made peace with the kitchen that I have, and what a difference this has made to my life.

My small, pokey kitchen has come alive. Removing a cupboard had made room for an old, pine larder. It has oceans of room. I now have separate compartments for everything. The tumble dryer and a cupboard have been placed against the opposite wall, giving me more space. I now have more wall space to show off a plastic CD holder housing a display of cards, crystals, stones and dried flowers. And I finally treated myself to a dishwasher. But, unless there is order in my kitchen, having a dishwasher doesn't necessarily help. Bringing order into my kitchen has brought order into my life.

At a writers' retreat in Wales the chance to cook a meal with a group of strangers reminded me of what I needed to do. Our cooking was made easy by the wonderful selection of meals, complete with lists of desserts, contained on index cards in a small box. As we went through the list there was so much choice: paprika chicken, vegetable lasagne with a crumble topping, ginger and vanilla ice cream. Each recipe made my mouth water. Imagine, I could have this same feeling in my own kitchen – it would make life easier and mealtimes less hassle.

- Sit down now and write out 20 of your favourite recipes. Use cookbooks for soul food and favourite recipes – make it fun.

- Include side dishes, like coleslaw, fried mushrooms or plantains on your menu cards, which can bring a meal to life.

- Add a dessert and a drinks list to each menu plan.

- Then place them all in a box or container.

THE SOUND OF MUSIC HEALS

'One of the mainstays which fostered mental stamina for the more than 40,000,000 Egyptian/Ethopian descendants that crossed the Middle Passage was the ability to feel the Spirit of God through emotions, songs and dances.'

THE AFRICOLOGY OF CHURCH MUSIC, AFRICAN HERITAGE STUDY BIBLE

While food nourishes our bodies, music nourishes our souls.

The healing, soothing sounds of the old spiritual songs, whose words and rhythms carried in the wind the ancient beat of the drum, gave my ancestors a temporary respite from their pain and suffering.

To my people, music was a way of life. So, when they were forcibly removed from their lands, they took their music with them in their hearts. And music has survived.

Music is an ancient healing therapy that has existed since the Creation. Even silence has a musical rhythm of its own. In the stillness of my bed at night I hear the creaking of the floorboards, the sound of the wooden furniture breathing, the hissing of the radiator. Within, I hear the beating of my heart, the rumbling of my stomach, the intake and exhale of my breath. In the quiet of the early morning, on the top floor of my inner-city flat, I am greeted by the shrill dawn chorus of larks, blue tits, sparrows, robins, and blackbirds all harmonising in the stillness. Most of all, I can hear the clear, calm voice of my soul. Music and silence go hand in hand, like the energies of yin and yang. We need both to bring harmony into our lives. Whilst there is sacredness in silence, there is also sacredness in music. Music is a great teacher, a healing therapy to mend a wounded heart, an encourager of faith, a provider of inspiration. Music is the creative spirit's song.

Music has the power to seep into places where words cannot reach. A note can open the doorway to a heart which was closed. It can travel down to the depths to touch a sinking soul. Music is holy. Whenever my mother was upset or worried, she would start singing. She would sing whilst she was cooking, over the bathtub whilst she washed her clothes, or whilst she was ironing.

We knew not to talk to her at these times. It was as if she had drawn a sacred space around her that we could not enter. Even when we tried, we wouldn't receive an answer. It was only the change of tone in her voice that told us that she had heard us. I believed singing was my mother's meditation, stilling her, quieting her, taking her to the centre of her being and connecting her with God, cleansing her soul and allowing her to return, knowing that as a child of God she was protected and safe.

Certain songs can reduce me to tears, because music works in much the same way as cranial therapy. It releases past hurts and pain trapped in the deep tissue of the body.

Music can penetrate us, releasing emotional pressure. This is why I often re-emerge from a crying spell after listening to a song feeling clearer and lighter. Music is my safety net in which I can release my feelings. Now I understand why my mum sang so loudly in the bathroom whilst she washed her clothes. This was her way when she was upset, stressed or simply overwhelmed – to metaphorically wash away her pain with sound.

Some pieces of music fill me with feelings of happiness and joy. Others remind me of days gone by, a poignant moment with a past lover, or a friendship that I miss. Music is an amazing transformative conduit, which has the power to capture my whole life in its notes and rhythms.

Music is soul food for the subconscious, a divine blessing, a gift graciously bestowed upon us earth angels. Just imagine for a moment a world without music . . . Yes, I thought you might feel that way.

We can use music as a spiritual tool. Whether it is the simple clapping of hands to cleanse the energy of a room, the beating of a sacred drum for a sacred dance, or the sound of singing to drive away negative energy from the body, music is a tool that can assist us on our spiritual journey.

TONING

Julia Cameron, in her book *The Vein of Gold*, describes toning as, 'an ancient spiritual technique that is very centring. Done vocally it creates harmonies that calm the spirit and still the mind.' I have always found singing a very centring act. I loved being in the choir throughout my school years but, after I stopped attending church, I lost touch with the spiritual virtues of singing.

I came into contact with toning at a workshop in Ohio that I attended in 1995. On the last day we did a wonderful exercise where we toned the chakras. Each centre was cleansed by breathing through the repetition of the following mantras:

Roof chakra: **Vam**   Throat chakra: **Ham**
Sacral chakra: **Ram**   Third eye chakra: **Lam**
Solar plexus chakra: **Yam** Crown Chakra: **Mmm**
Heart chakra: **Om**

We began by balancing the base chakra and followed this by balancing the rest of the chakras moving upwards. This exercise has a wonderful, grounding feeling to it. The breathing allows a cleansing process to take place.

Toning is the music of our heart that marks our entry into sacred space. It is the musical opposite of silent meditation. Toning opens the body, making it a receptive vehicle for the spirit within.

THE POWER OF MUSIC

Ancient healers knew the power of music as a spiritual aid. Music is a great filter for our emotions. It can awaken emotions or deepen them. There are times when all I want to hear are slow love songs, usually when I am missing a loved one or when I am healing a broken heart. I play the same record, over and over again, until a shift occurs internally which will eventually manifest externally. At other times all I want to listen to is fast, uplifting music, and at still other times I only crave the silent symphony of nature. My choice of music exactly reflects my emotional and spiritual state of being at the time.

Our bodies have a deep connection with music. Indeed, the sound of a favourite tune has been known to wake people out of deep comas. When my nephew was on life support, we played his favourite rap tunes by his bedside. People in churches sang hymns and prayed for him. Music played a large part in his healing.

Dance is music's soul partner. Together, they make magic. One of the best courses I have ever done used music as a healing vehicle. We would begin each workshop with dancing, to unlock resistance and to loosen up. Both music and dance open the body. As spiritual tools, they can take us beyond this temporal dimension. Music and dance can transmute and shift negative energy from the dark to the light.

Now music is an integral part of all my therapeutic work. Now I listen for music that connects me to my emotions, touches my soul and awakens my spirit. I listen for the positive words of the songs that share people's life experiences. When I sing a hymn in church I delight in knowing that I am singing a prayer. Without music in our lives, where would we be?

SELF-DISCOVERY EXERCISE
Musical Autobiography

MUSIC CAN PUT us in touch with the events of our lives. For instance, I once met an old friend in a record shop. We stood chatting as I searched for a compact disc. Holding a copy of an old Whispers CD in his hand, my friend started searching for a favourite tune. Intuitively, I knew which tune it was. 'Are you looking for *I'm the One for You?*' I asked. We laughed as we realised that we both loved that song. I shared with him what the tune reminded me of.

About 17 years ago, I had attended a soul weekend away at Caister Sands. Staying in caravans and partying all night long was my idea of having fun. A last dance in a caravan at 5.30am with a handsome young man was unforgettable. In the smallest amount of space we stepped, hopped, grooved and glided our way through every beat of this tune. We danced it out, leaving no part of the song untouched. When I got back to London I searched high and low until I found that record. Every time I hear that tune it still brings back sweet memories.

Memorable songs and tunes provide us with a musical score for the key stages and transition points in our lives. For example, certain hymns remind me of my days growing up in the church and of school assemblies. A Luther Vandross song reminds me of so many weddings I have attended. Certain reggae tunes can conjure up a vivid image of the exact party I was at, where I was standing, what I was wearing, and my state of mind. I can remember as far back as when I was 16. Such is the powerful vibration of music.

How about putting together a collection of music that tells the story of *your* life?

◆ If your parents are alive, start with them. What music did your mother listen to when she was pregnant? If your parents can't remember, ask them what particular music reminds them of you. Think back over your life, picking out memorable songs that mark significant times.

◆ Set a day aside to listen to your collection. Enjoy your trip down your musical memory lane. Music is as important to the memory as a diary, photograph album or family video. It keeps our memories of the past alive.

◆ Have a sort through your music collection. Divide it up into different categories. Here are some suggestions:

— Love songs
— 'Pick me up' songs
— 'Keep me going' songs
— Warrior women songs
— Gentle, soothing songs
— Relaxation songs
— Songs to clean to
— Songs to dance fast to
— Songs to give birth to (literally and metaphorically)
— Songs to fall asleep to
— Songs to make love to

◆ Get to know and appreciate your own personal music library. Listen out for new additions.

CHAPTER 11

Still Waters Run Deep

Meditation is like rain to the earth, pollen to a flower.
It is food for your spiritual soul.

'WISDOM COMES TO those who listen.' These
words echoed through the silent passages of my mind as I quietly
meditated one morning. For most of my life, listening had not been
my strong point. But when life got too much, when I felt I couldn't
go on, it was the art of listening that saved me.

SACRED SILENCE

In the past, I did not listen because I was too busy talking, too busy
working, and too busy telling everybody else what to do. Listening
requires stillness. And stillness allows us to open ourselves to the
deeper recesses of our intuitive, creative and spiritual self. In this still
place, we can connect with the depths of our being. And in those
depths lie an ocean of treasures that will soothe and heal our spiritual, mental, physical and emotional selves.

I spent a lot of time during my early years being silent. One of the
benefits of this was that my mind was always abundant with ideas. I
remember waking up early, before anyone else in the house, and
changing around my entire bedroom – wardrobe, bed, the lot. I

would dust and clean, and then sit down and write a story. I followed the voice that spoke within me during my silent times.

I also spent a lot of time reading. Reading was my escape from the world. I was a regular visitor to our local library – sometimes as often as four times a week. In my teenage years, this preoccupation with books soon turned into a preoccupation with people. Being around people meant that I didn't have to listen to myself. I avoided quiet time with myself because I knew that I would have to listen to the truth.

Yet silence always provided me with answers and solutions to problems. Because I intuitively knew this, I kept distracting myself from finding that quiet place within me. For this reason, when I was first introduced to meditation it felt very uncomfortable. I would fidget, and my mind would be over-run with thoughts. I would end up feeling that I hadn't done it right because I hadn't experienced a beautiful idyllic vision or been on the receiving end of some great message from God.

I had huge expectations of meditation. I just couldn't deal with the simplicity of it all. I couldn't accept that, in the humbleness of silence, without any pomp or ceremony, in the depths of my own being, lay the answers.

BEGINNING TO MEDITATE

In silence your intuition works powerfully. Silence is a spiritual act, embedded in most ancient rituals throughout the world. If you have not meditated before, or are having difficulties meditating, I suggest that you start by creating a simple silent ritual in your daily life. All you need is a block of time, say 15 minutes each day, and something to sit on. This is all that is required.

Notice if you are feeling uncomfortable at this suggestion. Often the ego starts to get scared at this point because it is aware of where you could be heading. Be firm with yourself. Ensure that there are no distractions, and begin.

Sit with your eyes closed and connect with your breathing. Do not speak, just tune in your awareness to what is happening around you. At first your mind may be full of thoughts: What are you going to cook tonight? What will you have to do at work tomorrow? Allow your thoughts to flow by. The more you practise this exercise, the more you will notice that your thoughts decrease and a different voice begins to take over. She may be a voice you hear from time to time, or she may be a voice you are very unfamiliar with. Whatever the case, listen to the wisdom in her words and just be.

Once you have familiarised yourself with the sacredness of silence, you are ready to move on to meditation. I want to focus on the simple healing power of meditation because, in my experience, successful meditation still appears to be a challenge for many. Women often say to me 'I don't know how to meditate' or 'I find it difficult to relax' but meditating is like learning to drive a car – it requires practice. You will have some bumpy rides, experience a few rocky roads, before you become confident. After a while, all experienced drivers are able to drive without paying undue attention to the actual mechanics of driving the car. The actions of driving become automatic. Meditation works in much the same way. You turn up, surrender and give yourself over, as you make a deeper connection with your soul. And each time you do it, it becomes easier.

Meditation is a healing ritual. 'Medi' means 'to heal'. 'Ta' means 'to take or have'. And the suffix 'ation' means 'action or result'. So meditation is a tonic for your soul.

Like the roots of a tree, meditation takes us to the foundations of our being. Each breath we take is like a kiss of life. With each breath we exhale, we can let go of our rubbish. When we don't meditate our being becomes weak. We waiver. We are unsure and uncertain. Our roots become entangled with weeds, which keep multiplying as we desperately struggle to control their growth. It is only when we take time to tend our roots, by being still and meditating, that our leaves begin to grow and flourish.

Our leaves are the spiritual, emotional, physical and mental aspects of our being. Challenges are presented to us and all around us things disintegrate. But, if we stay centred, if we meditate and open ourselves to our own internal power, our spirit, like the roots of the tree, we will weather the storm.

THE BREATH OF LIFE

Meditation connects us with our God, the Creator, and the higher power in our life, through the healing energy of breath. Breath is the one element that separates us from death. We cannot live without its healing presence in our lives. It is the umbilical cord between life on earth and life in another world. Yet many of us take something as simple as breath for granted, forgetting its vital importance.

In meditation our goal is to become more conscious of the way we breathe. Some of us breathe fully into our lungs, sending oxygen to all the cells in our bodies. Others take short, sharp breaths, cheating ourselves of the rewards we could gain from correct breathing. We each have a limited number of breaths we will breathe during our lives. Yet we are short-changing ourselves by not breathing fully.

A car will not run unless it has petrol. In the same way, breath is the fuel the body needs to keep it going. I was once told by a mechanic that I had created a serious problem in my car engine because I had only been filling my car with a minimal amount of petrol each time I visited the petrol station. This was, in fact, an accurate reflection of the way I was living my life at the time. When we don't breathe correctly, it can have a drastic impact on our spiritual, emotional and mental well-being.

Correct breathing expands our minds and raises our spirits, providing insights and inspirations that can strengthen and transform our lives.

Breath calms our emotions. When I am angry, tense and frustrated, my breathing becomes shallow and restricted. I tense my body and my brain acts accordingly. When I breathe correctly the breath dissolves the anxiety, making room for positive thoughts and emotions. When we breathe we feed our bodies with oxygen. When we exhale we get rid of all the toxins.

We cannot see our faces in running water. In stillness and silence, meditation allows us to travel deep within and make contact with our spirit selves. Over time, you will notice that meditation has the magical power of creating more time. Meditation is an important healing ritual that not only enriches our spiritual selves but also has great influence on other aspects of our lives. When we meditate we can transcend time. By meditating, and connecting with the centre of ourselves, we create the space for greater harmony and balance in our lives.

Breath cleanses our emotions and meditation is the tonic that keeps us sane in a toxic world. Through meditation we become daily visitors in the wonderful house of God.

SELF-DISCOVERY EXERCISE
Cleansing Breath

THE BEST TONIC for your body is a slow deep breath. Deep breathing circulates oxygen throughout your body. Breath is your life force ebbing and flowing. Use breath to cleanse your body and mind and replenish your spirit. Begin with a cleansing breath exercise.

◆ Sit on a chair with your back straight. Place the palm of your right hand over your stomach. Inhale, taking a slow, deep breath. Pull the air down and feel it circulating around your stomach. Your stomach should expand outwards as you breathe in.

◆ Now push the air back out by exhaling slowly and deeply. Your stomach should pull in as you release the air you are holding inside.

◆ Repeat this seven times, inhaling and exhaling. Do it slowly and with clear intention. Fill the breath you inhale with cleansing energy. Visualise the breath cleansing, as it travels through your body. As you exhale, imagine all the toxins and negative emotions being released.

◆ When you have finished sit quietly for a few moments and listen to your breath before you rise.

SELF-DISCOVERY EXERCISE
Balancing Breath

BALANCING BREATH connects with the power of the solar plexus chakra and third eye chakra. It cleanses and brings about harmony between the left and right sides of the brain. It is sometimes known as 'power breath'.

◆ Using the thumb on your right hand, press your right nostril closed and breathe in slowly through your left nostril.

◆ Send the breath down to your stomach area. Hold the breath there and quickly close your left nostril with the third finger on your right hand. Hold both nostrils closed for a few seconds.

- Gently release the pressure on your right nostril and breathe out slowly, still keeping the left nostril closed.

- Take a deep breath in through your right nostril, keeping the left nostril closed. Hold the breath in and close your right nostril. Hold both nostrils closed for a few seconds. Open your left nostril and slowly let the air out again.

- Rest quietly for a moment before moving on to your meditation or sacred space.

SELF-DISCOVERY EXERCISE
Word Power Breathing

THIS EXERCISE IS very powerful. It tones the skin and relaxes the muscles around the mouth. It also relieves stress, tension and anxiety. Working on the throat chakra, it also clears the way for you to express what you really want to say. Try it – it really works.

- Open your mouth as wide as you can and take a huge deep breath in. Really fill your stomach region.

- Now exhale the breath by pushing the sound 'AHHH' out from the back of your throat as you pull your stomach in.

- As you let out the sound 'AHHH', visualise any negative emotions and feelings being released.

CHAPTER 12

The Courage to Dream

Your dreams are visions questing to be given life in your waking reality

Have the courage to dream
Your own dream,
Not the dreams of your ancestors, your family,
Your parents, your friends,
Your own divine dream,
Live your dream from the purest
Part of you.
Keep stoking its fire,
Massage it with passion,
Breathe magic into it,
Move the thoughts of your
Dreams into words on the page,
Utter them through the walls
Of your mouth.
Give them life by taking action,
Have the courage to live your own dream.

EVERYONE HAS DREAMS, whether they are conscious of them or not. Daydreams are the journeys we embark on as we close off from the conscious mind and move towards the land of the unconscious. Dreams are the same journeys in our sleep time. We also have dreams in the sense of ambitions and aspirations.

MAKING DREAMS INTO REALITY

Dreams alert us to our hidden desires, opening us up to what we want for ourselves and what we want to become. Dreams are the voice of our Soul Purpose. The images and thoughts of our desires become the blueprint of our dreams.

Your determination to realise a dream, when consciously worked on, becomes a powerful force that works externally to manifest the details of your dreams in physical reality. As you work towards your dreams, they work towards you. The more steps you take towards realising your dreams, the clearer they become. You must actively work on your dreams, otherwise they will just stay in your head.

When I was a young girl growing up I was full of dreams. From the age of eight I was clear that I would become a teacher and later on a journalist. Back then, I instinctively knew how to create and visualise what I wanted for myself.

I wanted to write, so I wrote. I won second prize in a writing competition at my local library. I wanted to be a presenter so I got up and did something about it. Eight years later I featured in an interview on Janet Street Porter's London Weekend Television show. Next I presented a live spot as a guest young journalist on Maggie Norden's Capital Radio Sunday afternoon programme.

I became really passionate about journalism. I lived and breathed it. I decided I wanted to train as a journalist so I applied to do a national qualification in journalism. I sat the entrance test with over 300 other hopefuls on a rainy weekday morning. I hadn't confided in anyone about what I was doing. I hadn't sought advice from any teachers or friends. So, when I turned over the entrance test papers, I got a shock. The questions required greater knowledge than I possessed at that time. I did my best but failed to secure a place. This was a big blow to my self-confidence.

Then I did a U-turn. I buried my dreams and did no creative writing for another six years. Instead I threw myself into academia, achieving my 'O' and 'A' level qualifications and a BA Honours degree in Government and Politics. I used it as a hiding place. Those were lonely years. On the surface I looked like a successful teenager doing all the right things. Inside I felt empty. The more qualifications I gained, the more unfulfilled I felt.

Then one weekend I found myself on a retreat for black counsellors. I sat at the front of the class drinking in the workshop leader's every word. I was hungry for spiritual sustenance, some soul food. I had reached the point where I knew I had to work through some of the traumas of my childhood.

Even though I had buried my dreams, my unconscious mind had kept them alive. That weekend witnessed their rebirth. I broke through my denial of my inner aspirations and desires. I faced up to my fears, took courage and wrote. My words became a flowing river. I heard the call of my earlier quests. I surrendered to the spirit of my childhood dreams. My sense of failure had paralysed me, making me shut off from the excitement and enthusiasm of what I really wanted for myself. I would no longer let fear be my guide.

LIVING YOUR OWN DREAMS

Our dreams need to be acknowledged; they require us to recognise their existence. And we need to be brutally honest with ourselves about whose dreams are we living.

My parents dreamed of making a better life for themselves and their children. They certainly achieved this physically and materially but sometimes I wonder at what cost to their own spiritual and emotional needs. My parents' generation often put aside their own personal desires in favour of the 'collective vision' – a better life for their families and for their children.

My mother's personal dream was to become a nurse. I often tease her and say she should have been a doctor. The energy with which she discusses our ailments, and the way she always checks whether I've taken my daughter to see the doctor at the first sign of sickness, is enough for me to believe that that is what she should have been. But her dreams somehow got buried amongst raising six children. I really wish she could have pursued those aspirations but I believe the energy of her untapped dreams was transferred to me.

Imagine my mother's disappointment when I completed my degree in Government and Politics and became . . . a youth worker. Not an employee in an office with a smart suit and briefcase. No, each morning I'd rush out of the house, wearing jeans and trainers. I knew I had shattered my mum's dream of what success looked like.

But it was an important lesson for us both. Living my parents' dream was becoming a burden. Whilst I acknowledged and honoured the fact that they had achieved their dreams for our family, I had to live my own.

Dreams are the seeds we plant in our imagination that can grow into the real images of our everyday lives. Like plants, dreams require nurturing. They need warm, protective, safe places in which to grow. Time and patience are great friends to a dream. They patiently stand by as it develops, grows and matures.

NURTURING YOUR DREAMS

We can bring life to our dreams by writing them down. By writing down one of our dreams we give it its first breath. The writing adds sound and vibration to the silent movie. To intensify my dreams, I create collages using images from magazines and newspapers. These become the individual frames of my inner movie, depicting my vision for the future.

Your dreams give birth to your Soul Purpose, and it is the visible manifestation of your dreams which sets your purpose in motion.

Don't let your dreams pass you by. Dreams fill you with hope – the wonder of what awaits you if you only dare to look. Dreams hold the key to the truth of your being. They are the motion pictures of your Soul Purpose, in full colour with digital sound and wide screen – a panorama of your life. They are the torch that lights your path as you travel in the true direction of your Soul Purpose. Your dreams are visions questing to be given life in your waking reality.

INTUITION AND DREAMS

Intuition is the spirit-powered sixth sense that is always working on your behalf. Before something happens your intuition will often tell you about it, in the form of a voice, or a symbolic message, or a dream.

It is difficult for your intuition to get through if your internal frequency is blocked with negative thoughts and emotions. When you create harmony and balance in your life your intuition responds more energetically. It's always there working for you, but now its vibrations will become clearer and sharper. I'll share with you a story of how my intuition worked powerfully on my behalf.

I was near the end of my pregnancy. I had been told that I was due to give birth on 6 August 1988. The summer of '88 was a hot one. I enjoyed taking life easy in those last days. The heat, although uncomfortable at times, was welcome. An incident in the flat I was sharing at the time had led to me temporarily returning to live at my parents' home. The cause of my return was a rift between my flat-mate and I.

At first we had got on fine. We lived our own lives and had no problems sharing our communal areas. But all this changed when we decided to share a telephone line. My flatmate started making calls to Barbados on the shared line and refusing to pay for those calls, so we fell out.

To cut a long story short, three months before the end of my pregnancy my flatmate drew a knife on me and threatened to use it. Now I definitely knew it was time to go home.

So, for the last couple of months of my pregnancy, I relaxed in the safety and comfort of my parents' home. The day before I was due to give birth I woke up out of a powerful dream. Even though I could not recall the full details of the dream I remembered the message that I had heard throughout it: 'Jackee you must get up and go and visit your flat and you must do it now.'

Rising from my bed, I went into the dining room and the kitchen. The house was empty. I was hoping to check out what I had dreamt with someone. But, with no one in, I had only myself to listen to. The message would not go away.

Before long, without even realising it, I was preparing myself for the journey to my flat, which required taking two buses. I had listened to my own voice and I was trusting it. I moved slowly. It was another beautiful, hot day. Something was on my side. As I reached the bus stop, the bus arrived. As I crossed two major roads to catch my connecting bus, it arrived. I was definitely being supported in getting to my destination.

As I walked up to the door of my flat I could feel the butterflies in my stomach. I had no idea of what awaited me. Before going to stay with my parents I had secured both my rooms so I half-knew that my possessions would be safe. I stood for a few seconds at the door before I put the key in, trying to centre myself.

A few seconds later I was pushing open the door. It was dark and

I slid my hand along the wall to turn the light switch on. I couldn't make out what it was but there was something wrong with the carpet. The stairs were covered in what looked like white powder. As I slowly climbed them, one by one, I realised they had been sprinkled with flour. I called out but there was no answer.

I could feel the fear beginning to take over and in the distance I could hear the sound of running water. It was coming from the direction of the bathroom. I pushed open the door and entered. The plug was in the sink, the tap was on, and the water was slowly dripping over the side. I turned the water off. Then, I saw that the water in the bath was just about to overflow too. I was still confused as I turned off both taps.

As I explored the rest of the flat I realised that the entire carpet had been sprinkled with flour. In a second I understood what had happened. My flatmate had done this. Then I noticed that the doors to each of her rooms were ajar. I pushed each one and entered. Both rooms were empty. She had moved out, but not before attempting to ruin the carpet and flood the place out.

The delay between her departure and my arrival must have been a matter of about 15 minutes. If I had arrived any sooner I would have walked into her in the flat. Any later and the damage to the flat would have been done.

The combination of my dream and the power of my intuition had prevented damage to my flat and harm to myself. On the morning of 6 August, I gave birth to a beautiful baby girl. This truly was a new beginning.

I had dreamed what the Native Americans used to call a medicine dream. The medicine dream brings the person a completely accurate vision of the future. To the Native Americans, it was of the utmost importance to trust and follow the message of the medicine dream. We should do the same.

SELF-DISCOVERY EXERCISE
A Pocket Book of Dreams

I WAS BURSTING WITH energy after the full moon ritual I had just performed in Tucson, Arizona. I couldn't get back to sleep. In fact I had no desire to do so. I wanted to be creative. I had a copy of the

African American women's magazine *Essence*. I decided to find pictures in it that reflected my dreams and aspirations.

The book I had intended to use now seemed too large. I wanted something that was pocket-sized, that I could carry around in my bag and refer to easily. I had just the thing. Purchased a while back, I had held onto it, knowing that its usefulness would at some point become clear.

A painting of an effervescent woman dancing was the first image that leaped out from the pages of *Essence*. I wanted to dance with life, both physically and metaphorically. Soon I found more and more images that reflected the energy of my dreams. I cut out a section of biographies of writers who had contributed to the magazine. I wanted to work on realising my dream of becoming a writer, so I cut out a small photo of myself and stuck it on the contributors' page of my pocket book of dreams.

An article by a Bajan, an African American sister was included. I felt a kinship with her. I wanted to feature as a descendant of Barbadian parents on the same page. So I included the piece in my pocket book of dreams to inspire me to work towards manifesting this dream.

My pocket book of dreams could travel with me anywhere I wanted. Its constant companionship would remind me of where I was heading. It would inspire me when I needed encouragement. It would grow with me as I grew.

I found the perfect photograph for the front cover. It was an image of a young girl aged about 14, jumping, with her hand raised to the sky. Her face said it all: 'Yes, I've done it!' The affirmation on the back read:

> Dance to the rhythm of life,
> Celebrate being,
> Touch the sky,
> The Wind and I.

To create your own pocket book of dreams you will need: a small blank, preferably hard-back book with plain pages, a selection of magazines or photocopied images from books, glue, scissors (optional) and a pen for writing down affirmations.

♦ Give yourself one or two uninterrupted hours.

♦ Find your images and tear or cut them out.

◆ Glue in your images and write affirmations beside them – these are now the blueprints of your dreams and desires.

MEDITATION
Dream Canyon

I WAS INSPIRED to write this meditation by a beautiful painting entitled *Dream Canyon*, by Sally J. Smith. I gave this meditation the title Dream Canyon, forgetting that this was in fact the title of the painting. The image of lying in the pool and seeing one's reflection both below and above symbolises how our dreams reflect what is happening, has happened, or will happen in our waking life.

◆ Prepare your dream space. Light a perfumed candle or your favourite incense, or burn an aromatic essential oil in an oil burner.

◆ Lie down comfortably, close your eyes, take a deep breath and relax. Allow yourself to become more and more relaxed.

◆ Place your right hand over your stomach area to ensure that you are sending your breath to the area of the solar plexus.

◆ Let your mind slowly clear as you wait for your dream meditation to begin.

> You find yourself standing at the entrance of a huge range of reddish-brown rocky mountains. They loom large above your head, silent in the clear blue sky. The air is quiet, the earth beneath your feet warm. You take several deep breaths. Pause for one minute.

> You hear a voice calling your name. The sound stirs a feeling in your soul and you move steadily in its direction. The path winds slowly uphill. After a five-minute walk you rest for a while on a boulder. Pause for one minute.

> You hear the voice again. This time the voice sings your name. The singing echoes beautifully around the canyons. It bounces off the rocks like electricity. You find yourself responding. You sing your name, and the call and response of your two voices make beautiful music. Pause for one minute.

You feel water beneath your feet. Ahead of you, the rocks have formed steps that allow the waterfall to flow gently down. You are not afraid. You move boldly on. The higher you climb, the more the waterfall flows. You stop and take a drink of the water. The taste of the water melts in your mouth and refreshes your body, quenching your thirst. You rest a while. Pause for one minute.

You move on ahead. You know it is not much further now. You begin to feel a chill. You realise your skin is bare. Just ahead of you, you see a scattering of stones. One by one, you gather seven fairly large stones. Close by is a bundle of wood. You place the stones on the earth, forming a sacred circle. You place the wood inside the circle. Just then you notice two small white stones lying side by side. You pick them up and rub them together. Miraculously, you create a spark. You rub the stones over the wood and the fire lights. You lie on the chocolate-coloured smooth rock surface and rest for a while but you don't sleep. Pause for one minute.

You decide to continue your journey. The rock steps begin to descend. You follow the path. You find yourself in a pool of turquoise-blue water. You dip your fingers into the water. It is warm. Beneath the water is golden sand. It feels comforting and inviting. You lie on your side with half of your body immersed in the water. The bottom half of your body, and the canyon above you, are clearly reflected in the water. You are not afraid.

You tell yourself: 'I will remember all that comes to me in the dream time, memories from the past, happenings in the present, visions of the future. All objects, people or animals I will take note of, for they are my messengers. The dream canyon will protect me.' You sense a presence beside you. You know it is the voice. She whispers that she will protect you. You are safe. You close your eyes, relax and go within. Pause for seven minutes.

Now you awaken from this dream. The sun is shining high in the sky and directly on your skin. You feel alive; you rise and sit for a few minutes, gazing at your reflection in the pool. You say a prayer, thank the spirit guide of the voice and begin your descent. Pause for one minute.

You look behind you. The fire has burnt out. You move ahead, thinking about the images in your dream, until you reach the bottom of the canyon.

◆ Now it is time to wake up. At the count of one to seven, open your eyes and stretch your body.

◆ Take your time and remember all you have experienced. Pause for seven minutes.

◆ In your Soul Purpose Journal write down all the things you experienced, messages you received, and symbols or images that came to you. What do you believe to be the message or the meaning behind your dream?

Create Your Own Dream Canyon Meditation Tape

◆ Record the words of the meditation onto a blank cassette, leaving space for the pauses.

◆ Even better, use your favourite piece of music as background.

This is a wonderful meditation to enhance the power, magic and beauty of your dreams. Enjoy.

MEDITATION
Acorn

THIS MEDITATION helps affirm your dreams into existence.

◆ Relax, enter sacred space and close your eyes.

You find yourself sitting underneath a huge oak tree. Take a look around. As you do, notice that you are surrounded by a forest of beautiful trees of all kinds. Stay seated on the ground, with your back against the tree, and drink in the view.

On the ground are hundreds of acorns, some small, some large. Select one and hold it in your left hand.

Imagine yourself inside the acorn, like a baby inside the womb.

— What colours do you see?
— What sounds do you hear?

In this place of your birth you hold all the potential of your life. In it you hold your dreams and the declaration of your Soul Purpose. It is imprinted in your soul. Fill yourself with the words and images that come to mind.

Now you are ready to plant your acorn in the soil of Mother Earth. Walk until you find a suitable spot.

Imagine the seed growing, expanding, pushing its roots down into the earth, sending its branches and leaves upwards and outwards. Imagine that, as the acorn grows and expands into the oak tree, so do your dreams.

Visualise the oak tree in front of you. In its branches are shimmering reflections of your dreams. Climb the tree and touch them, one by one.

Now slowly begin your descent. When you are back on the ground, stand before the tree with your arms outstretched and say aloud:

'I am the roots and the fruits of my tree of life.'

Stay with the tree. Pause for two minutes.

You can revisit your tree of life at any time. Watch it as it sprouts new branches bearing the blossoms of your dreams.

Give thanks as the tree's roots deepen, mirroring the more meaningful relationship you have cultivated with yourself.

♦ When you are ready, return to the room, relaxed, calm and centred.

♦ Give thanks for the blessings you will now receive.

SELF-DISCOVERY EXERCISE
Create a Dream Collage

USE YOUR DREAM collage to light your path as you discover your creative desire and ultimate dreams.

♦ Choose one dream goal or aspiration you want to work on. Collect strong inspiring images from magazines that illustrate it.

♦ Find a happy, smiling photograph of yourself.

♦ Create your dream collage on a large sheet of poster paper and place the photograph of yourself in the middle.

♦ Display your collage in a space in your home where it will be seen every day. A good space is in your bedroom. Let your dream collage be the last thing you look at every night and the first thing you wake up to every morning.

SELF-DISCOVERY EXERCISE
Dream Space

WE DREAM MORE intensely and deeply when we are relaxed. We can encourage this by paying attention to our sleeping arrangements. Bedrooms are the major holding places of dreams. Encourage their magic by creating an environment to support this. Create your dreamtime space.

You will need: your pocket book of dreams (see page 186), a candle, an oil burner (burning with your favourite essential oil – orange, ylang ylang and rose are good ones to try), pen, pencils or crayons, an object or sacred item (such as a crystal or stone) to focus on, before you drift off to sleep.

♦ Take a relaxing bath (see the bath rituals in Chapter 4).

♦ Drink three glasses of spring or mineral water before you retire. Put a glass of water under your bed or nearby to help you dream more clearly.

- Light your candle (but make sure you remember to blow it out before you go to sleep). Burning a candle in a glass jar is the safest option.

- Now ground yourself. Lie in bed with your feet and arms stretched out. Have your pocket book of dreams by your side, as you will need to use it as soon as you wake. (I have to write down my dreams immediately after I wake, otherwise I instantly forget them.)

- Hold the crystal or stone in your left hand (which receives energy into the body) for a few minutes before you drift off to sleep. Allow your mind to relax and unwind. Blow the candle out when you are ready to go to sleep.

- As soon as you wake, write down as much as you can remember about your dream.

- After seven days read what you have written. Look out for common links and themes in your dreams. Ask your intuitive self to reveal the hidden messages. Dreams speak to us of our futures.

SELF-DISCOVERY EXERCISE
Creating Your Personal Dreamtime Oasis

WE CAN ENHANCE bedtime rituals by paying attention to our sleeping arrangements. The bedroom, our sanctuary from the rest of the world, is the energy container for our dreams. It is our personal retreat where we can recharge our batteries and make deeper connections with ourselves through our dreams.

Is your bedroom an inviting space that encourages you to relax and deepen into your dreams? Take a mental inventory of your bedroom. We are now going to work on transforming it into your dreamtime space. This exercise can be carried out over several days.

- Begin by clearing any clutter from your bedroom. If you have a television be brave and remove it. Or cover it with a cloth. Do the same with your computer.

- If possible, clear the room of any books or papers. Hang up or put away any clothes that may be lying around.

- Take a good look at your bed. Is it fit for a queen? Or is it a lumpy mattress that has been causing you discomfort for many years? In many parts of Africa, a bed is a highly valued piece of furniture. In some regions beds were carved from the trunks of sacred trees, and decorated with images representing the connection between human beings and the spirit world. A new bed may be out of the question. But you can transform your bed by simply changing the sheets and other bed accessories. Add some brightly coloured cushions and a cover that stimulates your imagination.

- What about the images on your wall? A friend I stayed with in Tucson, Arizona, had a wonderful dream collage directly in front of her bed. I spent most of my waking time staring at it. What images could you add to your room that would help intensify your connection to your own dreams?

- What about the aromas in your bedroom? Pleasant scents can improve mood and sleeping patterns. Burn your favourite scents in an oil burner to enhance the atmosphere in your dreamtime space.

- Add flowers or plants to your bedroom. (I buy flowers every week to lift my spirits.) Bring things into your bedroom that connect you to the earth, like stones, pebbles, shells and fossils.

- If your walls are drab, why not add some colour? Sarongs are cheap and make wonderful hangings.

These are just a few ideas to get you started. Let your imagination run wild and create a dream space that is right for you.

Once you have created your dream space, why not try the following exercises?

SELF-DISCOVERY EXERCISE
Sky Watching

THIS IS A GREAT exercise especially when you are at home and need time out doing nothing.

♦ Relax your body but stay alert. Have your curtains partially or fully open, depending on the level of privacy you feel comfortable with.

♦ Stay mentally alert but allow yourself to drift as you watch the sky at night. Maybe the moon is out? How many stars can you see?

♦ Do nothing else for 15 minutes but explore the vast expanse of the sky.

♦ Tell yourself you are now ready to go to sleep. Ask specifically for what you want to explore in your dream:

— Ask if you can have a dream that will put you in touch with your true feelings.
— Suggest that the solution to a particular challenge you may be facing will appear in your dream.
— Before you fall asleep, repeat several times 'I will remember my dreams.'

♦ Have your pocket book of dreams under your pillow or close by. Dream memories can be as fleeting as a breath of fresh air. As soon as you wake, before you do anything else, write down as much as you can remember about your dreams.

SELF-DISCOVERY EXERCISE
Dream Pillow

TO HELP RECALL your dreams, drink a cup of tea made with the herb mugwort before retiring to sleep.

♦ To make your pillow, you will need a piece of material 12 inches by 6 inches. Choose a piece of fabric that you like. Go for a fabric that feels lovely when brushed against your skin. Velvet or satin would be ideal. Have ready some items to decorate your pillow, such as crystals, moon shapes, beads and shells.

◆ Next you will need 50g (2oz) of dried mugwort and an aromatic herb like lavender, comfrey, or camomile.

◆ Stitch or glue your decorations onto the outside of the material. Then turn it inside out and sew up the sides and most of the top. Leave a hole, add the dried herbs and stitch the remainder of the top.

◆ Bless your pillow and smudge it, or place it on your altar with a rose flower on top.

◆ Before you go to sleep hold the pillow for a few minutes whilst meditating on your dreams. Sleep with your dream pillow near your head.

SELF-DISCOVERY EXERCISE
Lost Dreams

THIS EXERCISE IS about excavating buried dreams and desires. Excavating your dreams can reignite a long-lost passion or love. It can also rekindle deep memories of what you really desire for yourself.

◆ Answer the questions as quickly as possible. Don't think about them. Writing quickly kills our inner critic and quietens our logical voice.

◆ List five things you loved doing as a child.

◆ List five things you always wanted to do as a child (these could be things you really wanted to do but never had the opportunity to do).

◆ List five things you would really love to do but are too frightened to try.

◆ List five things you would do in your life if there was absolutely nothing holding you back.

◆ List five things in your life that you would love to be remembered for.

SELF-DISCOVERY EXERCISE
Dream Quest

THIS EXERCISE WILL help you on your way to manifesting or unearthing your buried dream.

◆ Write down one dream that you really desire.

◆ Write down one thing that would make you feel that you have achieved this dream.

◆ Write down an action that you could take within the next seven days to move you closer to your dream.

◆ Write down what you will do to celebrate the achievement of your dream.

◆ In three years' time, where do you visualise yourself in relation to this dream or other dreams?

◆ What gift will you receive as a result of the manifestation of this dream? For example, would realising your dream put you in touch with your leadership, your compassion, or your creativity?

◆ Write a note to God/your higher power giving thanks for connecting you to your dream.

SELF-DISCOVERY EXERCISE
Dream Life Writing

HOW WILL YOU get what you really want if you don't allow yourself to dream about it? Dreams enable us to imagine our hidden desires and untapped talents. For this exercise you will require a pen and your pocket book of dreams.

Dream life writing is best done in the early morning when you rise or just before you retire to bed. It's a wonderful way to start and end your day.

- Set the clock for 20 minutes and write without stopping. Just let the pen keep moving across the page.

- Write about what your dream life looks like: the colours, the sounds, and the smells. Awaken your dream through all your senses.

- Don't censor what you write, even if it doesn't seem to make sense. Through the writing, you are moving back the barriers created by your logical mind which prevent you from getting in touch with your hidden desires.

- After 20 minutes read through what you have written. Sign your name at the bottom and date your entry.

- Put a note in your diary or calendar to re-read your dream life writing piece in 40 days' time. Reflect on what progress you have made. Are there any surprises?

RITUAL
Night-Time Storytelling

As A GIRL, I loved having bedtime stories read to me. When this was not possible I read them myself. I still love to read at every opportunity and I have been able to pass my love of stories on to my daughter.

In ancient times the African oral tradition used stories to keep a village's history and traditions alive as well as to pass on messages about life and the spiritual world.

- For this ritual, you need to research or find a bedtime story that opens your heart and rekindles your spirit. Or, even better, why not write your own.

- Record your story onto a tape, perhaps starting the tape with a piece of music and ending the story in the same way.

- Create your own personal bedtime storytelling ritual. Press 'play', lie back, relax and enjoy.

CHAPTER 13

The Rhythmic Moon

I AM FASCINATED by the moon. I often lie on my settee and gaze at it in wonder. On certain nights, particularly around the full moon, I am filled with an extraordinary energy. It's as if the moon is speaking to me. I wake in the middle of the night with a surge of creative energy. I move around my flat sorting things out. Unfinished letters are completed; creative ideas flow; a messy flat is suddenly organised.

Other times – particularly at points in my life where I have become disconnected from myself and my spirituality – the full moon creates a different energy within me. Going through my journal notes, I have observed a pattern: I am either energised, or I get into arguments with loved ones, or even strangers, when the moon is full.

THE PHASES OF THE MOON

According to the divine laws of the universe, the moon is the keeper of feminine energy. In spiritual terms the moon is referred to as Mother Moon and the sun as Father Sun. At the time of the full moon, women have enormous magical powers and intuitive insight. We can learn to tap into this power at will. When the moon passes through its phases of waxing, waning, dying and rebirth (as a new crescent), we can feel these changes physically, emotionally and psychically.

The first phase of the moon, waxing, where the moon gradually grows larger until it becomes full, lasts for about nine and a half days.

The full phase is the next nine and a half days. It is a time of nurturing and fulfilment, a time of things blossoming and bearing fruit, a time to give birth to new projects and new ideas.

The waning stage, when the moon appears thinner and thinner and later in the night, is the final nine and a half days. It is a time of inner reflection and withdrawal. Women often feel a strong desire to retreat, to toss out old ways, habits, beliefs and projects, and start again. The waning stage was traditionally a time for women to rest and be quiet in their lives.

The dark of the moon is the three- or four-day period when we cannot see the moon at all whatever the weather. During this period the moon is moving out of the old cycle (waning) and into the new cycle (waxing). We can use the cycles of the moon to connect with our own inner rhythms. The dark of the moon is an opportunity for women to explore aspects of the hidden self. It also suggests a time of rest and retreat from the world.

THE SACRED CYCLE

The menstrual cycle is connected to the waxing and waning of the moon. Also linked to this are the five to seven days of menstruation. 'During menstruation women become psychically open,' says Vicki Noble, in her book *Shakti Woman*. 'In ancient times women were able to access vision and power when they bled. They were held in reverence by men and the community.'

Many ancient ceremonies revolved around women and their cycles of bleeding and ovulation. When communities of women live close together their cycles tend to merge and they bleed around the same time.

In North America, Navaho girls mark their coming of age – their first period – with an initiation process. Girls are isolated while they fast and prepare corn bread for the community.

The menstrual cycle is a powerful phenomenon, a gift bestowed upon women. Menstruation itself is the body's way of releasing old blood. It is a cleansing process. For five to seven days the body goes through a releasing cycle.

Because of women's disconnection from the power and magic of menstruation, and because of the build-up of pain associated with periods, we often think of the cycle as an inconvenience rather than a joy. But I really believe that, as women, we should reclaim the menstruation cycle as a time for celebration. Tremendous energies and forces are available to women during this sacred, profound time of the month.

Facing the intense power and magic available to us during menstruation is the key to unleashing our power. When we truly connect with our menstrual power we are not nice girls any more. We are true to how we really feel. We express our sexual, emotional and creative selves from the depths of our wombs. We are wild women. We move through our shadow selves, releasing, learning and growing, as we get closer to the light of who we really are.

The next time you feel irritated as your time of menstruation draws near, see if you can give yourself the space to truly express yourself. One way to do this is to hold a moon ritual.

Celebrating our cycles together as women at the time of the full moon can move us closer to each other. At moon rituals we can chant, fast, relax, keep journals, dance, or simply be quiet. The following rituals and exercises explore how to go about holding a moon ritual, how to keep your own Moon Journal, and how to nurture your relationship with Mother Moon.

RITUAL
Full Moon – Outdoors

THIS RITUAL CAN be carried out on your own or with a group of sister friends. You will need to be outside, preferably near a tree. You will also need a piece of fruit (like an apple or a pear) and access to the earth so that you can bury the core of the fruit. Don't worry if the full moon is not visible to the naked eye. It is there.

The moon signifies feminine energy which is about giving. When the moon is full it is time to say thank you for everything that has happened to you over the 28 days of your cycle.

♦ You will need an apple or pear, or a crystal, stone or seeds, some dried sage or lavender, and some food to use as an offering to the land. Have everyone gather together. The first thing you must do is enter sacred space to honour the Creator, yourself and the power and magic of what you are doing.

- Once you have entered sacred space, all conversation is part of the ritual. Allocate someone who will read out the steps or guide the group through the ritual. If you are doing the ritual on your own, either memorise the steps or have them written down in point form on a card or sheet of paper. Better still, simply trust your intuition.

- Take seven long, deep breaths, feeling the muscles in your body relaxing. Allow your body and your thoughts to unwind and slow down. Take as long as you need for everyone in the group to feel centred and focused before you begin.

- Call upon each member of the group to say a few words of supplication or a prayer. Next, ask each individual to say out loud everything she is thankful for receiving over the last 28 days. As each person says their thanks, ask each in turn to take a bite of the apple or pear and pass it on to the next woman in the circle. Or allow each woman to hold a moonstone – a silvery white stone – or some seeds to represent new life. When all the thanks have been completed, bury the core, stone, crystal or seeds in the earth below the tree.

- Next, each woman in turn will share aloud their intentions for the next 28 days. What is their focus? What do they intend to achieve? If you are out in the open, you may wish to sit or lie on the land to soak in the magic and the power of Mother Moon and Mother Earth. Alternatively, stand with your arms open and allow the light of Mother Moon to bathe you and fill your being.

- Always leave Mother Earth a small gift to thank her. Sprinkle the earth around you with some dried sage or lavender.

- Declare the circle open and end with a blessing or prayer.

- A really good way of completing the ritual is to invite all the women to immediately write their thoughts and feelings about the moon ritual and their intentions for the next 28 days in their Moon Journals. Some women may wish to draw or paint or express themselves through other creative art forms.

◆ Have someone indicate when sacred space has ended. Give each other hugs and share food that has been prepared beforehand. If any women are menstruating at the time of the full moon, have them come together and serve the food for the women of the circle. The healing hands of these wise and powerful women will bless the food at this sacred time.

The menstrual cycle should be a sacred time for all women throughout the world. A time to cease all activities and come together. If you start to create this healing space for yourself and others around you, in time your daughters and their daughters will return to our ancient customs.

Instead of an intrusion, women will then begin to see monthly menstruation as a time of healing, cleansing, celebrating and inner nurturing. By connecting with the different energies of the moon we can enhance our connection with our own bodies. We are beautiful, powerful and wise women. The moon is a vital force – open yourself to its power and let it work for you.

RITUAL
Full Moon – Indoors

FULL MOON RITUALS can be performed outside or indoors. Tune into the energies created by the rhythmic moon. For this ritual you will need: candles, incense, flowers, aromatic oils, journal, pen and creative materials such as markers, paints and magazines to use for collages.

This is best performed on the night of a full moon or new moon. Preferably choose a room in your home where it is possible to see the full moon, even if it is not visible to the naked eye.

◆ Cleanse the room. Light the candles and incense. Adorn the room with flowers. Burn some oils and have all your other items laid out ready.

◆ Ensure that you won't be disturbed.

◆ If there is a window in the room, open it as wide as you can tolerate.

- Close your eyes and take seven deep, cleansing breaths. Take a few minutes to centre and ground yourself before entering sacred space.

- Spend as long as you like in silence, looking directly at the moon. If the moon is not visible, visualise an image of the room radiant in her light. The powers of Mother Moon are still magically at work even if she cannot be seen.

- Remain in this space for at least ten minutes.

- Say aloud or silently a prayer of thanks for everything you have received in the last 28 days. It's easy to forget to say thank you for the small wonders and everyday miracles of life.

- When you have completed your thanks take seven deep, cleansing breaths and relax.

- Now turn to your journal or your creative materials. Write down your thoughts or create a collage that illustrates your new goals and desires for the next 28 days. If you have created a collage, use lots of colour to increase its power and impact on your consciousness. End by writing out a list of affirmations and a prayer of thanks and place these somewhere in your collage.

- Take seven deep, cleansing breaths and relax.

- Say aloud a blessing or prayer of thanks for your goals and desires as if they have already been received.

- If you can, go outside and give thanks to Mother Moon. Spend a few moments each day for the next 28 days looking at your list and/or collage.

RITUAL
Full Moon – Ocean Ritual

THIS RITUAL IS best performed at sunrise or midnight, at the time of the full moon, by the sea. Always take precautions: stay close to the shore and let someone know where you are.

- Allow the radiance of Mother Moon to bathe you in her healing powers and gaze upon the waters of Yemoja, Goddess of the Sea. Watch Yemoja shimmering in the light of the full moon and be renewed.

- Take a quick dip in the water. Don't linger long.

- Say a prayer of thanks and connect with the energy of the moon and the sea.

- Follow the instructions for the Full Moon – Indoors ritual (see page 203).

- After performing the ocean ritual bring a platter of fruits as an offering of thanks to Mother Moon and to Yemoja, Goddess of the Sea. At the end of your prayer of thanks give your gift to the sea.

- When you have finished, return to your room and complete the remainder of the ritual by writing down your desires and goals for the next 28 days and/or create a collage.

RITUAL
Moon Bath

WATER IS CLEANSING and healing. Living in urban environments often means we do not have access to natural water, like the sea, river or streams. A bath is the next best option.

Prepare the required items beforehand. You will need: candles, flowers, bath salts or essential oils, and some incense.

- The flame of the candle represents the universal life force. It also represents your spirit. Allow this light to embrace you.

- Decide on what colour flowers you wish to use. (I usually buy orange or yellow flowers because I am from the deity of Oshun, Goddess of Love, Beauty and Sensuality, deriving from the Yoruba tradition. The new moon is her mirror and the sacred drum her womb). Cut some of the heads of the flowers and use them to decorate your bath water and bathe your skin.

- Add bath salts scented with essential oils to fragrance your bath. (I use orange, jasmine and patchouli fragranced bath salts which I prepare myself). Or simply add three drops of orange, two drops of jasmine and two drops of patchouli essential oils to your bath, mixed with a base oil, such as almond oil. Swish the water around. Burn frankincense, jasmine or myrrh incense.

- Play some gentle music in the background or simply relax in the healing vibrations of silence.

- If you have a window, open it. I feel more connected to the ritual and to Mother Earth when my window is open. The darkness of the night and the mellow breezes soothe and caress me.

- Variations on this ritual include cleansing with sea salt which can be purchased from good health food stores. Salt is excellent for cleansing – a salt bath releases the toxins from the body. Pour 1kg natural sea salt into your bath and relax.

- Repeat the following chant seven times:

'I release myself from negative experiences
of the past.
I embrace the lessons they have taught me.
As Mother Moon shines down on me, I look forward
with joy to the lessons before me.
I am divine, I am blessed, I am joy.'

- When you have finished anoint your body with an aromatic massage oil. To make your own aromatic massage oil, add three drops of orange and three drops of geranium essential oils to three tablespoons of a base oil. Add orange peel to the blend. It is warming and soothing to the skin and you will end up smelling wonderful, with skin as soft as a baby's.

- Keep your Soul Purpose Journal by your bed, to write down the dreams and creative ideas which will flow as you sleep. On awakening, give thanks for the beginning of a new day.

SELF-DISCOVERY EXERCISE
Moon Journal

JUST AS IT IS important to write in a journal during the day, keep-ing a reflective record of your feelings, emotions and moods during the evening and night can provide you with valuable insights into yourself. The more in tune I become with Mother Moon, the more closely I am able to identify the phases of the moon with my own mood swings.

◆ Buy yourself a large, plain, hardback book to be your Moon Journal.

◆ Then go through old magazines, and other journals looking for images that reflect the moon and its relationship with women.

◆ Now make collages on about ten individual pages, scattered inter-mittently throughout the diary, to constantly keep you in touch with the power and magic of Mother Moon.

◆ Place your favourite image on the front of the journal and create a vibrant cover with your name and 'Moon Journal' on it.

◆ Copy the dates of the new and full moon into your everyday diary and get a wall calendar on which to check the phases of the moon.

◆ Commit to writing a journal entry each evening which explores your day. The focus will be on surveying the different feelings and emotions that you have experienced throughout the day. You will also write about how you feel each evening.

◆ For each journal entry write the day of the week out in full, the date, and the month. In the right-hand corner draw a symbol depicting the phase of the moon. If you only have the dates for the full and new moon that's fine. Get accustomed to using the symbols of the moon to signify the phase it is in:

The new moon or dark moon

 The crescent moon (waxing)

 The first quarter moon

 The Gibbous moon (the bulging moon before she is full)

○ The full moon

◗ The waning full moon (getting smaller)

◑ The last quarter or waning half moon

◖ The balsamic moon (waning crescent moon)

A woman's connection to the moon is very deep. The different phases of the moon speak to us of change, of birth, fullness, dissemination, disappearance, rebirth and new growth. She gently takes us through from new to full, full to dark, and dark to new. The moon's rhythms affect the earth's tides and women's menstrual flow.

Writing in your Moon Journal is an opportunity to delve deeper within. Write of the fire that burns in you. Write of the love you wish to share. Write about your dreams as if you were to live them from this moment on. On the pages of your Moon Journal you can share your deepest desires and your darkest secrets. The words on the pages of your Moon Journal are just between you and the moon.

Every month read over the pages of your Moon Journal. Notice the connections between how you feel and the phases of the moon. Do they correspond? Take note of when your menstrual cycle begins and when it ends.

For almost six months I began menstruating on the first day of the full moon or the night before it. In the private space of our Moon Journal we can nurture our hidden desires and bring to life the fullness of our being by celebrating all that we are. Write in your Moon Journal under the full moon.

RITUAL
Moon Writing

MOTHER MOON CALLED me in my sleep. I knew I had to be up at 6am for our trip to the mountains. But my body decided otherwise. Like clockwork at 4.20 I was up. My waking and sleeping times had become an ingrained pattern. I could no longer put it down to jet lag. The daytime did not entice me to write in the same way that the stillness of the night did. The silent conversations of the night heavily outweighed the bustle of the day. I had found my true mode for writing. I welcomed her with open arms.

The moon sat on her throne, pregnant with fertility. Her companion star in the left-hand corner shining bright. The stars were out in force. The whole scene felt magical. Intuitively I knew my ancestors had developed the same relationship with her. Her light had lit their paths across hills and mountains, plains and valleys, oceans and seas.

For a moment the thought of leaving Tucson saddened me. But I knew I had to create this same magic back home, in London. What was comforting was that the same Mother Moon here in Tucson would be the same Mother Moon who would greet me from the top floor window of my flat when I returned home. Only now our relationship had changed. We had created a synergy between us, acknowledging each other, sourcing each other in the magic of the night.

This exercise is a must for all budding, aspiring writers and artists and for those wanting to tap into their creative spirits.

It is best performed on a full moon. If the full moon isn't visible to the naked eye, do the exercise anyway. Her loving feminine energy will sense your desire and find you.

If you cannot perform the ritual outdoors, do it at an open window in your home facing the moon.

If you are going to work outside you will require: warm clothing, a blanket, pen and paper, and two or three lanterns (just enough so you can see to write).

Whether outdoors or indoors, you will need creative materials (such as paints and crayons). Visual and creative artists may wish to paint, draw, sew or sculpt in place of writing.

- Centre and ground yourself. Enter sacred space.

- Connect with Mother Moon and breathe in deeply, pulling the breath right into the solar plexus chakra. This is your power centre, the birthplace of life, purpose and creativity.

- The moon is a direct link to this region of a woman's body. Through your breathing, it will leave you abundant with physical and creative energy.

- Set yourself a time limit for your writing.

- Have your pen or creative materials ready. Don't worry about what you are going to write or create. When I first sat outside under the moon I never had any idea what I would write about. I just trusted and let my pen move across the page.

- Sit quietly under the gaze of Mother Moon if she is visible. Start writing or connecting through your chosen art or creative form when you feel moved to. (I sometimes sit in silence for 10 to 15 minutes before I write anything at all.)

This ritual is a great starting place. Just flow with it. Don't try to work it out. Surrender to the process and let Mother Moon take care of the rest. I believe all artists and spiritual warriors (that means you) should get drunk on this moon writing ritual. It is an energising drink for your spirit and good food for the soul.

SELF-DISCOVERY EXERCISE
Moon Cycles and Moon Dreams

FOR THE LAST YEAR my periods have coincided with the full or new moon.

- Chart your periods for the next three months and how they relate to the different phases of the moon.

- Notice your changing moods, your energy. How does the moon affect you?

- Keep a log in your Moon Journal of your dreams at the beginning of the full moon, the new moon and when the moon disappears.

- Do your dreams increase or decrease during the different phases of the moon?

RITUAL
Moon Libation

A LIBATION IS an ancient African ritual. In the past it was performed in reverence for the wisdom of the ancestors. Priests or elders
traditionally poured libations.

Rum, vodka or spring water is poured from a specially designated
vessel onto the soil of Mother Earth. The elder or priest would traditionally perform this by going down onto their right knee. Energetically, the right side of the body carries the vibration of giving.

At many of the weddings I attended as a child, before the speeches
were made, an elder (usually a man or the master of ceremonies)
would pour gin, rum or vodka onto the hall floor as a way of starting the proceedings. This always fascinated me. Even though it was
not explained in any detail I now understand that what I witnessed
was an ancient tradition which has survived into modern times.

I performed this moon libation ritual on the night of a full moon
in the Tucson valley in Arizona, and it created a healing between
myself and the spirit of one of my grandmothers who I did not get
on with. I hope it will move you also to honour the positive wisdom
and spirits of your ancestors who paved the way for you to be here.

Mother Moon sat potently in the sky, her feminine energy shining down on me. I sat directly under her gaze, mesmerised. Her light
lit a long path in front of me. I placed four night-light candles in a
beautiful aquamarine pottery dish. But they were no competition for
the awesome light that shone from Mother Moon. One bright, lone
star had taken courage and positioned herself right above Mother
Moon's head.

This was the same Mother Moon who had lit the ocean as it carried away my ancestors (who were imprisoned against their will and
taken from their homeland). Yoruba, Goddess of the Sea cradled the
souls of those for whom the sea became a burial ground. On many
nights only Mother Moon could have provided any solace for their
pain. How they must have longed to have been back on the soil of
their homeland. Mother Moon saw it all. I felt humble in her presence.

I felt moved to pour libation. I had filled my vessel with spring water.
I spent a few minutes in silence as I grounded and centred myself.

I began by calling out my own name, Jackee Cheinu Sataya Holder. I called my name three times, each one louder than the one before. The power of my name caused my inner self to vibrate.

I called out the names of my grandparents on my mother's side (Stanley Earle Morgan and Cleopatra Earle) as I poured the spring water slowly onto the earth. I asked that the goodness of their hearts should walk with me, before me and beside me. I poured again. Next I called the name of my grandfather on my father's side – Joe Tate.

As I called the name of my Paternal grandmother, Ursula Tate, I burst into tears. I had not expected this. The intensity of my sobs surprised me. I spoke these words aloud before I realised what I was going to say: 'I know there was love for me in your heart even though you did not always show it to me.' The tears poured.

I stood still and remembered my grandmother. She had arrived in England in about 1966. In all the time she stayed with us I don't remember her ever giving me a good word. She had returned to Barbados within two years. Her time spent in England had been unhappy. When she died it did not pierce my heart as I felt it should. My tears were a release from this pain.

I had so wanted my grandmother to accept me. As a child I was confused by her obvious dislike of me. Over time I had come to accept that my grandmother was going through her own pain. I needed to free myself from this particular generational inheritance. That night I felt that my heart was at peace.

The moon was slowly disappearing behind the trees, taking its light with it. I closed the libation with a prayer and sat in silence, thinking only of my grandmother.

In the background the wind chimes at the front of the house began to sing. I believe this was my grandmother's voice whispering in the wind. I know she heard my call.

For your own libation you will need: a vessel or pot to hold the libation offering of spring water (this vessel should be used only for this purpose); a healthy, thriving plant if you are unable to pour the libation directly onto the earth; the names of your ancestors (direct family members) if you are aware of them, or the names of ancestors from the past; a small offering of dried sage or lavender as a way of saying thank you to Mother Earth as you close the libation.

RITUAL
Moon–Sun

IT IS 4AM. Tucson is asleep and I am awake. Whilst sitting and gazing at the moon this ritual intuitively comes to me. It is best performed at the time of a full or new moon. This is a good time to pull things together. Many people feel abundant with energy. Things fall into place. The new moon brings inspiration. She is vibrant with potential.

The pen moves on the page and I begin to write a thank-you note for all that I am grateful for.

When I have finished writing I tear the page from my journal and place the thank-you note on the earth with a stone to hold it in place. I place the note in the west under the direct gaze of the moon. I remember, as I am doing this, that energetically the west is the place of the ancestor's spirits.

Next I write down a list of my intentions for the next 28 days. I deliberately use the word 'intentions' as I commit to open myself to the evolution and unfolding of that which I desire. I let go of my need for things to happen in the way I think they should. I am aware I have no attachment to the outcome. I have a desire to learn and grow from the value of each experience.

It is early morning now. The moon has begun to disappear as the sun begins his ascent. I place the intentions under a rock or shell directly in the path of the sun. I believe the masculine energy of Father Sun will provide the energy for the unfolding of the intentions. I leave my intentions outside for several hours to be soaked in the rays of the sun.

- If you don't have access to a garden or the earth, work indoors in a space in your home where you can view the moon as it sits in the night sky.

- Instead of placing your thank-yous and intentions on the earth, stick your paper directly on to a windowpane, with the words facing the moon and the sun.

- After several hours collect your thank-yous and intentions and place them in your Soul Purpose Journal.

- After 28 days re-read what you have written. What has unfolded?

SELF-DISCOVERY EXERCISE
Moon Lodge Menstruation Cycles

UP UNTIL THE birth of my daughter who I had when I was 26, my menstrual cycle never bothered me. To be more precise, I never bothered about my menstrual cycle. Most of the time I saw it as a rude interruption to everyday life – a few days of my life each month that I just had to see through. To have noticed it any more than that would have been to have acknowledged the inner work-ings of the body I inhabited, which I went to great lengths to ignore.

My abuse at the age of seven was a violation, an infringement of my sacred space, my internal temple. I did my best to alleviate the pain by paying very little attention to my body and its needs. Giving birth to my daughter changed all of this. It began with the first nine months of pregnancy. I underwent a major transformation in my relationship with my body. Overnight I moved from treating my body as a hollow shell to worshipping it as a holy temple. The advent of the birth had created a sense of awe, a wonderment, a feel-ing that I was about to witness a great miracle.

My body was going to be the vessel through which all of this would take place. Suddenly all I could think of was nurturing it with nourishing, healthy food. Suddenly my body became a work of art, a miracle machine that was so advanced that it could produce life. I worshipped and adored my body from head to toe.

I can't say that I really missed my periods during this time but when they returned my relationship with them had also changed. Firstly, I welcomed the fact that they were a monthly declaration that I had not conceived. I was not mentally or emotionally ready for another child. And the presence of my menstrual cycle slowly began to remind me of the fact that menstruation is a time of release. I began to allow myself to fully explore the broad range of feelings and emotions that welled up inside me before, during and following my menstrual cycle.

Before having a child I could honestly say I never experienced period pains. When other women spoke of their discomfort I could not directly relate to what they experienced. I believed, on reflection, that this was just a sign that my body was in shock. I did not feel, because to feel would have been to remember the painful emotions that I had buried deep within the recesses of my muscles. My subsequent giving birth had fully opened the doorway.

Whilst I had done what I considered invaluable work on releasing my past hurts, the physical reality of becoming a mother marked the final release. From that day I subconsciously gave the message to my body that it was okay to feel.

Now I am right in there with the ebbs and flows of my menstrual cycle. I surrender, as much as I can, to the impending darkness that often swoops down on me days before my menstrual cycle is about to begin. I try to stay centred and grounded at the start of my cycle when my energy begins to drain. And I reach a rising crescendo towards the end of my cycle when my energy increases, often in direct response to the vibrant energy of the full moon.

Sometimes I stay in darkness for the entire duration of my cycle but I am learning to be gentler with myself. I have noticed that my spiritual and emotional growth spurts are closely linked to the dark moons of my menstrual cycle. Whilst I am in this space it feels as if I will never get out. I feel depressed. I take my negative energy inward. Often it feels as if nothing in my world is going right. The more I fight and try and put it right, the longer I take to get out of this space.

Recently I have come to accept that it is okay for me to sometimes be in this desolate space. It is a reflection of my authentic self for me to feel my anger, to gush out my pain. I have quietly acquiesced to the fact that to surrender is a rite of passage. Now I am no longer surprised when one day the light suddenly breaks in and I emerge feeling enlightened and full of energy. It was precisely this realisation that led me, two years ago, to create a three-day weekend workshop entitled 'Retreat to Advance'. We women need spaces, healing places, either inside or outside our homes to which we can retreat.

Ancient women knew this and practised the ritual of women resting at the time of their menstruation. They understood fully the notion of advancing to retreat.

In these modern times we need to find ways of integrating the healing rituals of the past into our daily lives. Moon lodges can play this vital role, because I believe that the only way forward for us, as women, is to come together in healing circles and sacred spaces. Reclaiming moon lodges in our communities will be paramount in our renewal of ancient rituals and in our collective and individual healing.

SELF-DISCOVERY EXERCISE
Moon Lodge

IN THE PAST, moon lodges were sacred places where women gathered during their menstruation. In ancient times women were relieved of their duties during menstruation. The 'menses' (as it was known) was honoured as a sacred time for women. It was a time of rest.

Being connected to the moon, the menses was a time for women to share their dreams, visions, intuitions, talents and experiences. Traditionally, women were not allowed to prepare food or participate in sacred rituals because it was believed that this was a time for women to nurture themselves. Over time this has been superseded by the belief that women were considered unclean by men. For modern-day women taking time out may seem impossible. But ask yourself – how does the thought of being able to retreat, if only for a couple of days, during your menses sound to you?

There is no doubt that, as women, we need to reclaim many of the rituals and customs of the past. When women come together we create a collective, powerful, healing energy. Think about times when you have lived around or with women. Did you notice how you tended to menstruate together? This is a natural reflection of the rhythm of our energy when we join.

In *Daughters of the Moon, Sisters of the Sun* Wind Hughes describes the building of a moon lodge for women on Bainbridge Island:

> We wanted a place to go to hold celebrations, a place to retreat and to be alone, to revitalize our connection to ourselves and the Great Mother, and a place to go when we were bleeding on our moon cycle. It is a place of women's energy. No men can go there.

Thirty-five women raised the money to build the moon lodge, in a forest on a friend's property. Before building began, the women together visualised what the moon lodge should look like. On opening their eyes, the women drew what they saw and hung all the drawings on the wall. Although most of the women had never seen a moon lodge their structures were predominantly round. Everyone shared the building of the moon lodge:

The floor is carpeted and the walls covered with beautiful cloths. There is a wood-burning stove with a hearth, altar, lovingly made of mosaic tiles inlaid with pieces of glass, old stones, shells, crystals and beads in circular and spiral designs.

On the altar were incense, candles, photographs, feathers, stones, poems and even a vial (a small container often made of glass) containing someone's menstrual blood. Other objects in the moon lodge on Bainbridge Island included a life-sized mannequin of a crone (a female elder or wise woman), and a six-foot fabric 'Yoni' sculpture symbolising the vagina as a reminder of creation and the door to life. A journal was available for anyone to write in, and there were small musical instruments and drums. Pillows and blankets were available for anyone who wished to spend a night in this special place.

Just writing about the Bainbridge Moon Lodge makes me feel like I want to be there at this very moment. But why shouldn't women anywhere come together to create moon lodges of their own?

Perhaps one of you has an attic or garden shed that isn't been used. Is there a space in a room in one of your homes that could be easily transformed? What about a space under the stairs? Or what about seeking a room in a community centre that is underutilised? The possibilities are endless. When we positively come together in harmony and love just about anything is possible.

- To set up your own moon lodge, first bring together a circle of sister friends who wish to commit to its creation.

- Decide on how you will fund-raise for the creation of the moon lodge. You could hold car boot sales, organise a fundraising event, get women to make donations.

- Set aside a time when you can meet collectively to meditate on finding a space for your moon lodge.

- Collectively visualise what your moon lodge will look like.

- Share your drawings.

- Spend time designing the interior of your moon lodge. Draw on each other's creative, artistic and intuitive skills.

- Spend time creating your moon lodge.

- Have an opening ceremony for your moon lodge on the night of the full or new moon.

- You may wish to include the following sacred objects/items in your moon lodge: old stones, crystals, candles, flowers, alabaster shells filled with herbs for smudging, photographs, moon post-cards, poems, beautiful cloths, sweet-scented oils, altar/sacred space, journals/paper, crayons and markers, a holy book, a collective diary for journal entries, images of women, a sacred drum and other instruments, pillows, blankets and quilts, bottles of mineral water, mirrors, a small tape recorder, incense.

MEDITATION
The Baobab Tree Moon

THE SACRED MOON tree appears repeatedly in ancient teachings. The Baobab Tree Moon meditation takes you on a journey to your inner self. It is a voyage of connecting with spirit, igniting the mysterious powers of the moon and bringing to light the wisdom of the baobab tree.

The baobab (pronounced 'bayobab') tree is one of the oldest living trees on earth. It is known in African legend as the Tree of Life. It provides shelter, fruit, and bark for baskets.

> You are standing on the seashore gazing outwards. A gentle breeze caresses your skin as you take a series of deep breaths.
>
> The moon hangs pregnant in a silver, grey sky. Her light makes shimmering shadows on the sea.
>
> You begin your walk along the shoreline. At same points you clamber across rocks – you can do this easily. At other times your feet sink into the warm, inviting sand and your walk is effortless.
>
> Ahead you notice an entrance to a small cave. Sweet-smelling flowers surround it. You pause for a moment and savour the scents.
>
> You enter the cave. You are not afraid. The walls are white, shimmering stones that light your path. Ahead you can see a faint light. You follow the path downwards towards the light. Pause for one minute.

The path goes deeper and deeper. The light gets brighter and brighter. You find yourself at a small entrance which you have to crawl through. The hole is exactly the right size. You have no problem pushing yourself through. Pause for one minute.

You enter a cavern. It is full of light. In the middle stands a tree abundant with small pear-shaped leaves. The tree stands tall and goddess-like. She fills the space with an aura of confidence and inner knowing. The cavern walls loom high; you stretch your head and realise the top is open and the moon is beaming in. Pause for two minutes.

You bend down on your knees and drink from the pool that surrounds the tree. As you do, you notice the crystal-clear reflection of your face. A voice within you begins to speak. Ask yourself this question: 'What three things do I need to bring the spirit of my life alive?' Sit quietly as you listen. Pause for three minutes.

Say your thanks aloud and begin your descent back out of the cavern. You arrive back at the entrance of the cave. You thank Mother Earth and pick a flower from the entrance. You walk back over the rocks, to the seashore. You wish to give an offering to Yemoja, Goddess of the Sea. Stand silent at the shore, listening to your inner thoughts and remembering the words that were given to you. Pause for one minute.

Give your offering and then, at the count of one to seven, open your eyes. You will remember everything that was said to you.

MEDITATION
Soma Plant Moon

THE ANCIENT AND LEGENDARY SOMA plant is a sacred plant that is reputed to grow in the light of Mother Moon. It blooms infrequently and only at night under the light of the moon. From the new moon to the full moon the soma plant grows one leaf until, at the full moon, she is complete with 15 leaves. When I read about this plant I was fascinated by just how strongly she was guided by the rhythms of Mother Moon. As the moon waxes (increases), so does she. As the moon begins to wane (decrease), the soma plant loses one leaf each night until, at the dark of the moon, she has lost all of her leaves and is ready to grow new ones again.

We women can visualise the soma plant in order to tune into our essential being as we become intimate with every crevice of our bodies. We women, descendants of ancient seers and healers, hold great knowledge and wisdom about what our bodies need. As we grow and develop, our bodies grow and develop with us. On the surface, as we age, we appear to lose the looks of our youth, our figure, our vitality. But each apparent loss is replaced by a more deeply rooted treasure such as greater wisdom, deep inner knowing, maturity and acceptance of self.

Like the moon, the cycle of womanhood wanes. Each transition, from maiden, to mother, to crone, requires us to lose that which we no longer need. Like the soma plant losing its leaves, we lose energies, feelings and attitudes which we no longer require for our growth. With each new leaf that we grow, we gain qualities and energies needed for the next stage of our development as we move towards a total embracing of our higher good. These are the necessary gifts, blessed by the fullness of the moon, bestowed upon us for the next phase of our life's journey.

In this meditation you use the 29½-day cycle of the moon. For the first 15 days of the month you visualise a new leaf growing. And for the next 15 days of the moon's cycle, you visualise a leaf dying. Or you may wish to carry out the whole meditation in one sitting, as follows:

- Lying down on your back, with your arms at your side and feet slightly apart, take five deep breaths and slowly release. Take several more deep breaths, each time slowly releasing the air as each section of your body begins to relax.

- Lie still for about 10 to 15 seconds, then slowly breathe in and in your mind visualise a vibrant 15-leaf soma plant on a moonlit night. Take your time. The plant is tall and elegant, stretching upwards towards the light of the moon. Each leaf is open, resembling an outstretched hand.

- Take a deep breath, and exhale slowly. One by one, you will fill each leaf with an energy or quality you wish to bring into your life. Begin by bringing the desired outcome as an image or feeling into your mind. Breathe a golden sphere of light around the energy or feeling, slowly blow the energy into the first leaf and place the leaf gently at the bottom of your right foot.

♦ Take a deep breath, and when you are ready bring the second energy into your mind. Breathe a golden sphere of light around it, as above, and place the leaf gently at the bottom of your left foot.

♦ Repeat the same process for each leaf, placing leaves at different points on the body as follows: two leaves on the entrance to your sexual organs, two leaves covering your womb, two leaves covering your heart, two leaves covering your throat area, two leaves covering your third eye, and the final three leaves covering the middle of your head.

♦ When you have placed the final leaf on the crown of your head, exhale slowly and lie silent for five minutes as you experience the different energies vibrating through your body. (A variation on this would be to visualise placing a new leaf each night on the different parts of your body.)

♦ Now turn your attention to the moon. Breathe slowly in and out seven times as you drink in the image of the moon.

♦ Next, begin at your crown (the top of your head). Take a deep breath and bring to mind an emotion, a feeling or a particular aspect of your life that you wish to release. Visualise the feeling evaporating as the leaves shrivel up and die, one by one. Slowly exhale as you watch each leaf die. Bring to mind another feeling or emotion that you wish to release and do the same, until all the 15 leaves have been released. (A variation on this would be to release a different emotion each night through the death of one leaf, over 15 nights.)

♦ Lie still and say a prayer of thanks. Take seven deep breaths and exhale slowly. When you are ready bring your attention back into the room. Why not spend a few moments writing in your Moon Journal? Use this meditation to bring about changes, to release the past and to chart your connection and relationship with the rhythms of Mother Moon.

SELF-DISCOVERY EXERCISE
Alleviating Menstrual Cramps

THIS NATURAL REMEDY can help ease menstrual cramps.

* Take 25ml (1fl oz) almond or sunflower oil and mix with two drops of each of the following essential oils:

   — Clary sage
   — Marjoram
   — Lavender

* Gently rub the blend on your abdomen or lower back.

* You can also burn the following essential oils in an oil burner to help soothe pre-menstrual tension:

   — Bergamot
   — Lavender
   — Camomile
   — Ginger

CHAPTER 14

Sacred Spaces

OUR HOMES ARE our personal sanctuaries, our retreats from the world, where we are free to express our spiritual and creative selves. But, with our hectic lives, it is easy to forget to create special or sacred spaces within our homes. Finding that sacred space in your home brings its magic alive – it may be a seat by a window that lets in the morning sun, or a specially designated table or chest.

Sacred means 'holy', a place where you consciously or unconsciously invite spirit in. Churches provided my earliest experience of sacred places. I would get a warm, wonderful feeling and a strong desire to be quiet whenever I entered a beautiful church. The silence always had a calming effect on me. Years later, I experienced the same awe and wonderment as I stood in the sacred temples at Luxor and beside the pyramids in Cairo. One is intuitively touched by the energy of a holy or sacred place.

SURROUNDED BY THE SACRED

Many of us believe that sacred spaces only exist in buildings we visit, that have been created by other people. It is easy to bypass the sacredness in the buildings and places that surround us. Moving beyond the traditional meaning of 'sacred' allows us to appreciate the grace and sacred energy around us all the time.

An impromptu walk in my local neighbourhood brought this point home to me. Instead of my normal practice of driving I decided to walk to my destination. I had been writing all day and I knew the fresh air would help clear my head. As I walked, I began to tune into the buildings I passed. I stopped to admire a beautiful Edwardian house on the corner of the road. The detail on this house was exquisite – the intricate designs on the brickwork, the many different shaped and different sized windows. There was even an oval window I had never noticed before. Then came the prize discovery. Even though I drove past this building nearly every day I had never before noticed the roof garden at the top of the house. I drank in the beauty of this house, imagining what it must have looked like when it was first built.

As I continued on my walk, I made even more discoveries and I took great pleasure in admiring the many different ways in which people honoured and decorated their homes. Each home sent out a personal message or statement about the people who lived there. One house had a beautiful money tree in its front window that was stretching its branches in every possible direction. Another house had a branch with red leaves in a tiny crystal glass bottle which was perched daintily on a windowsill. I was amazed at the number of homes with beautiful stained-glass windows. Whenever I go to a church I spend ages studying the designs on the stained glass. Stained glass has always held a special magic for me. Now I realise there is no reason why I should not bring some of that magic alive by having stained glass in my home.

Of course synchronicity was playing its part. I had just finished editing this chapter on sacred spaces. And my walk was showing me exactly what I needed to make this section of the book complete. The best was yet to come.

As a young girl, I had always wanted to visit the windmill that I had heard was still standing in Brixton. Even after seven years of living in the area and seeing the sign, I had never once made the effort to visit it. But on this particular day I looked across the street and there in front of me was a sign saying 'Ancient Monument'.

I felt a shiver of apprehension as I walked up the street. I expected to see the windmill looming large in front of me. A part of me wanted to turn back but my legs just kept on moving. As I approached the end of the road there was still no sign. By then I began to doubt that it was still standing. Then, as I reached the corner, I felt my heart skip a beat. There it was – a huge, silent shadow on the grassland, overlooking the council estate and the children's playground.

I could smell its age, feel the ancientness of its being. Its silence spoke of wisdom and of time. It was built in 1816 and it was still completely intact. For a moment I felt as if I was on a movie set, as I imagined people farming the land around the windmill, at home in its natural habitat. I felt humbled by it. I had connected with the sacredness and the beauty of my everyday environment and the simple things within it. All I needed to do was open my eyes and look.

CREATING A SACRED ALTAR

Creating an altar gives you a specifically designated sacred space in your home. Traditionally, an altar is housed inside a building and a shrine is created outside. Your altar is your personal symbolic place of worship, the visible spiritual centre of your home. You can use your altar as a place to meditate, to pray, to seek inner guidance, or simply to be still.

For my first ever altar, I found a space under the large window in my bedroom. This was an ideal spot, as I loved to watch the sky and the clouds during the day and the stars and the moon at night. You can house your altar on a small shelf, on a windowsill or mantelpiece, under your dining-room table, or in a favourite box or chest. Once you have decided on the location of your altar, you will need to cleanse the space in which it is housed to consecrate it as a place of honour in your home (see the space cleansing ritual on page 237).

CLEARING CLUTTER

Clutter seems to have a natural affinity with the corners of my living room. I can smell it as soon as I enter my flat because clutter definitely carries an energy of its own. Before we begin any space cleansing, we must attack the clutter in our homes.

Your space cleansing will have better results, the more thoroughly you clear your clutter beforehand. Clutter is like a wound that must be exposed to the air before healing can begin. Otherwise, we end up ignoring the real problem and simply covering the wound with sticking plaster. Our lives today are full of clutter, draining our energy on conscious and subconscious level. Consciously, I get easily irritated by the sight of a growing pile of papers on my living-room floor. Subconsciously, I take myself to task for not having cleared it in the first place.

My home has a wonderful energy when it is orderly and free of clutter. By the same token, it has an unpleasant aura when it isn't. Both states are an accurate reflection of the way I am feeling about myself at the time.

Hiding your clutter is not the solution. Clutter plays games with the subconscious mind. You may consciously think that, because your clutter is hidden, you will automatically feel better. Think again. The subconscious mind goes to work, having conversations with your inner thoughts and berating you for accumulating and hiding all that clutter. Your clutter may be out of sight but it's certainly not out of mind.

Our emotional clutter works in much the same way, begging to be released. If kept unreleased, it plays havoc with our state of mind. Cleaning has always been one activity I have used to help shift my emotional clutter. When I lived at home with my parents I used to enjoy the weekly Friday night ritual of cleaning our house. I always felt good afterwards, both in myself and in the space.

Now, if I want to shift my energy, I grab the mop or broom. Somehow the rhythmic action helps me release unwanted energy. The left side of my brain responds to the physical action of sweeping. Because I go into automatic mode, I am now free to think and explore my subconscious, and the right side of my brain, the intuitive and creative side, comes to life. The two meet and, amazingly, they can have a conversation without having to complete for control. In that space I can work through issues and be open to any idea that pops into my head. And at the same time I am cleaning and clearing the space that I live in.

If I am stuck with my writing I know it is time to clear some clutter or go for a walk. Often a simple task, such as clearing a drawer or filing away papers, will be more than enough to blast me through the writer's block. Over time I have learned to ask the question: Am I clearing clutter as a way of distracting myself from completing my task, or do I need to clear clutter in order to remove a block?

Once you fully understand the reasons for clearing clutter, you are ready to begin your space cleansing.

A WORD ABOUT TELEVISIONS

I was rearranging my living room when it suddenly dawned on me that televisions have taken the place that traditional fires, and altars, once held as focal points in millions of homes around the world.

The television occupies a space where everyone can see it. In most households every evening the family sits huddled round and glued to the set. Imagine if that family was gathered around a log fire or a sacred altar instead. Picture the children lighting candles, and saying a prayer, before the family gathered to simply spend quality time with each other.

Television has played a big part in reducing communication and human interaction. You may not be aware of the fact that a television sends out powerful signals for up to three days after it has been switched off. This is partly why many people cover their televisions with a cloth or hide them in cupboards, when they are not in use. When I removed my television set from my bedroom, almost immediately I felt an energy change. My bedroom was transformed overnight into a quiet retreat. It became my sanctuary. I started taking more care over the room, I enjoyed going to sleep there, and slept much better. I also noticed that I remembered my dreams much more clearly and in more detail. Try removing the television from your bedroom (if you have one there) and notice what it feels like. Or place a quartz crystal on top of your television to reduce its magnetic energy.

A VISIT TO OMISADE'S TEMPLE

My dear friend Omisade was excited. She had finally finished creating the sacred cupboard space in her home. I was happy for her, as I visualised a small cupboard with shelves lined with crystals and candles and other sacred objects. She enthusiastically invited me to visit the cupboard whenever I wanted to. But I really had little understanding of just what she had created until I went to her home on New Year's Day.

The party the night before (20 people packed into my living room) and the cleaning up afterwards had taken its toll. When I woke up very late on New Year's Day I knew that I needed a spiritual revival.

I had awoken to see a full moon rising like a great woman warrior from the drifting clouds in the evening sky. She was so beautiful, so majestic. Five of us had performed a moon ritual on New Year's Eve. I felt my spirit calling me to reach within. But I knew I needed some help.

I followed my intuition and before I knew it I was on the phone to my friend Omisade. We chatted for a few minutes and then said our goodbyes. It felt incomplete but I couldn't work out what it was I wanted to say, ask for, or do. Five minutes later the phone rang and there was Omisade inviting me over. I jumped up, packed some lamb curry I'd already cooked, grabbed a plantain, and made the short journey to her home.

I was totally unprepared for what greeted me. Omisade told me to centre myself, gather my pens and paper, and make my way up to her bedroom. By now I was curious, but pretty positive that I would find myself in a few minutes sitting in front of a small cupboard with some lighted candles and meditating.

But from the moment I entered the room I knew I was in for a treat. Omisade was kneeling on the floor, holding back a blue flowing curtain that led into what I can only describe as an underground cupboard in her bedroom. As I went in, I was humbled by the sheer beauty and brilliance of the space. Here, in the heart of South London, my sister friend had created the most divine sacred space I had ever been blessed to enter. This sacred space was later renamed, by my daughter, Omisade's temple.

Her temple had in fact been a cupboard packed with black bags full of clothes. But she acted on her vision and transformed this cupboard full of clutter into a sacred space. The temple was about two and a quarter metres long and about two metres wide. There was ample room for me to stretch out comfortably on the floor, which was covered with my favourite rug in an array of browns, yellows and oranges. (I had begged Omisade to try and find a similar one for me.)

The walls were painted with a beautiful scene of a tree with a rising sun, and in the distance the seashore. This scene spanned three of the walls, wrapping you up in the vibrancy of its colours.

Against each wall were rows of assorted candles, nightlights, scented oils and incense burning. The aroma in the temple was heavenly. In the background a tape recorder played healing music.

This was a sacred womb space. As I explored my surroundings, I discovered a small treasure tree painted on one wall, from which hung jewelled baubles. From a corner of the ceiling hung a golden eagle and some light-blue frosted candles.

This was the most divine way to welcome in the first day of the New Year. Omisade had reminded me that our homes need not be static temples. She had proved that it is within all our capabilities to transform the darkest corners of our homes and fill them with light and love. I lay on the floor, basking in the sacred energy that had been created in an ordinary home, on an ordinary street. I wrote, meditated and gave thanks.

The next day, four of us were to be found in sister Omisade's home waiting our turn to spend quiet time in the temple. I have visions of people queuing in the future for their turn in Omisade's temple.

Towards the end of my time, my daughter Aida came in. She couldn't stop saying how wonderful she found the space. 'Mummy,' she said, 'we can clear out the walk-in cupboard in my bedroom and do the same.' I looked at her in surprise. Our children are our greatest teachers. In my own home I, too, have a walk-in cupboard which is full of clutter. It is dying to be transformed. The words of my daughter hit me with their wisdom.

Take a good look around your own home. Maybe, if you look close enough, you too have a space in which you can build your own temple of love. Your sacred space can be as big, or as small, as you wish. Dare to make it just as you desire it.

Thank you, Omisade, for so lovingly sharing your life and your home with me and reminding me of how greatly we can expand, and create what we want, beyond our wildest dreams.

MAINTAINING SACRED SPACE WITH MOTHER EARTH

Mother Earth is God's gift to humankind. She is our home, resplendent in her beauty, abundant with nature's riches, and awesome to the eye. She is forever changing, growing, dying and giving birth. Mother Earth is indeed heaven on earth.

Mother Earth is alive with spiritual blessings to nurture our souls. She cradles us in times of sorrow and supports us in times of joy. When things are hectic, a walk through her fields and forests brings calmness and serenity. Through the changing seasons, she brings the gift of change. She feeds us daily with the fruits of her soil.

The trees, the mountains, the stars, the sky all hold messages for us. If we look to them they can help us to make a deeper sense of our world. Mother Earth longs for us to fully honour her, touch her, and sense her. Deep down, we all long to be with her.

Standing on the shores of her seas refreshes ailing spirits. Hugging a tree gives us energy from the roots of the earth. As the wind whispers through the leaves, the voices of our ancestors speak. My feet on the soil, the carpet of the earth, connect and strengthen me as I am reminded of the journey my ancestors made so that I could be here.

I cannot be without her. My home is surrounded by trees – oaks and elms, an apple tree – making me feel blessed. I rise to the sounds of the birds that reside outside. From my kitchen window, I watch the hustle and bustle of the grey squirrels, as they go about their daily work.

My day begins peacefully as I watch the changing colours of the morning sky – the purple haze that greets the orange of the rising sun. This is nature painting beauty on my soul. I cannot live without the richness of earth space.

Connecting with our earth space is a wonderful tonic, promoting greater balance and harmony in our lives. It feeds our energies in the face of ever-increasing demands. Nature is the keeper of change. She flows through change with confidence. In nature there is no holding on, just a natural, graceful surrender.

It was as a result of connecting with Mother Earth that I discovered I had a passionate love and respect for trees. The spiritual energy of trees is very strong. Trees have spent many years on Mother Earth and therefore hold great memories from the past. They remind us of how, in days past, our ancestors honoured their relationship with trees. Old sayings like 'touch wood' show that our ancestors had a deep respect for trees.

Recently, while out with my daughter and her friend, I parked my car in front of a funeral parlour. As I gathered together my belongings, the girls were looking through the window. They did not seem greatly impressed by the gravestones displayed in the front window. My daughter's friend's comment was: 'When I die I don't want a tombstone. I want a tree to be planted where I am buried. As the tree grows, people will remember me.' She was so right. In the past, trees were planted on burial sites so that the spirit of the deceased could live on in them.

I have developed a close connection with two trees. One is the baobab tree, which is native to the African plains. It is a magnificent tree that can grow up to 20 metres tall and 10 metres in diameter. It is reputed to live for many years and its fibres can be used to make cloth, rope and paper. I have a very special image of the baobab in my pocket book of dreams. It is a sacred space, decorated with cushions, under a tree which, to me, is the ancient baobab tree. I have visualised myself meditating in this sacred space, meeting my Board of Life Directors and listening as I am guided by their counsel.

The other tree I am strongly connected to is the elder tree. I first came across it about five years ago. I met a friend for lunch and we sat under a tree in a small park. When we were leaving I noticed a plaque which gave a history of the tree. It simply said that the elder tree was known as the witch's tree and that, in the past, when witches were being hunted, they disguised themselves by changing into the form of an elder tree. Since that time I have tried to find out as much possible about the elder, which is also the source of one of my favourite drinks – elderflower water.

More recently, I was sitting in my local library, finishing off the manuscript for *Soul Purpose*, when I turned to the bookshelf behind me and noticed a book of names. I decided to look up my first name 'Jackee' and my surname 'Holder'. Amazingly, Holder was a German name, originally given to people who lived near an elder tree.

I am fascinated by the unique shapes of trees. Some trees take the forms of beautiful goddesses with their branches outstretched, as if they were two large, welcoming arms. Others seem full of hair and look as if they are laughing at you. Some are shy and retiring and seem to hide behind other trees. To Native Americans, trees are the standing people.

Like human beings, trees carry their own aura and have different healing properties. The oak is a tree of strength, providing us with the power to respond to challenging situations. The silver birch provides clarity of vision for the over-stimulated mind. The willow connects you to your deepest feelings and the weeping willow, no doubt, to your tears.

If you want to connect with a tree, begin by gently moving into its aura. Move up under its branches. Don't be afraid. Approach it much as you would on a hot summer's day when you would eagerly seek its shade, away from the hot sun. Stand or sit close to the trunk. Say a blessing and ask the tree's permission to take from it. Quieten your mind and relax. Either sit with your back to the tree or hug the tree.

Feel the texture of its trunk. Observe the shapes on its bark. Surrender yourself to the tree, then listen and remember what you hear.

Once you have completed your connection, say thank you to the tree. Leave it a gift (bury a small stone or crystal in the earth beneath it, leave a feather or a strand of your hair, or sprinkle sage or rosemary around its base). What was the message you received? If the message appears unclear, give it time to be made clear to you. Simply remain open and the message will come through.

SACREDNESS IN EVERYDAY LIVING

When I was young I used to believe that miracles always had to be large and eventful, and that sacred things only happened when ordained by someone else. I often overlooked the sacredness in my everyday life. Writing *Soul Purpose* has allowed me to absorb and appreciate these smaller but no less important miracles.

There were times during the writing of this book when I just had to stop and do something different. It was in those moments of watching a video, or an old film, that the perfect line would often jump from the screen and land in my lap. For example, the lines 'Get busy living or get busy dying' and 'Hope can set you free' struck me when I saw the film *Shawshank Redemption*. And, from *Young at Heart*, starring Doris Day, the following line hit me: 'A man decides his own destiny, if he has enough courage or ambition.'

It is in these moments that I take in and appreciate the smaller details in life. I have time to notice the joy that can be gained from simple things. From this place, the subconscious mind works powerfully to weave together the information that we need in the most enchanting ways. Suddenly the song you've always wanted to buy (but of course you didn't know the name of the song or the artist) is played on the radio. That's the magic of small miracles.

When I sit and think about it there have been so many touching moments in life when I have been filled with joy. If we rush, we can easily miss these rich and meaningful moments. They can bring greater depth to our lives and they usually cost nothing.

For instance, I recently delighted in the surprise of finding three cowrie shells embedded in the most sensuous, fragrant soap given to me by a dear friend. Waking up at 6am, just in time to watch the unfolding of a purple and red sky, is an almost perfect start to my day. Witnessing the joy on my nephew's face on Christmas day as he shares the fact that his best ever present is being home with his family (he is in a wheelchair as a result of an accident). Or seeing my sister's enthusiasm as she retells the story of staying up all night to read the dream book I gave her as a gift. A chance meeting with my old primary school teacher touches my heart. She was kind, caring, inspiring and a creative wizard. When I tell her about my book she hugs me and tells me she wants a signed copy. As I go for a walk in my local neighbourhood, I take in the creativity with which people are decorating Christmas trees outside their homes. Using a new library for the first time, I find two books which are just what I am looking for.

Why not look back over the last seven days of your life? Tease out those sacred moments. It may have been an unexpected conversation, or just a quick glance. We often don't know when these moments will come. We just need to be open to receiving them.

'Miracle' is a Latin word, meaning 'when a wonderful thing happens'. What miracles have you overlooked or forgotten? If you're stuck, why not start with 'Today another miracle took place – you lived to see another day.'

BUYING MEANINGFUL ITEMS IS GOOD FOR THE SOUL OF YOUR HOME

I love rummaging through other people's junk – I always get excited in anticipation of finding the one item that I really want. But this is not about collecting more clutter. Whenever I buy something, I always try to stick to the principle of giving something else away.

For example, I had my old sofa for 12 years. It was a plain sofa but it had an iron-frame sofa bed inside that I could use when guests slept over. For years I complained about my sofa, but just never got around to buying a new one. However, I did manage to purchase a huge wicker chair which I loved, although it made my sofa look even drabber. One day, as I was driving past a second-hand shop, there it was – the matching sofa to my wicker chair. I reversed my car, ran into the shop, and bought it. What was interesting was that this happened just at the time that I had made a commitment to buy myself a new sofa. None of the new sofas that I looked at did anything for me. With its newly made cushions, this second-hand purchase was not only exactly what I was looking for, but it was also an item of meaning in my home.

I have endless stories like this. One afternoon I pulled over at the sign of a Christmas jumble sale. My interest in an antique dinner service set led me to explore one stall in particular detail. The price was right but some of the plates were chipped. Then my hands almost accidentally found a polaroid camera that I had not noticed before. I could feel my heart racing. I had wanted a polaroid camera for months, to use in my creative work with groups. The camera had its own case, and the guarantee and instructions were enclosed. I asked the woman behind the stall if it was working – it was. Not only that, it still had a roll of film inside! When she told me the price I thought I was going to fall over – £1 – for a gift that meant the world to me.

And it didn't end at that stall; I also purchased an old-fashioned, glass lemon-juice squeezer for 20p, which sparkled when it came out of my dishwasher. The final miracle happened just as I was about to leave. About a year before, I had purchased a gold, square-shaped decanter bottle with protruding squares on the front. I loved this bottle. And everyone who came to my home commented on it. Before I knew it I was standing in front of a stall selling its exact double. I bought it immediately for £2.50. My impromptu visit to the jumble sale had blessed me with an armful of treasures.

The real joy of second-hand browsing is never knowing what you're going to come across. But it also helps to go hunting for what you want with an open mind. For example, I wanted to purchase an old 1950s kitchen cabinet with lots of small cupboards and a pull-down flap for my kitchen. Within weeks I came across three or four in shops, but they just weren't right. Then, on my way to the dentist one afternoon, I passed a second-hand shop – and there it was, the ideal cabinet. I decided to stop on my way back. It was as lovely as I had thought. It was partly stripped, showing the lovely pine wood that had been hidden under coats of white emulsion. However, I allowed the rudeness of the shop owner to put me off purchasing it.

For a week the cabinet stayed on my mind, especially as it would have been ideal for storing my kitchen utensils and magazines. I decided to visit the shop the next morning. To my complete amazement, it had not been sold. I bought it. It was only after I paid for it that I realised exactly what I had purchased. The owner of the shop was in a better mood, he complimented me on buying such a nice piece of furniture, and told me its history. Apparently Lord Loom (who later became famous for Lloyd Loom chairs) had made the cabinet. I was delighted, not only with the history of the piece, but with the beautiful object which would now be a central feature in my small but creative kitchen.

I also bought an old set of scales with a huge wicker basket sitting on top. It looks wonderful sitting on top of my kitchen cabinet and I'm going to put stained glass in two of the cabinet doors. When we fill our homes with furniture and items which have deep meaning for us we fill our homes with love.

But remember that there is a thin dividing line between compulsive buying and purchasing an item that you instantly know is right for you or your home. Here's how I work it out.

Firstly, don't be afraid to take some time out before you part with your money. Some of my best buys have not been bought instantly.

If you can't wait to get it home and are so excited that you just have to tell others about it, it's a sign that you're on the right track.

Don't be afraid to suggest a lower price for an item. When I have suggested a price based on what I could really afford at the time, it has always been accepted. I've also received lots of free gifts from shops where my energy has inspired people to give me things.

Decide on how much you will spend before you go shopping. For instance, at my impromptu jumble sale visit, £5.20 was all I spent. Many of us can easily squander that amount on cigarettes, alcohol and junk food. But that £5.20 bought items that have given me more than £500 worth of joy.

Whenever I go shopping in a supermarket I set a limit in my head as to how much I'm going to spend and I always stay within that limit without working it out as I go along. Do the same when treasure hunting for second-hand bargains.

Keep an eye on shop displays and interiors of buildings for creative ideas for your home. For example, I have a simple but effective display of dried flowers hanging in my kitchen which I have personally dried. Likewise, when I saw cards displayed in a plastic hanging CD holder in a shop I was inspired to use the same idea, but instead I displayed shells, crystals, stones, starfish and flowers. Friends have enthusiastically used the same idea in their homes.

Make a list of what you really need for your home. Once you become clear about what you need, you will be amazed at how quickly the objects appear on your travels.

Before you part with your money, ask yourself: Does this item possess beauty and in what way will it be useful? For instance, having purchased a number of beautiful bottles, my collection is now becoming too large. So I've decided that I can lovingly give them as gifts filled with scented bath salts and wonderful-smelling massage and body oils. I am giving the same beauty to others that drew me to the items in the first place.

Letting something in means letting something go. Always get rid of something when you buy or find something new.

Don't forget to cleanse second-hand items. Smudge clothes and furniture with incense or a smudge stick (cedar or sage cleansing stick) available from local health food and New Age shops. Wash down furniture with Florida water (available in ethnic grocery stores), or water mixed with the juice of a fresh lemon.

The world is full of all the materials we need to make our homes into creative and spiritual sanctuaries. What you give away could be someone else's treasure. In the same way, what they give away could be yours.

Old and abandoned items can be transformed as you touch the soul with which they were originally created.

SELF-DISCOVERY EXERCISE
Sacred Space Tasks

TO GET YOUR life moving both physically and mentally begin to clear out the clutter in your home. Remember clutter is always a sign of energy that is stuck – often a reflection of some aspect of our lives.

♦ Clear a cupboard or drawer in your home.

♦ Start a journal entry in your Soul Purpose Journal with the words: 'My sacred space would look like . . .'

♦ Have an evening in and watch no television. Instead, listen to the radio, read a book, create a collage, or work through some of the exercises in *Soul Purpose*.

♦ For a month, throw one thing away every day. Yes, one thing every day. If you don't use it, and it doesn't bring beauty into your home, let it go.

SELF-DISCOVERY EXERCISE
Beauty and Order

EVERY DAY DO something to make your surroundings more beautiful. Give your environment tender loving care.

- ◆ Put fresh flowers in your bathroom.

- ◆ Place a photo that you love on your desk at work.

- ◆ Change a room around.

- ◆ Play beautiful music while you do your housework.

- ◆ Burn your favourite incense.

- ◆ Open a window and let fresh air in.

- ◆ Light a candle and enjoy a candlelit meal.

- ◆ Clean your windows and put a vase on your windowsill.

- ◆ Draw the curtains and let natural light into your home.

RITUAL
Cleansing Your Space

TO CREATE a sacred space, you first need to cleanse it.

Cleansing Yourself

Having a salt bath before you begin will cleanse and allow you more open to the sacredness of your room.

- ◆ For a salt grounding and cleansing bath, dissolve 450g (1lb) sea salt and 450g (1lb) Epsom salts in a bath full of water.

- ◆ Soak in the solution for half an hour.

- Relax and visualise the salt drawing away all the negative forces and energy trapped in your aura. Your aura is the electromagnetic field which surrounds your physical body. Some people are able to psychically see the aura as a light with several colours shimmering through it. Others will feel or sense the aura. When we say things like 'I've got a good/bad vibe about X' it is often a sign that we are sensing the person's aura.

- Once you have completed your bath, you are ready to begin cleansing your space. Ground yourself by taking a few minutes to be still. Connect with your breathing and reflect on the aim of what you are about to begin. Perform your space cleansing and the setting up of your altar in silence, maintaining sacred space throughout.

Smudging the Space

We will begin by smudging the space. I suggest using a smudge stick of cedar wood, sage or sweet lemon grass, frankincense or lavender incense. When cleansing a room, incense is only effective as long as its aroma is in the air. Smudging (by using a smudge stick or by burning herbs) will last much longer.

Smudging originated amongst the Native Americans. My first experience of smudging was ten years ago whilst I was on a retreat in California. A Native American healer was amongst the group gathered high up in the mountains. She explained that she would smudge us all to clear away the negative energies from around our auras. The combination of burning sage and lemon grass created a delightful aroma in the fresh, crisp mountain air.

Sage is traditionally used in cleansing ceremonies because of its purification properties. It is often referred to as the 'wise old woman'. Lemon grass is said to clear away negative thoughts and is traditionally used in sweat lodges, and purification and healing rituals.

- To create smudge smoke, place the herbs in a metal container in which it is safe to burn them using charcoal to assist them to burn or simply light a smudge stick.

- Once the herbs are alight, blow the fire out and the herbs should continue to smoke.

- Begin by smudging yourself. If you are cleansing the room with someone else present, ask them to smudge you. They can do this by moving the smudge smoke, from the top of your head, downwards and around one side of your body and then up the other side and back to the top of your head.

- If you are on your own, raise the smudge smoke to the top of your head and fan it all over your body.

- Say a prayer or a blessing whilst you perform the smudging ritual. The following works well:

'Open my heart, open my eyes, clear my thoughts. I am now a channel of light. All the energy I need is here. Blessed be.'

Blessing the Space

Now you are ready to bless the room or space. We will do this by carrying out a ritual based on the Native American offering to the four directions: east, north, south and west.

- To work out where each direction is, place yourself in the corner of the room directly facing where the sun rises. This is in the east. Once you have located the east, you can work out where the other three points are.

- Begin by facing the north. Blow the smoke in the direction of the north and say aloud:

'I call upon the spirit of the north, the place of my dreams, the birth place of my ancestors, the burial ground of my soul.'

Take a deep breath.

- Now turn to the east. Blow the smoke in the direction of the East and say aloud:

'I call upon the spirit of the east, the home of my spirit, the birth place of my true self.'

Take a deep breath.

- Now turn to the south. Blow the smoke in the direction of the south and say aloud:

'I call upon the spirit of the south, home of my inner child, let me tap the power within.'

Take a deep breath.

♦ Now turn to the west. Blow the smoke in the direction of the west and say aloud:

'I call upon the voices of my ancestors, the goodness and oneness of their spirits.'

♦ Take a deep breath and relax. Now you are ready to move on to the next stage of your space cleansing.

♦ Stay centred and maintain sacred space. Using your smudge stick or by burning herbs, take the smoke into each corner of the room. Centre yourself in each corner of the room before you begin.

♦ Fan the smoke from the ground upwards towards the ceiling of the room. As you do this, your intention is to clear away negative or stuck energy which may be present. Negative energy loves to gather in corners.

♦ You may wish to repeat an affirmation or say a prayer as you perform the smudging of the room. For example:

'All negative energy is transformed. The air is free.'

Repeat in each corner.

The Seven-Day Cleansing Ritual

Now you are ready for the seven-day ritual. Seven days is ideal, as it means the room is cleansed on a deeper level. Performing it over seven days is not essential.

We use either salt or eggs for this stage because they soak up negative energy. (In African and Caribbean communities we have traditionally used onions, garlic and lemons in much the same way.)

For space cleansing my preference is salt which is a sacred and healing earth element. In ancient times salt was considered to be as precious as gold.

Salt also has a number of purifying elements. Salt in the sea has been known to clear skin ailments. As a teenager I suffered badly with eczema. When I was 16 I went on holiday to Barbados. I was told to swim in the sea as much as I could. My eczema completely cleared up. I attributed this to the salt in the sea. I use salt in my bath to clear toxins from my body. I have also developed a special relationship with sea salts through the aromatic bath salts that I make. When purifying your home, use natural sea salt or rock salt crystals.

- Before using your salt in this ritual, it is customary to bless it. Place the salt in a bowl and say a prayer or blessing over it to invoke its healing elements.

- Place a pinch of salt or one egg in the easternmost corner of the room. Then do the same in each corner of the room.

- Leave the salt or eggs in the room for seven days.

- On the seventh day collect the eggs and place them in a carrier bag. Ensure that they are not broken. Dispose of the eggs by burying them in the earth.

- If you have no access to earth, dispose of your eggs by flushing them down the lavatory. Salt is best disposed of by sprinkling it on to the earth. If you can get to natural flowing water, dispose of the salt there. Some teachings suggest vacuuming up the salt but I prefer to give it back to the earth.

- Now you are ready to set up your altar. Select a time when you will not be interrupted. You may wish to set up your altar when there is a full or new moon, at sunset or at the time of day when you were born. Have all the physical objects that you wish to place on your altar ready, so they can be cleansed beforehand.

Cleansing Objects for Your Altar

- Cleanse your crystals in a bowl of water to which you add sea salt for between 1 and 24 hours. Crystals love to bathe in the light of Mother Moon or the warm rays of Father Sun. Put them out on a balcony or windowsill on the nights of a full or new moon, if you wish. Alternatively, wrap your crystal in a piece of silk for storage and protection. You may also bury your crystals in the earth for 1 to 24 hours, or longer. Burying in Mother Earth neutralises your objects.

- Natural rock crystals, such as amethyst and rose quartz, don't fare well if left in salt water for too long. Instead, cleanse them in mineral water and place them in the direct light of the moon or sun.

♦ For a speedier cleansing, smudge your crystals with frankincense, myrrh, or a natural Indian incense such as *nag champa*.

♦ Always use mineral water for cleansing and for use on your altar.

♦ The objects you may wish to place on your altar might include any of the following: crystals, photographs of family members, a special bowl to hold water, a sacred feather, images of guides, a spiritual teacher, or an image or symbol that represents a higher power or the god/goddess of your heart. You may also wish to place a copy of a holy book on your altar. Silver is an excellent metal to use. Have you ever noticed how silver turns black on some people? This is because it picks up energy, positive and negative.

♦ The four elements – earth, water, fire and air – should ideally be represented on your altar. Candles represent fire, incense represents air, crystals represent the earth, and water, itself. Think about how you might want to represent the four elements on your altar.

♦ Find a wooden table for your altar, smudge it and wipe it with Florida water. I cover mine with a white cloth. Choose a cloth that speaks to you and use this only for your altar and nothing else.

♦ At this point you may wish to light a candle. Use a white candle to bring in the light or purple to call in the energy of spirit. Follow your intuition.

♦ Smudge all your sacred objects in preparation for placing them on your altar. Now is an ideal time to perform a meditation or visualisation. Visualise the power and healing energy of each sacred item, then place it on your altar, blessing it as you do so.

♦ If you have a vessel of water on your altar you may wish to add a few drops of your favourite essential oil to it. Change the water on your altar every seven days. You can energise the water by pouring it between two glasses before placing it on your altar.

♦ Finish off with a prayer of protection and give thanks for the sacred space and energy you have divinely created in your home.

This is simply a guide – you don't have to follow it religiously. Allow yourself to be open and listen to the voice of your intuitive self. However, try to ensure that you cleanse your space as deeply and effectively as you can.

Over time, the sacred objects on your altar will either expand or decrease. Don't be afraid to remove or replace items. I have broken down my altar five times and started again, since my very first altar seven years ago. As we let go, we grow and move on from people and objects. Having an altar has given me space to connect with my spiritual self. It has supported my spiritual awakening in a very big way. Remember, sacred space is all around us and within us. We can enter it at any time. The door is always open.

SELF-DISCOVERY EXERCISE
And Her Eyes Were Watching God

THERE IS A tree at one of the entrances to my local park. Its branches have all gone but it is still glorious. One day I decided to really explore this tree. Her trunk was enormous. There was no way I could hug her in one go, she was too large. She was naked and resplendent. The words 'There is beauty in nakedness' flashed across my mind. This tree represented transformation. In spite of having been stripped bare, she still carried the energy of rebirth.

Some months later I learned that she was in fact one of the oldest trees in the park. Apparently she had been struck by lightning in a great storm. They say lightning is the earth's way of bringing sacred energy to a place. I believe she has been touched. Inside, she is still alive. They say that in time we will see her give birth again. I love this tree so much that I named her And Her Eyes Were Watching God, after Zora Neale Hurston's book. I have a photograph of her for my pocket book of dreams.

A naked willow tree catches my eye. As I approach her, I see a shallow eye in the centre of her trunk. It sparkles in the drizzly rain.

- See how many 'eyes' you can spot on trees as you walk past them.

- Everywhere in parks there are trees standing in circles. Circles are symbolic – representing the womb, the earth, the sun, the moon, and the orbits of the planets. How many tree circles have you noticed in your local park?

♦ Two new estates were built on my road and in both cases the trees – especially two willow trees – were not harmed. Keep an eye out in your local area to see whether trees are protected when new buildings are being erected.

CHAPTER 15

Ancestral Messages

Ancestral Messages Chant

Ancestral powers,
Blood blessing Mother Earth,
Footsteps buried in the sand.
Ancestral sounds,
Speaking to me in my sleep,
Calling my soul.
Ancestral voices,
Sweet whispers in the wind,
The drum beats to the pitter, patter of rain.
Ancestral knowing,
Hearing my calling, going,
Not knowing where I am going, just trusting.
Ancestral memories
Of the way we used to be,
The life we left behind.
Ancestral dreams of visions awakened,
Knowing I must act to CRE-ATE the future.
Ancestral guide,
Guiding me through the labyrinth of life.
An invisible hand,
Always protecting, reaching for my inner soul,
The soul who knows the truth of who I am.
Ancestors smile each day as I move closer to joining them, when
    my purpose here is done,

On the other side.

We owe it to our ancestors to claim the birthright of our purpose. After all, their very existence is the reason why we are here.

I ONLY FOUND out recently that my grandmother on my mother's side was named Cleopatra. No one had ever mentioned this to me before. Everyone called her by her nickname, which was Claris. My grandfather, her husband, was a tall, handsome man who went by the name of Stanley Morgan. He had money, horses and servants. I know very little about Cleopatra and Stanley. But I believe the memory of who they were is flowing through my bloodstream and is alive in my subconscious.

When I was a child the Egyptian queen Cleopatra always fascinated me. At the time I didn't know that my own grandmother had been named after her. What was it about my grandmother that moved her parents to give her this name?

I only saw my maternal grandmother on a few occasions when I went on holiday as a child to Barbados. During my last visit she was sick in bed, having had one of her legs amputated. As I write this piece I am struck by how much of our past we let slip through our fingers. I have come to realise that, like a tree, I need to know my roots, my foundations.

I was the last member of my family to see my paternal grandfather alive. And I was the last one to see our oldest living relative Aunt Delcina before she died recently. Both times I was unable to get the family history on tape. I am praying that the ancestors will speak to me in another way. And they have. On her last visit to Barbados to attend my Aunt Delcina's funeral my mother arrived back with a stack of papers. These papers contained the names of members of my family going back to the early 1900s. They also contained the death certificates of generations of my family on my mother's side. A cousin in Barbados is in the process of researching the family tree.

I wonder if my grandmothers sat on the seashore, watching the sun set and thinking about the purpose of her life. Was she happy with her life? Did she have a sense of purpose? I chose to come into this family lineage. I ask myself what memories of my family I carry in my bones. I know I have work to do. My ancestors paved the way for me – otherwise I would not be here, doing what I am doing. Their past is my future. Everything has happened for a reason. I have no doubt of that. By honouring them I am simply thanking them for all the work they have done.

My mother's name is Celestine which means 'celestial or heavenly'. There is also a beautiful crystal, bluey-silver in colour, that is called a celestine. Where did the idea for my mother's name come from? What were the unconscious thoughts behind it? Perhaps the angels stood over her birthing and ordained that it be so.

My mother has lived up to her name. She has raised six children in a challenging environment, and experienced what I call a nervous breakthrough (as opposed to a nervous breakdown) when she was pregnant with my last two sisters (twins) in 1970. Her breakthrough disrupted our family life. I took on a lot of responsibility, as the oldest girl, and I loved it.

Throughout my teenage years my relationship with my mother was rocky. I didn't understand her and she didn't understand me. I thought she was a hard, tough woman. It is only now I am realising that my mother's outer shell is tough, to protect the soft, sensitive being that she really is. In that way we are truly alike.

My mother has been through a lot. Her culture and upbringing are deeply ingrained in her being. She has been an incredible homemaker, extremely organised and creative, and with a fierce love for her children. Her faith and belief in God has been her rock. It has forced her to review her life and begin to love herself again. Nowadays she goes to exercise classes, is a member of a senior citizens' club, has a very healthy diet, and will come and spend a day in the spa with my sisters and me and relish the pampering of her body. It's amazing how things change.

She also has a wonderful relationship with my daughter. It is very comforting to see them when they are together. Our healing can happen in so many ways. Under every difficult, challenging, negative experience is a blessing in disguise. My mother has learnt to live again. The ancestors must be smiling.

My mother is also a dreamer, a woman who sees. I believe she has always needed guidance with this power. She used to frighten me with the negative things she dreamt about. I remember her always warning us not to do such and such because she had dreamt about it.

My sister Martha and my daughter Aida are also dreamers. My memory tells me we have always had women with second sight in our family. Our role is to harness and nurture these gifts of the third eye and inner knowing and use them for our highest good.

The ancestors are at work – weaving the web, creating the stories. They have walked this far. Now it is up to us to walk the rest of the way. Each of our footsteps will become memories implanted on this earth, capturing the history (or herstory) of our families. We are the makers and the shapers of the future. It is our job, as spiritual beings living a human existence, to complete our life mission here on earth.

ANCESTRAL ALTARS

It was a bitter, cold, October morning. But the sharp air on my face did not lessen the warm glow in my heart. As I waded through the Welsh fields full of cow dung, I couldn't hide my excitement. I, the one black face on a writers' retreat in Wales, could not hold back my eagerness to get to the sea.

Our task was to perform a writing ritual using the four elements. Back at the retreat centre, we had been told about the importance of preparing ourselves in sacred space. I found myself in the beautiful garden, sitting on the steps. I prayed and sat quietly with my thoughts. This process helped immensely in enabling me to ground and centre myself for the journey ahead.

The walk of almost a mile did not take long. Arriving at the sea was a bit of a surprise. We could not see her as we approached. Then we rounded a corner and there she was, greyish-white, salt spray rising from the waves. I stopped in my tracks and gave thanks. The landscape before me was a fusion of sea and sky.

Our first task was to gather driftwood for the fire we would build. There was plenty around. As I gathered the pieces of driftwood, I noticed the abundance of stones on the shore. These were beautiful stones. I intuitively felt I had to have some with me. Their colours varied between greys, reds and oranges. And each stone had its own unique markings. Some called my name. Without even thinking about it, I began to fill my pockets with the stones. Each one was chosen, for what I wasn't sure, but I knew they needed to be with me. The rest I took to the fire where we made a sacred circle of stones and placed the wood in the centre.

Within minutes we had created a raging fire. The feeling of standing by the sea, surrounded by all of the elements – earth, water, fire and air – brought my body and spirit to life. I stood and basked in this union, feeling the energy rise up within me from my vagina to my heart. A combination of the smoke and the sacredness of what we were doing brought tears to my eyes. I drank in the joy of the moment, my ears loving the sounds of the gushing waves and the gentle breeze on my earlobes soothing me.

Bliss bathed me and I knew I was at home. In that moment I felt that I had connected with the power centre inside myself. My soul had opened up, Mother Earth was energising me, I was being refilled. The earth is our friend; she will replenish our energies and bring our spirits alive whenever we call on her.

Most of us stood around the fire in a circle. The fire was glowing, and her flames brought a welcome heat. I watched as the flames embraced the different directions. I then said that I would like to dedicate the starting of the fire by carrying out a Native American tradition of calling upon the four directions. Amazingly, the sun was behind me. So, from its position in the east, it was easy to locate the four directions.

Some months back, after reading a wonderful spirit-filled book for writers entitled *Soul Between the Lines* by Dorothy Randall Gray, I had written my own dedication ceremony to the four directions – the north, the south, the east and the west. So I pulled my dedication out of my pocket and performed the ritual, saying the words as we stood facing each of the directions. I was ready to go wherever spirit needed me.

Now it was time to write. We all wandered off in different directions. I sat on a small rock facing the sea. I sat there for what seemed like ages. I couldn't write. All I wanted to do was gaze at the rich tapestry of earth's elements that surrounded me.

I decided to walk. My feet took me directly to the shoreline. I clambered across boulder after boulder, moving closer and closer to the edge of the sea. Suddenly I found myself standing on a boulder totally surrounded by water. It was just the sky, the sea and me. I stood on the boulder, facing the sea, hugging myself. As I looked up to the sky I gave thanks. I was so happy; in fact I was overjoyed. I felt at one with the universe, with God, with the goddess inside me. This was not a feeling money could buy, or that anyone else could give me. This was priceless (yet it is a feeling that any of us can have whenever we want). My soul opened as I stood there, pouring thanks into the universe.

Suddenly I had a sense of *déjà vu*. I turned my head and looked back towards the shoreline. Then I stared at the rocky wall behind me and the image came through. I was standing looking back at the caves where my ancestors had been held captive before they were taken like cattle to the ships. I watched them walking out, frightened, into what must have seemed terrifying at the time – the sea. I heard their screams. I felt their pain. By now my tears were gushing. I was there with them. I don't know how long I stood there, as I lost all sense of time. Then, as quickly as it had come, the feeling left and my body was overcome with a sense of quiet peace. I stood with my arms outstretched and prayed. The tears came back but now they were tears of joy.

A gentle voice calling my name brought me back to the present. One of my tutors was standing some distance away, smiling at me. 'It's time for us to go back now.' I didn't want to leave this place. I knew the ancestors had spoken to me. My journey had connected me to my people once more. It had connected me to myself. My soul was pleased.

I walked towards my tutor. Her words as I walked beside her were, 'You looked like a priestess standing there.' I didn't say anything, but my eyes spoke, acknowledging her words. As we walked back, I stopped to sprinkle sage into the sea. We made our journey back to the centre.

On returning to my room, I intuitively placed the stones I had collected from the sea in a circle by my bed. The circle had a powerful presence; I liked its energy. I took the stones home with me.

Within days of arriving back home, I decided to create a new altar in my bedroom. I began taking the existing one apart. I felt a sense of urgency about getting the new one in place. I wasn't sure why, but I just followed the strong feeling that I had.

My new altar was like no altar I had created before. I had placed the stones in a circle on some brown mudcloth from Gambia. In amongst them was a light-brown stone candleholder that I had purchased whilst on holiday in Tucson. In the centre of the circle I placed a purple, scented candle on a beautiful hand-painted purple dish. I ceremoniously lit the candle and sat in silence with my new altar. The fragrance from the candle hugged my room almost as a way of saying thank you. This new altar felt solid, sure of itself, as though it had been here before.

A few months later, while reading an article about working with the ancestors, I realised what I had created. It was an interview with Malidoma and Sobonofu Soma (African healers and keepers of ritual traditions) which clarified the significance of my experience by the sea and the setting-up of my new altar. In the article Malidoma and Sobonofu said that stones were the primary elements of shrines or altars and it was important to collect or choose stones that speak to our souls in some special way. When I read their final words everything made sense:

'Stones represent the spirit of our ancestors.'

Magic had taken place that day; the spirit of my ancestors had been at work. What I had created was an ancestral altar.

SELF-DISCOVERY EXERCISE
Setting up your Ancestral Altar

SETTING UP AN ancestral altar means you are honouring the spirit of your ancestors for the good they have done, and saying thank you for the fact that they lived so you could be here.

◆ First cleanse the space where your altar will be and set up your altar in sacred space. A mantelpiece is often a good place. Then arrange some or all of the following items:

◆ Stones representing the souls of your ancestors.

◆ Items that represent your cultural traditions. Those of African heritage or origin may wish to place an African mask on their ancestral altar. The African craftsperson, or artist shaman, often carved the spirit of the ancestors into the wood of the mask. On my ancestral altar I have three cowrie shells. I use cowrie shells because of their historical importance in Africa where they were used firstly as currency and secondly for their powers of divination.

◆ A vessel containing soil or earth from the land where you live.

◆ A bowl or vessel containing water. Water represents purification and peace and is the container of emotional energy. I also have a bottle of sacred water collected from a stream where we performed a head blessing ritual on a healing retreat. I have used it on my altar and for the pouring of libations.

- A candle – to represent the light and the wisdom of your ancestors that is always there for you.

- A bowl of fruit (food for your ancestors). Include some soul food items.

- Flowers, preferably white, or flowers that your ancestors were familiar with.

- Photographs of deceased family members.

- Objects of special significance given to you by past family members.

- Keep a record of the names of your family members. (You may wish to memorise them.) On her last visit to Barbados, where she was born, my mother brought back the death certificates of many of the deceased members on her side of the family. I am now able to call on the names of great-great-great-grandparents.

- Use the ancestral chant (see page 245) to call upon the spirit of your ancestors. Read a passage from a holy book, say a prayer, and call out the names of your ancestors as and when it feels appropriate. By honouring your ancestors, you are closing the gap between yourself and the spirit world.

RITUAL
Burying and Planting

OUR ANCESTORS HONOURED and respected the healing powers of Mother Earth. This earth, physically and spiritually, is humankind's most precious gift. Yet, over centuries, we have been responsible for the abuse of Mother Earth. Though she is abundant in riches, we have pillaged from her and not given back. As we approach the new millennium, the dawning of a new age, it is time for us to renew our relationship with Mother Earth. It requires a reclaiming of past collective ancestral memories whose cultural traditions honoured Mother Earth.

My vision, then, is to find myself, on 1 January 2000, burying and planting. There are two reasons for this. The first is to help bring about the collective shift of consciousness that I believe will take place globally on that day. I also want this ritual to mark the 37 years I have spent on this earth. As I dig into the soil of Mother Earth, I want to give thanks to the spirit of my ancestors who walked before me and for the souls of the guides and the teachers who walk with me.

Secondly, as I write, I recognise that I am already the past and the future is already in existence. In a short time, future generations will be viewing us as their ancestors. When they make contact with Mother Earth what will they find? When their hands unearth a gleaming crystal, will they understand its healing power? Will they honour the plant that has been lovingly placed in the earth under the light of the full moon? These, to me, are the things that matter; that, in pursuing my own spiritual enlightenment, I also leave a rich source of inspiration for those in the future.

So, what is the difference between burying and planting? A burial marks an ending. As we bury our dead deep down in the soil of Mother Earth, we are returning them to her. I was reminded of this so beautifully one December morning as I stood with a group of mourners at the graveside of a dear friend who had passed away.

Her coffin was resting by the side as a group of her male relatives began placing the soil into her grave. After a while one could see that the men were growing tired. A group of women, including me, were standing randomly together. None of us was dressed for digging so it was strange that in a matter of minutes seven women or more had taken over the entire task.

I had never done anything of the kind before. In fact I did my best not to attend funerals in the first place. Yet something strange and beautiful happened that day. The more I shovelled the earth the stronger I became. At times I felt as if I had travelled through time, as if I had done this before. Suddenly my connection with the earth became a healing experience. As we women moved the soil the rest of the crowd sang, urging us on. It was as if intuitively we had made a pact long before our arrival that this would be how we would mark the ending of a friend's life on this physical earth.

As we placed the earth onto her coffin we each silently said our prayers. I had made a blend of sea salts sprinkled with essential oils. The smell lingered joyously amongst the soil as I sprinkled it on. The connections with Mother Earth created a healing vacuum through which we could transform our pain. The act of burial itself sacredly honoured and marked the passing over of our friend's life.

Burying marks an ending. Planting, however, marks our desire to produce new life or to begin again. You can plant a new plant, a tree, or a list of your desires. I planted a purple amethyst at the foot an oak tree in my local park. I felt like a little girl again as I buried the gemstone snugly in the warm earth. As it is my birthstone, I know that it will hold great healing power for me. And, as the oak brings strength, I pray that it will fill my gemstone with strength and my life also.

With all this in mind, why not try this simple ritual, using the gifts of burying and planting in your own life, to assist you on your journey? You will need to bury your pieces of paper in soil.

◆ First make a list of all the fears, feelings, emotions and physical challenges that have blocked you on a piece of paper.

◆ Gather together any old journals you are ready to release. (I have realised that my old journals hold powerful memories of the woman I was in the past. They do not reflect the woman I am now.) Ceremoniously burning your journals can mark a closure of your past self. If you have a lot of paper build a small bonfire. Bury the ashes into the soil or earth. Close by saying a prayer, asking for help and guidance in reaching your highest good and realising your Soul Purpose.

◆ Sing, drum, dance – whatever you feel called to do – but within your chosen form include praise and thanks to your higher power.

◆ Find a sunny spot or a place near water for your planting ceremony (this is not essential).

◆ Begin by writing down words and sentences that affirm the experiences you wish to bring about in your life, the qualities you wish to develop, grow, bloom and blossom throughout the year.

◆ End with a written vision of your Soul Purpose, as a testimony to the path you wish to follow for the remainder of your life here on earth.

◆ Plant some seeds or a crystal to represent that which you wish to bring about.

◆ Give an offering to Mother Earth.

◆ Say a closing prayer.

Remember God is everywhere – in the trees, in the flowers, in the sky. God is here. And when we touch Mother Earth we touch God.

SELF-DISCOVERY EXERCISE
Ancestral Inheritance

OUR ANCESTORS HAVE given us so many good things but we are also affected by the pain and the baggage we may have inherited. Use the following questions to seek out tne roots of any negative emotional baggage that has been passed down through the generations of your family. In your Soul Purpose Journal write down the first intuitive response that comes into your head.

- Describe a way of behaving or a problem that has been passed down through the generations to your current family.

- Where and how did the problem begin in your family history?

- How does this family inheritance show itself in your present family relationship?

- What does it stop you and your present family from doing?

- When this problem is transformed (seen in a positive light) what gift does it bring you?

- What was the reason for the inheritance being passed on in this way?

- What do you believe was the original lesson of the inheritance?

- If you were to let go of this ancestral inheritance, what changes would you make in your own life?

SELF-DISCOVERY EXERCISE
Healing Past Ancestral Blocks

USE THE FOLLOWING guided visualisation to assist you in healing past ancestral hurts that have been passed down through the generations. It's best if all your immediate family can join you. But, if not, just gather as many as possible and visualise the rest.

- ◆ Centre and ground yourself and enter sacred space.

- ◆ Visualise a gathering of seven generations of your family. Ask your higher mind to take you and your family and all your ancestors back to the place where the hurt originally occurred.

- ◆ Ask that all who are gathered to centre and focus their awareness. Ask that each person goes within and makes a commitment to wanting to be there.

- ◆ Bring before you the members of your family involved in the original hurt.

- ◆ Ask them to simply state the cause of the hurt.

- ◆ Ask them to say how they would have liked the matter to have been resolved.

- ◆ Ask everyone present to visualise the original incident as if they were physically present at the time. Tell them to smell it, sense it, feel it in their bones. Everyone, from the past to the present day, is to participate in this part of the process.

- ◆ Now have the whole family clan hold hands. Together the whole clan is going to breathe out and release into the universe the memory of the old experience and all those that followed it. On the count of seven, visualise the old experiences being released through the breath of all those who are gathered.

- ◆ Now have a new, positive, healing image of the whole family replace the old memory, which has been erased.

- ◆ Have the whole family clan join hands and, together, on the count of seven, visualise breathing in new memories of how things will be from the present moment and into the future.

- ◆ At this point, family members may wish to sing, dance, drum or whatever they need to do to celebrate the transformation of the family inheritance and the removal of the block.

- ◆ Ask everyone to form a circle. Call upon the oldest member of the clan present. Tell everyone that you will now plant a tree to mark a new beginning. This will be the family tree. Under the shade of this tree, family members can call on the spirit of their ancestors. They can come to this tree and ask for guidance. Under this tree they can bring their tears.

◆ Assist the elder in the planting of the tree and visualise it growing and its leaves spreading over the heads of all that are gathered. The elder should complete the planting by pouring a libation at the foot of the tree. The ritual is closed with a family blessing.

◆ Thank everyone for coming. Close your eyes and, on the count of seven, all your family members from the past will disappear back to their resting place. Present family members will return to their homes. On the count of seven, open your eyes and come back into the room.

CHAPTER 16

Fuel for Your Spiritual Journey

PRACTICE AND ENGAGE in the rituals, meditations and self-discovery exercises in this book. See where they take you on your journey to self-knowledge. You are the holder of the key that will change your life. Others can guide you towards the door but you must put the key in the lock and turn it. Do the work that will open the door.

People will talk about you, attack you, whatever you do. If you stay stuck, they'll talk about you. If you make changes to your life, they'll talk about you. If you dare to be bold, do something different, they'll talk about you. So you'll get talked about, whether you keep your life the same or you make changes. Do whatever it takes to move your life on. Give yourself and others something to really talk about.

On your spiritual journey be prepared for your ego to fight for control, as it is threatened by your expanding consciousness. Spiritual competition is part of the journey's challenge. A teacher enlightened me about this a few years ago. And I now understand fully what she meant. Many of us enter into spiritual competition with each other. We compare our spiritual experiences to see whose is the deepest, who has received the most enlightened feedback from teachers, healers or gurus. We try to elevate ourselves above each other, based on our perception of where we are on the path. We covet our spiritual knowledge and understanding and choose to share only with those who acknowledge us based on what we know.

But spiritual competition is a sure sign of our own internal dysfunction. Spiritual growth is available to each and every one of us. We are all at the level that is perfect for us, right at this moment. The truth is, no one is necessarily any more spiritual than anyone else. We are all children in the eyes of the Father/Mother God. Instead, see yourself as a perpetual beginner, constantly open to learning and growing. Be excited about what lies ahead. Life is about learning. If there was nothing else to learn we would get bored. Keep your eyes focused on where *you* are going. Let God take care of the direction of others.

Embracing your Soul Purpose will often get other people's backs up. Instead of giving you warm, receptive feedback on your growth, your ideas, your painting, your new job, you will receive the opposite. Suddenly your best friend or your family will stop approving of you.

Before you start wilting under their disapproval, stop for a minute. Why not try a different approach? Instead of focusing on what you receive (in terms of other people's opinions and criticisms), focus purely on what you can give – in your work, in your creative activities, in your personal life. The criticisms will still be there but the sting will have gone. When you are rightfully embracing your Soul Purpose and serving the world, infinite approval will beam out to support you – even in the face of adversity and challenge. Seek approval from within, rather than from others.

Be prepared for others to pass you by, go beyond you in their achievements, and attain the success you have always wanted for yourself. This, I believe, is one of the most terrifying realisations on the journey. There will always be someone who gets there before you. And there will always be someone who will follow you. What is most important is that you get there. Take your attention off your position in the rankings or the ratings. Instead, focus on how you're going to do it, and simply get on with it. Countless ideas have been shelved because we're too busy focusing on what other people are doing. No one can take away your unique purpose. It is yours and no one else's.

Sometimes on the journey you will need to be patient. For instance, I was not ready to give birth to *Soul Purpose* until now. Before now, the birth would have been premature and you would have been reading a very different book. By surrendering to the process I allowed what I was meant to write come through.

Everything happens in divine time. Just trust the process and have faith. Everything will be taken care of.

Others passing you by have no bearing on what is rightfully yours. If you feel resentful or frustrated about someone's success, ask yourself 'What is it about what they have done that reminds me about what I haven't done?' What do you need to do right now to move a step closer to your own success?

If other people can achieve, it is a sure sign that you can too. Bless those who have started living their Soul Purpose. Remember, you do not know what it took for them to get there. By blessing them you are blessing yourself too. I love to send cards and letters to people who have moved to places I want to go. I do it from my heart. Try it. Basking in their success is an excellent way of encouraging yourself to get moving.

Practice, practice, practice. So many of us want to achieve in certain areas but we don't want to put in the work. When we show up for work, the universe will show up too. Only when we have laid the foundations can we rest, as the universe goes to work on our behalf. So-called luck is always a result of work done beforehand. For some of us, our preparation may have been done in another lifetime.

We are learning and teaching all the time. Through my work I feel blessed to have had the opportunity to learn so much from hundreds of men and women who have come into my life and I into theirs. Stay open to being a learner – keep the door constantly ajar. You might think you know all there is to know about your chosen field but, believe me, there is always more to learn. Being the expert puts us in a straitjacket. It leaves little room for curiosity. But the journey is never-ending, the possibilities are endless.

Pray, pray and pray again. This is one frequency that is never blocked and there is no tariff to pay. Keep in constant communication with the god in your life. Phone her every day. When things get tough, talk to her, when things are going well, talk to her. She is the best friend you could ever have. She is always there for you whatever your needs and whenever you need her.

Trust the process and it will all make sense.

Connecting with your Soul Purpose is an adventure. For the journey you will require an abundance of faith and trust and you will need a willingness to embrace spirit. Once you put your intention out there, two things will happen. Firstly the universe will start working for you, and secondly – almost as a safety check – you will be tested.

Don't be put off by the tests. My authority to do what I do (which was really about believing in myself), my credibility, my faith, spiritual practice and my integrity have all been put to the test. This is all part of the master plan. Now from where I stand I know that if everything I have was to be taken from me tomorrow it would not be the end of the world. I have complete faith in the knowledge that I am a child of God and I am loved.

God wants the best for you. Do you want the best for you? Be honest about what you really want from life. Too many of us are afraid of being up front about what we believe our Soul Purpose to be. Dare to reach deep down inside you and make contact with that which you were meant to do. Don't focus on what others are doing. Be glad and happy for their success. And keep reaching for your own.

Keep the ugly emotion of comparison at bay. By comparing, you simply dim the light on your own talents. There is only one person in your race and that is you. It really doesn't matter, for example, if a similar play to your own has been written before. Your play will have your own personal stamp on it. So what if someone else's voice sounds like yours. This is the voice you were blessed with so use it.

Sometimes I think we forget that the same god who plants the words into the heads of some of the greatest writers, or the sweet voices into the throats of your favourite singers is the same god who plants ideas into you. This shows in the poems that you, the poet, writes, in the articles that you, the journalist pens and in the works that you, the artist, creates.

If you have engaged in the exercises and rituals in *Soul Purpose* you will have taken time out to be still. And it is in the stillness that you will hear your own authentic voice and the voice of spirit. Nothing gets resolved in a panic. Go within to find greater fulfilment and happiness.

As I write these final words, I am walking in the park. It is a wet, rainy day but I do not notice. In fact it feels good. As I walk, my mind relaxes and my body unwinds. I stop to take in the beauty of a magnificent oak whose sprawling, glossy, green, leafy branches call me. She is the eternal mother, providing the perfect shelter for our next moon ritual. I visualise climbing her branches. I cannot wait. It is in stillness, meditation and communion with Mother Earth that we find our answers.

As I look back over my life, I am thankful for all I have experienced, both positive and negative. Those experiences have provided me with a fertile training ground. It is now up to me to take the lessons and learn from them. The same is true for you. Until we do, the lessons will keep coming back, showing up in different people and different experiences.

Take the lesson, bless the experience and move on. Release and let go of everything that no longer serves you. Keep stoking the fire, planting the seeds, writing the words and doing the deeds. You are the sower of your own harvest, the creator of your own dreams.

Take that leap of faith. Get up and sing, get up and dance, get up and write. Get up and do whatever it takes to turn your life around. The divine grace of God has more than enough love for us all. The god inside you wants you to win. I want you to win. There is nothing that would make me happier. So, as you immerse yourself in the continued realisation of your Soul Purpose, remember that you can do it, you can make it through. When you manifest your Soul Purpose in your life you provide another bright light, like a shining star, here on earth.

The tide is changing, the winds speak of change, the trees (the standing people who hold the wisdom and memories of the past) speak of transformation. When we boldly live the truth of our Soul Purpose, then this earth will truly be a brighter, more loving and joyous place.

Reclaim your heritage, the priceless gift bestowed upon you at birth. Through God, all things are possible. Rise up and take your rightful place on your throne.

May the gods and the goddesses shine down, on and through you forever and ever. Amen.

Blessings.

I am *Jackee Cheinu Sataya Holder*,
a ruling servant of God,
a disciple of power,
whose purpose is truth.

RECOMMENDED READING

A Course in Miracles, Penguin Books, 1985. (For more information, contact: Foundation for Inner Peace, PO Box 635, Tiboran, CA 94920, USA)

Afua, Queen, *Heal Thyself for Health and Longevity*, A & B Book Publishers, 1992

Arewa, Caroline Shola, *Opening to Spirit*, Thorsons, HarperCollins, 1998

Boyd, Julia, *In the Company of My Sisters – Black Women and Self-Esteem*, Penguin Books, 1993

Breathnach, Sarah Ban, *Simple Abundance: A Daybook of Comfort and Joy*, Warner Books, 1995

Brice, Carleen, *Walk Tall: Affirmations for People of Color*, RPL Publishing Inc., San Diego, 1994

Bridges, Carol, *The Medicine Woman's Guide to Being in Business for Herself – How to live by your spiritual vision in a money-based world*, Earth Nation Publishing, 1992.

Cameron, Julia, *The Vein of Gold: A Journey to Your Creative Heart*, G.P. Putman & Sons, New York, 1996; Later edition published by Pan Books, 1997

Cameron, Julia with Bryan, Mark, *The Artist's Way – A Spiritual Path of Higher Creativity*, G.P. Putnam & Sons, New York, 1992

Edelman, Marian Wright, *Guide My Feet – Prayers and Meditations for Our Children*, Beacon Press, 1995; Later edition published by Harper Perennial, 1996

Gawain, Shakti, *Creative Visualisation*, Bantam New Age Books, 1982

Gray, Dorothy Randall, *Soul Between the Lines*, Avon Books (a division of the Hearst Corporation), New York, New York, 1998

Gray, Miranda, *Red Moon – Understanding and Using the Gifts of the Menstrual Cycle*, Element Publishers, 1994

Hughes, K. Wind and Wolf Linda, *Daughters of the Moon, Sisters of the Sun: Young Women and Mentors on the Transition to Womanhood*, New Society Publishers, 1997

Jeffers, Susan, *Feel the Fear and Do It Anyway*, Century Hutchinson Ltd, 1987

Kimbro, Dr Denis P., *What Makes the Great Great – Strategies for Extraordinary Achievement*, Doubleday, New York, 1997

Kingston, Karen, *Creating Sacred Space with Feng Shui*, Piatkus Books, 1996

Linn, Denise, *Sacred Space*, Rider Books, 1995

Louden, Jennifer, *The Woman's Retreat Book: A Guide to Restoring, Rediscovering and Reawakening Your True Self – in a moment, an hour, a day or a weekend*, HarperCollins, San Francisco, 1997

Mariechild, Diane, *Mother Wit – A Guide to Healing and Psychic Development*, The Crossing Press, 1981

Moore, Thomas, *Care of the Soul – How to Add Depth and Meaning to Your Everyday Life*, Piatkus Books, 1992

Moorey, Teresa, *The Moon and You for Beginners*, Headway, USA, 1996

Paterson, Jacqueline Memory, *Tree Wisdom: The definitive guide book to the myth, folklore and healing power of trees*, Thorsons, HarperCollins, 1996

Reid, Lori, *Moon Magic – How to use the moon's phases to inspire and influence your relationships, home life and business*, Carlton Books, 1998

Satir, Virginia, *Self Esteem*, Celestial Arts, 1975

Schwartz, David, *The Magic of Thinking Big*, Pocket books, Simon and Schuster Ltd, 1995

Serure, Pamela, *The Three-Day Energy Fast – Get Calm, Get Clean, Get Clear*, HarperCollins, 1997

Taylor, Susan, *In the Spirit*, Amistad, New York, New York, 1993

Teish, Luisah, *Jambalaya – The Natural Woman's Book of Personal Charms and Practical Rituals*, Harper, San Francisco, 1985

Wade, Dr Brenda and Richardson, Brenda Lane, *Love Lessons – A Guide to Transforming Relationships*, Amistad, New York, New York, 1993

Vanzant, Iyanla, *Acts of Faith: Daily Meditations for People of Color*, Simon and Schuster, 1993

Vanzant, Iyanla, *In the Meantime – Find yourself and the love you want*, Simon and Schuster, 1998

Vanzant, Iyanla, *One Day My Soul Just Opened Up – 40 days and 40 nights towards spiritual strength and personal growth*, Simon and Schuster, 1998

Vanzant, Iyanla, *The Spirt of a Man – A vision of transformation for Black men and the women who love them*, HarperCollins, 1996

Vanzant, Iyanla, *Tapping the Power Within – A path to self-empowerment for Black women*, Writers and Readers, 1992

Wade Gayles, Gloria, *My Soul is a Witness – African American Women's Spirituality*, Beacon Press, 1995

Wall, Vicky, *The Miracle of Colour Healing – Aura-Soma Therapy as the Mirror of the Soul*, Thorsons, HarperCollins Publishers, 1995

Walsch, Neale Donald, *Conversations with God, Book 1 – an uncommon dialogue*, G.P. Putnam and Sons, New York, New York, 1995

Williamson, Marianne, *A Return to Love – Reflections on the principles of a course in miracles*, Thorsons, HarperCollins, 1992

INDEX